Long Overdue

Charles P. Henry

Long Overdue

The Politics of Racial Reparations

New York University Press • *New York and London*

NEW YORK UNIVERSITY PRESS
New York and London
www.nyupress.org

Library of Congress Cataloging-in-Publication Data
Henry, Charles P., 1947–
Long overdue : the politics of racial reparations / Charles P. Henry.
p.   cm.
Includes bibliographical references and index.
ISBN-13: 978-0-8147-3692-0 (cloth : alk. paper)
ISBN-10: 0-8147-3692-0 (cloth : alk. paper)
1. African Americans—Reparations—History. 2. African Americans—
Legal status, laws, etc.—History. 3. African Americans—Civil rights—
History—20th century. 4. Civil rights movements—United States—
History—20th century. 5. Reparations for historical injustices—United
States. 6. Racism—Political aspects—United States. 7. United States—
Politics and government—20th century. 8. United States—Race relations.
9. Slavery—United States—History.   I. Title.
E185.89.R45H46 2007
323.1196'073—dc22   2007023051

New York University Press books are printed on acid-free paper,
and their binding materials are chosen for strength and durability.

Manufactured in the United States of America
10 9 8 7 6 5 4 3 2 1

For my grandchildren—Ashlyn, Michael, and Tyler

Contents

Preface

Up to a few years ago, I had no interest in writing about reparations. Vernon E. Jordan Jr., an African American Washington power broker, former civil rights leader, and lawyer, was on my campus promoting his then just-released memoir, *Vernon Can Read!* During the question-and-answer session, someone asked what he thought about the issue of reparations. Jordan said something to the effect that he didn't think much about it because (1) he didn't need the money and (2) it wasn't going to happen. While the response drew chuckles, I felt it was flippant and unsatisfying on several levels. First, it raised but then ignored class issues that have arisen in the Black "community" since Jordan's days as a leader of the civil rights movement. Second, by framing it as being only about money, Jordan reduced a complicated issue to a simple payment that many reparations advocates themselves oppose. Third, by framing the question in a self-centered way, Jordan helped ensure that it would not happen and exhibited the kind of transactional rather than transformative leadership that have made many people cynical about contemporary Black leadership. In a broader sense, I couldn't help but think that the reason that reparations will not happen is as important as the reason that they will happen. Moreover, such predictions of failure ignore the positive aspects of identity and political community that could emerge from just the struggle itself.

Around the same time as Jordan's talk, I was routinely checking the book tables at the local Costco when I found Randall Robinson's book *The Debt: What America Owes to Blacks*. I was amazed to find a book on such a controversial racial topic in a mass superstore. Apparently, despite Jordan's dismissal, reparations apparently have arrived as a popular topic.

The combination of the two events made me start thinking seriously about the subject. Reparations have been an issue since the Civil War, but during my lifetime they have been promoted only by small groups of Black nationalists, such as Harlem's Queen Mother Moore.

Now they are moving into the mainstream. Even if Vernon Jordan is not interested, prominent members of the Black elite like Jesse Jackson, John Conyers, and Randall Robinson are. Nonetheless, despite their support and polls indicating African Americans' overwhelmingly favorable views, White Americans have been adamantly opposed to reparations. I find it ironic that the last two presidents—representing the two major political parties—would both travel to Africa and apologize to Africans for America's role in the slave trade but refuse to apologize to African Americans at home.

It has become evident that starting any conversation about reparations in terms of financial compensation due to Blacks, as Jordan did, quickly draws a negative response. This response usually is, Why should I have to pay for something I didn't do? But if the question is shifted from Who will pay the financial compensation? to Why hasn't there been an apology from the president and / or Congress for slavery and state-sponsored segregation? this often prompts a much more complex and tortured response. Many, including almost all our political leaders, have invoked the danger of resurrecting the past. Then in August 2005, Hurricane Katrina struck, and the history of racial segregation, economic disadvantage, and White fear was before our eyes and impossible to ignore. Yet for seemingly endless days, they were ignored as people, mainly Black, died. Then came the questions about race, poverty, and citizenship. This book is my contribution to that discourse.

Several people read earlier drafts of this manuscript, and I hope the end product meets their approval, even though they bear no responsibility for its shortcomings. These readers included Dianne Pinderhughes, Robert Allen, George Lipsitz, and Robert Blauner. Scharn Robinson was helpful on legal issues early in this process. I also want to thank the students in my graduate seminar on racial reparations, graduate student researchers Allen Caldwell and David Leonard, librarian Corliss Lee, and the staff in the Department of African American Studies at the University of California at Berkeley. I offer my thanks, as always, to my family and especially my wife, Loretta, for their love and support. Finally, my appreciation goes to Ilene Kalish and the staff and reviewers at New York University Press for their interest in and contributions to this work.

Let those who have been forgotten be re-remembered and let the healing begin.

Introduction

Insufficient Funds

In a sense we've come to our nation's capital to cash a check. When the architects of our republic wrote the magnificent words of the Constitution and the Declaration of Independence, they were signing a promissory note to which every American was to fall heir. This note was the promise that all men, yes, black men as well as white men, would be guaranteed the unalienable rights of life, liberty, and the pursuit of happiness.

It is obvious today that America has defaulted on this promissory note in so far as her citizens of color are concerned. Instead of honoring this sacred obligation, America has given the Negro people a bad check, a check which has come back marked "insufficient funds."
—Martin Luther King Jr., "I Have a Dream"[1]

Apology: The First Step toward Reparation

On May 16, 1997, President Bill Clinton offered the following apology:

The United States government did something that was wrong, deeply, profoundly, morally wrong. It was an outrage to our commitment to integrity and equality for all our citizens. We can end the silence. We can stop turning our head away. We can look at you in the eye and finally say on behalf of the American people what the United States government did was shameful, and I am sorry.[2]

Clinton's apology was made to those survivors of the government-sponsored Tuskegee experiment, in which scientists with the U.S. Public Health Service used 399 poor Black men with syphilis as guinea pigs. These state-sanctioned scientists were studying the effects of syphilis on the human body. Because the data for the experiment were to be collected from autopsies of the men, they were deliberately left to degenerate and die. They were never told that they had syphilis, nor were they ever treated for it. Instead, they were told that they were being treated for "bad blood" and were given free "medical exams," free meals, and free burial insurance for participating in the study. The experiment lasted for four decades, from 1932 to 1972, with dozens of men dying and infecting their wives and children. This milestone apology by President Clinton is an example of what I would call an *effective apology*. Furthermore, I would argue that this example should be used as a prototype for the long-overdue effective apology that the U.S. government should make for slavery.

What do I mean by an effective apology? An *effective apology* requires communication between the wrongdoer and the victim. If the victim is to forgive the wrongdoer, how he or she feels about the person who committed the injury must change. The wrongdoer must accept responsibility for his or her actions. If the victim forgives without good reason, he or she is accepting the violation and devaluation of himself or herself. Thus, an apology that leads to forgiveness is something over and above the punishment of a wrongdoer by a judicial system.[3]

How can a government official who was not involved in an unjust act apologize for it? No one can apologize or forgive by proxy. The Clinton administration had nothing to do with the Tuskegee experiments. Yet a distinction must be made between individual reconciliation and national or political reconciliation. A sincere apology by the duly elected representative of a people can mark an important first step in the process of reparation leading to national reconciliation, forgiveness, and healing.[4] Clinton's official apology as the president of the government responsible for those experiments was a first step in this process.

An apology does not mean, however, that the dispute is resolved. In most cases, it is only the first step in a reparation process that may involve restitution, compensation, rehabilitation, satisfaction, and guarantees that the action will not be repeated. In *Taking Responsibility for the Past: Reparation and Historical Injustice*, Janna Thompson writes: "Reparative justice concerns itself with what ought to be done in reparation for injustice and the obligation of wrongdoers, or their descendants or successors, for making this repair."[5] Accordingly, reparative justice is different from retributive justice, which focuses on the punishment of wrongdoers. I would argue that reparations are most appropriate in the case of African Americans for the "peculiar institution" of slavery, since the wrongdoers are either dead or difficult to identify. Reparative justice denotes a space between the vengeance of an abstract wrongdoer and forgiveness from an abstract victim.

Presidential Apologies for Slavery—In Africa

In July 2003, President George W. Bush traveled to Goree Island off the coast of Senegal. At this former slave-trading post, he gave a speech on the topic of slavery in America, citing the efforts of Frederick Douglass, Sojourner Truth, Harriet Beecher Stowe, and Abraham Lincoln to end the "peculiar institution." Agreeing with President John Adams, who called slavery "an evil of colossal magnitude," Bush said,

> At this place, liberty and life were stolen and sold. Human beings were delivered and sorted, and weighed and branded with the marks of commercial enterprises and loaded as cargo on a voyage without return. . . . One of the largest migrations of history was also one of the greatest crimes of history.

Those who survived the middle passage, Bush observed, "entered a society indifferent to their anguish and made prosperous by their unpaid labor." Commenting on the fact that slaves were property and articles of commerce, Bush noted,

> For 250 years the captives endured an assault on their culture and their dignity. . . . . Christian men and women became blind to the clearest commands of their faith and added hypocrisy to injustice. A republic founded on equality for all became a prison for millions. . . . Enslaved Africans heard the ringing promises of the Declaration of Independence and asked the self-evident question, "Then why not me?"[6]

Closing his remarks with a reference to contemporary race relations, Bush concluded,

> My nation's journey toward justice has not been easy and it is not over. The racial bigotry fed by slavery did not end with slavery or

with segregation, and many of the issues that still trouble America
have roots in the bitter experience of other times. But however long
the journey, our destination is set: liberty and justice for all.[7]

Reporters noted that Bush's speech was remarkable in that it deliberately shied away from making excuses, from exonerating the
slave owners and traders because they simply were doing what was
acceptable in the society of that time. They also observed that Bush
honestly appraised contemporary attitudes toward race. At least one
reporter hoped that Bush's Senegal speech would "be a turning point
in his nation's conversation about race, an acknowledgment by our
elected leader of the sins of the past and present, topped with a firm
belief that the problems can be solved, but the memories should never
be erased."[8]

Standing before his African hosts, Bush expressed regret for
America's role in the African slave trade, but he did not apologize to
African Americans for their enslavement. Senegalese President Abdoulaye Wade then reminded him that African nations need help
building their economies so they can overcome slavery's legacy, stating that "all Africans are asking for is infrastructure so Africans can
work."[9]

An almost identical scenario took place a few years earlier in 1998
when President Clinton made the same pilgrimage to Goree Island
and expressed similar regret to his Senegalese hosts for the United
States' role in slavery. He also "regretted" U.S. support for oppressive
dictators during the cold war, tolerance of apartheid in South Africa,
and, during his administration, inaction during the 1994 Rwandan
genocide. Clinton, however, was even more explicit in his refusal to
apologize to African Americans.[10] Earlier in Uganda, however, Clinton
had come close to an apology:

> Going back to the time before we were even a nation, European
> Americans received the fruits of the slave trade. We were wrong in
> that as well, although I must say, if you look at the remarkable dele-
> gation we have here from Congress, from our cabinet and adminis-
> tration, and from the citizens of America, you can see there are many
> distinguished African Americans who are in that delegation who are
> making America a better place today.[11]

One African American member of the delegation, Maxine Waters, the chair of the Congressional Black Caucus, said she would prefer an apology from Senator Jesse Helms (R-NC) than one from President Clinton. She remarked, "I don't know what you say about these kinds of things; do you say that every president should apologize?"[12] Joseph Ndiaye, curator of Maison d'Ésclaves and Goree's undisputed authority on slavery, had a different response: "If President Clinton would like to do that, as the Pope did here, it would be fine. . . . I think it is very important for people not to forget what happened."[13]

What is it that takes American presidents of both parties to Africa to express regret for the slave trade? After all, the president of Benin traveled to Baltimore to apologize to African Americans for African complicity in the slave trade.[14] Wouldn't it be more meaningful for the American president to express regret at Old Point Comfort, Virginia, site of the first arrival of African slaves, or Richmond, Virginia, capital of the Confederacy, or Natchez, Mississippi, or any of the other large slave markets that dot the American South? Perhaps it would be more fitting to apologize from the Neshoba County fairgrounds in Philadelphia, Mississippi, near where three civil rights workers were murdered in 1964 and where President Ronald Reagan launched his 1980 presidential campaign with an appeal to states' rights.[15]

Remembering and Truth Telling: The Second Step

If an apology is the first step in a reparations process, then finding out or remembering the truth is the second step. In our time, truth telling has often taken the form of "truth commissions," established for a short period of time to investigate a pattern of abuse that occurred in the past. These bodies are officially sanctioned by the state to investigate the past and make recommendations for the future. They respond to the victims' specific needs and often provide a personal catharsis to those permitted to "tell their stories." They help reconstruct the past by filling in the blank pages of the historical record. They contribute to justice and accountability, sometimes leading to the prosecution of or even amnesty for the wrongdoers. Finally, they promote reconciliation and reduce conflict over the past by channeling individual desires for revenge into a broader and more constructive institutional context.[16]

Following the Civil War and Emancipation—and in the absence of truth and reconciliation commissions—Americans have had to sort out the relationship between *healing* and *justice*. White Americans in the North chose to heal the wounds with White Americans in the South. This politics of reconciliation, which took several decades and still exists in some forms today, forged a number of unifying myths to make it safe to remember the Civil War. This reconciliation between North and South did not, however, include Black Americans. Even at the fiftieth reunion of battle of Gettysburg in 1913, Black Civil War veterans were literally and figuratively left out of sight and mind. Fifty years later, Lincoln's "rebirth of freedom" had become Woodrow Wilson's forward-looking "righteous peace."[17] The Emancipation Proclamation and the Twelfth through Fifteenth Amendments to the Constitution, also known as the Civil War Amendments, granted Blacks citizenship in the "civic" nation but denied them membership in the "ethnic" nation. That is, the Civil War ended slavery but did not create equality. In short, to satisfy Whites in both the North and the South, Blacks were given citizenship but denied equality.

Whites, Blacks, and others assume the responsibility of historical obligations when they become citizens, whenever and however that occurs. A nation is an intergenerational community, and the existence of historical obligations is predicated on our moral relations to our successors. Our government's ability to make treaties, for example, is dependent on the belief that the agreements we make will be honored by our successors. But we are entitled to interpret the agreements of our predecessors according to our own ideas of justice.[18] We may know, for example, that our "founding fathers" did not include African Americans as citizens in the Declaration of Independence and the Constitution. If our political community is to continue to evolve, we must remedy that.

Many other countries, as well, are having difficulty dealing with the past because the past is still with them.[19] Memory of historical injustice is not a trivial matter to be swept under the rug in the name of progress. Memory or, more precisely, remembering is an important part of the identity of individuals and communities. The moral identity of a nation may be defined as the remembrance of those events that comprise its obligations and entitlements. Practices that require the living to keep the promises and contracts of the dead are inseparable from the value we assign to the self-realization of individuals and their ability to fulfill their responsibility to others.[20] The call for racial reparations challenges the official histories that ignore, explain away, or trivialize mass cruelties. Reparations thus are a way of democratizing history and hearing those voices that were silenced in the past.

Outline of the Book

Chapter 1 of this book gives the background of the political and legal histories of reparations and race relations in the United States. It looks at two presidential commissions on race as well as the how the courts and legislature have handled reparations and race relations. Finally, this chapter discusses the problem of American exceptionalism and how it has hindered productive changes in the United States.

Chapter 2 describes a series of historical events and the reparations efforts that they inspired. Rather than freezing history through categorization, this chapter uncovers the similarities and differences in reparations movements. How have the demands of reparations activists and the response changed over time? To what extent do reparations activists use the language of citizenship and inclusion? Do similarities or different themes dominate particular periods? Do the choices made by reparations proponents in one period constrain and limit future action in the next period?[21]

Chapter 3 compares the most widely known successful reparations movements, the case of Rosewood, Florida, with a similar but unsuccessful effort in Tulsa, Oklahoma. By focusing on two subnational or local events occurring at roughly the same time—the destruction of two Black communities by white lynch mobs—I hope to gain a deeper theoretical insight into the interplay of agency and social structure. Especially by posing counterfactual or "what if" questions, we can try to isolate and abstract the facts of each event that were judged both essential to its historical configuration and a significant historical cause of what followed. If the events are essentially equivalent but the claim for reparations resulted in different outcomes, what does that tell us about the reparations process?

The analysis of the contemporary reparations debate in chapter 4 uses a case study of the Civil Liberties Act of 1988, which is regarded by all as motivating the current efforts for African American reparations. How do the two claims compare? Are the contrasts between the two claims responsible for the different outcomes to date? Or are the deciding factors related to the mobilization of resources or larger social structural forces?

Chapter 5 profiles the 2001 World Conference against Racism as representing the increased importance of a global civil society and an international platform for the discussion of racial reparations.[22] I use social movement theory to examine reparations as a twenty-first-century manifestation of Pan Africanism. Although whether such a movement is forward looking or backward looking is a subject of contestation, most people would agree that it raises novel questions about national identity versus racial identity and constitutional law versus international law. And while the outcomes of such world conferences are often dismissed as meaningless, the primacy of the outcomes masks the benefits of the process. Such sites create a space for education, indoctrination, and the development of leadership. They can serve as a place of discovery, of expressing meanings and creating new identities. In short, they can serve as incubators of change.

Chapter 6 asks what would reparations look like and explores what has been accomplished to date. Museums are being constructed; cities and states are passing reparations-related legislation; and economists are estimating the costs of funding various reparations schemes. How can this process proceed in a way that helps the political community?

The epilogue discusses the impact of Hurricane Katrina on and the response to the reparations discourse. If President Clinton bemoaned the fact that his conversation about race did not imply urgency, then Katrina provides the crisis to motivate dialogue and action. The epilogue examines how that dialogue has been framed and the prospects for "repairing" New Orleans and the nation.

I

A Political and Legal History of Reparations and Race Relations

> We have given this issue [an apology] considerable thought over the course of the year. We conclude that the question of an apology for slavery itself is much too narrow in light of the experience of blacks over the course of this Nation's history.
>
> —From President Clinton's Initiative on Race: The Advisory Board's Report to the President, September 1998

The Politics of Reparations

Presidential Commissions

Beyond the apologies that have been made, such as they are, it is important to understand the political history of race relations and reparation in this country. The U.S. government has never convened anything resembling a truth and reconciliation commission to remember and seek remedy for the wrongs committed from the time of slavery to Jim Crow to today. There have been, however, numerous "study" commissions, and one of the most influential studies of American race relations was, in fact, not a government study. Concerned about the effects of urbanization on the increasing flow of Black migrants to urban centers following World War I, the Carnegie Foundation commissioned and financed the most extensive study of race relations in American history. The Swedish economist Gunnar Myrdal, with the help of a large staff and a number of consultants, conducted the study and published the two-volume study *An American Dilemma: The Negro Problem and Modern Democracy* in 1944.[1] The release of this study at the end of World War II proved to be fortuitous, as it gave the report attention it might not have received before the war.

Widespread urban violence in the mid- to late 1960s prompted a host of studies on race relations. Before these disturbances, social scientists did not seem interested in applying the new science of survey research to Black populations.[2] The most famous of these studies on race relations was the report by the National Advisory Commission on Civil Disorders, which was appointed by President Lyndon B. Johnson on July 29, 1967 (also known as the Kerner Commission after its chair, Illinois Governor Otto Kerner). In an address to the nation two days before he appointed the commission, President Johnson stated:

> Let us condemn the violent few. But let us remember that it is law-abiding Negro families who have really suffered most at the hands of the rioters. It is responsible Negro citizens who hope most fervently—and need most urgently—to share in America's growth and prosperity.
>
> This is not the time to turn away from that goal.
>
> To reach it will require more than laws, more than dollars. It will take renewed dedication and understanding in the heart of every citizen.
>
> I know there are millions of men and women tonight who are eager to heal the wounds that we have suffered; who want to get on with the job of teaching and working and building America. . . .
>
> And let us build something much more lasting: faith between man and man, faith between race and race. Faith in each other—and faith in the promise of beautiful America.[3]

Johnson's appeal for racial reconciliation was complemented by the commission's report calling for the following changes in the racial status quo:

- Opening up opportunities to those who are restricted by racial segregation and discrimination, and eliminating all barriers to their choice of jobs, education and housing.
- Removing the frustration of powerlessness among disadvantaged by providing the means for them to deal with the problems that affect their own lives, and by increasing the capacity of our public and private institutions to respond to these problems.
- Increasing communication across racial lines to destroy stereotypes, to halt polarization, to end distrust and hostility, and to

create common ground for efforts toward common goals of public order and social justice.[4]

The six-hundred-page report contained dozens of recommendations, ranging from education and employment policy to news media coverage and police actions. In light of today's views on taxation, perhaps the most remarkable recommendation is the commission's suggestion to raise taxes: "The major need is to generate new will—the will to tax ourselves to the extent necessary to meet the vital needs of the nation."[5]

In response to Johnson and the commission's calls for action was the sobering perspective of American racial history by sociologist Kenneth Clark, testifying before the commission:

> I read that report . . . of the 1919 riot in Chicago, and it is as if I were reading the report of the investigating committee on the Harlem riot of '35, the report of the investigating committee on the Harlem riot of '43, the report of the McCone Commission on the Watts riot.
>
> I must again in candor say to you members of this Commission— it is a kind of Alice in Wonderland—with the same moving picture re-shown over and over again, the same analysis, the same recommendations, and the same inaction.[6]

In fact, the commission seems to have shared Clark's pessimism in concluding that the "nation is rapidly moving toward two increasingly separate Americas,"[7] that neither the "existing conditions nor the garrison state" nor a state maintained by military power "offer[s] acceptable alternatives for the future of this country."[8]

Sounding much like Martin Luther King Jr. and the other civil rights leaders who called for a massive federal effort to end economic inequality, the commission recommended sweeping reforms in the areas of employment, education, welfare, housing, news reporting, and law enforcement: "Discrimination and segregation have long permeated much of American life; they now threaten the future of every American."[9] Lyndon Johnson was infuriated by the report, arguing that the commission ignored "the Marshall Plan we already have,"[10] Moreover, having identified White racism as "the proximate cause of the riots,"[11] Johnson faced a backlash from Whites, who wanted urban rioters punished rather than rewarded. Thus, bogged down in an increasingly expensive war in Vietnam, the most liberal president in U.S. history responded by creating another commission in June 1968. The National Commission on the Causes and Prevention of Violence, chaired by Milton Eisenhower, submitted its final report some eighteen months later, calling for annual increases in welfare expenditures amounting to $20 billion per year. But now that the United States was embroiled in the Vietnam War, the moment for such action had passed.[12] Moreover, Richard M. Nixon, who was elected president on a platform of law and order and was against school busing, had chosen the garrison state.

More than twenty years later, in 1992, Andrew Hacker's *Two Nations* contended that the Kerner Commission's prediction of a divided America was now a reality. Indeed, much of the social science data examining the impact of Reaganomics on African Americans endorsed his view.[13] Late in his second term, in 1998, President Bill Clinton responded to this racial divide by creating a presidential advisory board on race. Chaired by historian John Hope Franklin, the board was to assist the president in a year-long "great and unprecedented conversation about race."[14] But the board got a late start and its staff and the White House staff constantly disagreed. Conservatives complained that the board was not interested in their views, and some minorities argued the panel was skewed toward African American interests.[15] Whereas Franklin argued that the panel must examine the past, others wanted the focus to be on the future. Franklin also believed that Black–White relations had essentially shaped a paradigm that informed relations with all other people of color in the United States. Not all board members agreed, reflecting some of the same divisions as those in the public at large.

Some civil rights leaders and elected officials praised Clinton for his initiative but urged him to narrow the focus of his effort. Although Angela Oh, a board member, and Franklin maintained that reparations should be central to the commission's work, the president had ruled out reparations as not a "productive" issue for discussion.[16] The board did, however, deal with the issue of an apology for slavery. In a remarkable transcendence of the issue, the board concluded:

> We have given this issue [an apology] considerable thought over the
> course of the year. We conclude that the question of an apology for

slavery itself is much too narrow in light of the experience of blacks over the course of this Nation's history. . . . The apology we must all make cannot be adequately expressed in words, only in actions. We must make a collective commitment to eliminate the racial disparities in opportunity and treatment that characterize too many areas of our National life.[17]

Nonetheless, the actions called for fell far short of the recommendations of the previous race commissions..

The president identified four objectives for the advisory board:

1. Promote a constructive national dialogue to confront and work through challenging issues that surround race.
2. Increase the Nation's understanding of our recent history of race relations and the course our Nation is charting on issues of race relations and racial diversity.
3. Bridge racial divides by encouraging leaders in communities throughout the Nation to develop and implement innovative approaches to calming racial tensions.
4. Identify, develop, and implement solutions to problems in areas in which race has a substantial impact, such as education, economic opportunity, housing, health care, and the administration of justice.[18]

In contrast to the commissions created by President Johnson, Clinton's board limited itself largely to what citizens could do to heal the racial divide rather than what the government could do. An example is the following from the "Ten Things Every American Should Do to Promote Racial Reconciliation":

1. Make a commitment to become informed about people from other races and cultures. Read a book, see a movie, watch a play, or attend a cultural event that will inform you and your family about the history and current lives of a group different than your own.
2. If it is not your inclination to think about race, commit at least one day each month to thinking about how issues of racial prejudice and privilege might be affecting each person you come in contact with that day. The more that people think about how

issues of race affect each person, the easier it will be for Americans to talk honestly about race and eliminate racial divisions and disparities.

3. In your life, make a conscious effort to get to know people of other races. Also, if your religious community is more racially isolated than your local area, encourage it to form faith partnerships with racially different faith groups.[19]

Clinton's board cited the following as the most critical parts of the initiative:

- A President's Council for One America.
- A public education program using a multimedia approach.
- A presidential "call to action" of leaders from all sectors of our society.
- A focus on youth.[20]

None of these "elements" envisioned major expenditures, and there was absolutely no mention of taxation.

As Clinton himself complained, "It's very hard to pierce through the public consciousness and to do a sustained public education campaign in the absence of some great conflict."[21] Indeed, the persons he selected for his commission seemed to be a step removed from the political influence of Johnson's commissions.[22] In short, the president was admitting that only the threat of internal violence or external threat could move the majority of Americans to address racial inequities seriously.

It is not surprising that the only presidential initiative on race in thirty years ended with a whimper, its principal recommendation being for a presidential council on racial disparities. Yet without a crisis to motivate Whites or a specific focus such as reparations to attract Blacks, such efforts are purely symbolic.

Beyond the Symbolic

The general consensus among scholars of American politics is that the demand for civil rights for African Americans pushed race to the forefront of the political agenda, thereby realigning the two major political parties. The strong opposition of the Republican presidential candidate, Barry Goldwater, to the Civil Rights Act of 1964 clearly aligned his party with the tradition of White supremacy, whereas Lyndon Johnson's embrace of the civil rights movement firmly linked the Democratic Party with demands for Black equality. But even though Johnson beat Goldwater in a landslide in 1964, by 1968 the racial landscape had changed. The success of the former Alabama governor, George Wallace, in the presidential primaries in 1968 led Richard Nixon to adopt a "southern strategy," in which he changed the focus of the Republican Party by trying to secure the electoral votes of the historically Democratic southern states.

Although the realignment is apparent and the Republican success in using race as a wedge issue with voters is empirical fact, what is less obvious is the change in racial discourse. Because Black demands were framed in the civil religion that combines our fundamental political beliefs with our dominant religious beliefs, the civil rights movement was able to establish a norm of equality. No longer was it possible for the Wallaces of the world to campaign on blatantly racist appeals. Accordingly, in their calls for "law and order" and their attacks on "welfare queens" and big government, Wallace and his heirs began using coded references to race. So successful was this strategy that in 1980 Ronald Reagan could appeal to "states rights" from Philadelphia, Mississippi, the infamous site of the murder of three civil rights workers in 1964, and avoid being labeled a racist.

Academics have aided in this racial sleight-of-hand by creating the new categories of "racial conservative" and "racial liberal." Edward Carmines and James Stimson, for example, argue that "Goldwater was neither a racial bigot nor, in principle, a segregationist"; however, "his conservative ideology would not allow him to support government ordered desegregation policies."[23] They admit that his "racial conservatism" had a powerful appeal to the anti–civil rights forces that had been deserted by the national Democratic Party. What remains unclear is why Goldwater or any other person who is conservative in principle needs to have their racial views distinguished from their other policy positions. In fact, most of today's Black neoconservatives—who claim Goldwater as an ideological father—also accept the passage of the 1960s civil rights legislation as a positive good that makes possible a color-blind society. If one believes in limiting government action only in the case of race, does that make one a racial conservative or a racist?

Thomas and Mary Edsall make another interesting distinction in their influential work *Chain Reaction: The Impact of Race, Rights, and Taxes on American Politics*. They acknowledge that Wallace pioneered in shifting the political focus from Blacks' moral claim of equality to one of liberal elites punishing the White masses. Moreover, they believe this shift to the right brought no economic benefits to the White masses in the form of tax breaks. Nonetheless, the Edsalls manage to reframe the issue by positing the conflict as a larger debate over values rather than over White privilege. They state that the "rights revolution has focused on individual rights to the exclusion of traditional values like law and order, family, sexual conduct, joblessness, welfare fraud and patriotism."[24] Thus, in one fell swoop the Black demand for equality framed in the language of the Declaration of Independence and the Constitution, as well as the Bible, is removed from the pantheon of traditional values, replaced by racial code words invoking historical White stereotypes of violent Blacks, lazy Blacks, and immoral Blacks.

In his popular *The End of Racism*, Dinesh D'Souza uses these stereotypes to differentiate between racism and discrimination. He contends that Whites view racial discrimination today as a rational response to Black group traits and that Blacks are stuck in the old liberal paradigm of viewing such actions as an immoral assessment of individuals who do not conform to acceptable patterns of group behavior. D'Souza believes that we must separate White attitudes toward Blacks from Whites' treatment of Blacks. In the case of the former, D'Souza cites several studies indicating that White attitudes toward Blacks have dramatically improved in just over a generation. Many of these same studies note, however, that Whites refuse to support programs aimed at redressing past discrimination or regulating current discrimination. Unlike Myrdal, D'Souza believes that this gap between belief and practice is not racism but "rational discrimination." Store owners who keep young Black males out of their shops or cab drivers who refuse to pick them up, D'Souza asserts, are acting rationally and therefore are not racists. According to D'Souza, "prejudices and stereotypes are not intended to explain the origins of group traits, only to take into account their undisputed existence."[25] Moreover, rather than greater contact between groups leading to better relations, it often leads to greater prejudice. While not advocating a return to segregation, D'Souza concludes that "the relativist assumption that groups do not differ and that group generalizations are irrational turns out to be wrong."[26]

This remarkable shift away from liberal individualism and toward group-based discrimination has been labeled the *new racism* by some and *White nationalism* by others.[27] Analyzing racial discourse after the civil rights movement must include a discussion of the effects on it of globalization, privatization, and the mass media. Certainly, gender and class have assumed a central role in the contemporary discussion of racial identity. Yet in many ways, the "new" racism is much like the "old" racism. The same person who relies on group stereotypes to exclude Blacks from the home or workplace also appeals to individual rights to deny any accountability for reparations claims. In short, the historical framing of rights and responsibilities is *always* used to protect White privilege.

A Legal History of Reparations

The liberal individualism that America's founding fathers inherited from John Locke prohibits direct legislative references to group characteristics like race. The U.S. Constitution does not contain the words *Black* and *White*, and the infamous three-fifths compromise, created during the Constitutional Convention to count five slaves as three Whites for representation purposes in the House of Representatives, has more to do with Whites and White regional representation than it does with the character of slaves. Between 1836 and 1844, Congress formally adopted gag rules restricting the receipt of petitions opposing slavery and instituted a ban against mailing abolitionist literature to the South.[28] Fully 90 percent of legislative acts dealing with race fail to include the term *race*.[29] When the U.S. Supreme Court finally did directly address race in the *Dred Scott* decision of 1856, it was to state that the "Black man has no rights the White man is bound to respect."[30] Even though this decision was a major factor leading to the Civil War, it was not the denial of Scott's human rights that inflamed Northern opinion. Rather, it was the Court's denial of Congress's governmental power to regulate slavery that led to conflict. In short, the Court ruled that the federal government has no power to regulate private property even if that property is human. This tendency of the

Court to restrict governmental power when dealing with questions of race became one of its signature characteristics.

After the Civil War, the Fourteenth Amendment to the Constitution was passed explicitly to guarantee due process for former slaves. It states that all people born in the United States are citizens, regardless of race, and therefore deserve equal protection under the law, including the right to vote. The amendment was quickly expanded to include corporations, which then used it almost exclusively to protect corporate rights. The use of the "grandfather clause" to deny Black voting rights is an excellent example of the avoidance of explicit racial terminology in discriminatory legislation.

In contrast to corporations' willingness to embrace group rights is the fundamental unwillingness to recognize the different histories and problems of minority groups. There is ample recognition that the country is polyethnic, but great difficulty in accepting that the country is multinational. As such, national minorities may have special claims, such as reparations, demonstrating that a one-size-fits-all model of minority rights is both counterintuitive and counterproductive. In the 1954 *Brown v. Board of Education of Topeka* ruling, when the U.S. Supreme Court recognized for the first time that racial equality was socially determined, it did not call for a race-conscious redistribution of authority. In fact, desegregation plans usually led to the elimination of Black teachers and school administrators. Nor did the Court recommend any procedures for determining how the negative Black self-esteem it cited as the consequence of segregation was affected by desegregation. In addition, under the influence of *Brown,* other groups that might be termed national minorities have been treated in the same way as Blacks have. Accordingly, the autonomous institutions of Native Americans and Native Hawaiians have been attacked as forms of "racial discrimination" and "racial segregation."[31]

With the 1978 *Regents of the University of California v. Bakke* decision, race consciousness, not racial inequality, became the politically relevant aspect of race relations. By focusing on intentional standards like disparate treatment, decisions by the Rehnquist court succeeded in returning Whites to the center stage of legal concern. As political scientist Lorenzo Morris stated, "To institutionalize racism it was necessary to deinstitutionalize race."[32] Philosopher Charles Mills went even further, arguing that "to a large extent white supremacy may become independent of the feeling of racism" because "the system of ac-

cumulated, entrenched privilege can reproduce itself through motivation that is simply self- and group-interested."[33]

The legal scholar Randall Kennedy reminds us, however, that
even the most outspoken opponents of affirmative action on the high
court are not adverse to using racial criteria in the administration of
criminal justice. He notes that before 1986, the Supreme Court permitted prosecutors to challenge jurors on a racially discriminatory basis.
Chief Justice Warren Burger and then Associate Justice William Rehnquist dissented from the decision in *Batson v. Kentucky* that outlawed
such discriminatory racial challenges. Since that decision, both Justices
Anthony Scalia and Clarence Thomas have expressed their unhappi-
ness with the Court's efforts to prohibit all racially discriminatory pre-
emptory challenges. More to their liking was the Court's decision in
United States v. Martinez-Fuerte, which allowed the U.S. Border Patrol
to use "apparent" Mexican ancestry as a basis for determining whom
to question for purposes of investigating criminal trafficking in illegal
workers. Conservative justices found this action a "reasonable" use of
race that posed no constitutional difficulty.[34] Thus it seems that the use
of race is "reasonable" in criminal actions but "suspect" in aiding racial minorities.

Taking Reparations to the Courts

Without the political clout necessary to push reparations into the
policymaking arena, as demonstrated by Clinton's Presidential Advisory Board on Race, many proponents of reparations have turned to
the courts. Unlike past cycles of racial reparations, legal scholars have
taken the lead in framing the current discourse.

These legal scholars have clearly been influenced by the legal
claims filed by persons seeking reparations for past harms. These
scholars also cite the success that some Holocaust victims have had in
their claims against corporations for both stolen property and slave labor. Ironically, the Clinton administration played a key role in the
struggle for reparations for Holocaust victims. President Clinton appointed a special assistant, Deputy Assistant Secretary of State Stuart
Eizenstat, a Jewish American lawyer from Atlanta, to search the
U.S. wartime archives for proof of Switzerland's complicity with the
Nazis. The Senate held hearings, and in 1998, Senator Alfonse D'Am-
ato (R-NY) introduced legislation creating the Presidential Advisory
Commission on Holocaust Assets in the United States. According to

Michael Bazyler, although the money was coming from Europe and most of its recipients would be European, the movement for reparations was essentially a U.S.-based and U.S.-coordinated operation, with major support from the White House. In addition to numerous Clinton officials working almost full time on Holocaust restitution, nearly one thousand state and local officials in every state joined the campaign to persuade the Europeans to pay for their financial misdeeds during the war. These lawsuits eventually forced European governments to establish various historical commissions that have unearthed new and valuable information about war crimes against Jewish citizens.

The support of the U.S. government and politicians from both major political parties for Holocaust claims contrasts with their opposition to African American reparations claims or even to a study of the merit of such claims. In addition, Japanese Americans sued the U.S. government for their internment during World War II. As we shall see in chapter 4, their pressing their legal case helped bring about legislative action that resulted in the Civil Liberties Act of 1988, signed by President Ronald Reagan.

African Americans have filed lawsuits in New York, New Jersey, California, Louisiana, Illinois, and Texas seeking reparations (see table 1.1 for the statuses and types of reparations cases filed). Attorneys Ed Fagan and Daedria Farmer-Paellman, who filed most of these lawsuits, charged that institutions that owned, used, or insured slaves violated domestic and international law by conspiring to deprive the slaves and their descendants of their property. But a similar lawsuit, *Obadele v. United States,* was recently dismissed by the federal claims court.[35]

Another very prominent group of lawyers and legal scholars, including Charles Ogletree Jr., Willie Gray, Johnnie Cochran, Dennis Sweet, Adjoa Aiyetoro, and Randall Robinson, have filed many lawsuits entailing both public and private parties and at both the national and international levels. Ogletree divides the current reparations cases into three types. The first type is the federal lawsuits consolidated in the Northern District of Illinois that raise five claims: conspiracy, demand for accounting, human rights violations, conversion, and unjust enrichment. The defendants in this type of lawsuit are corporations, which contend that the plaintiffs lack standing and the events in question exceed the statute of limitations. A second type of lawsuit against

Table 1.1

Statuses and Types of Reparations Cases

Cases against a governmental entity		
1916	*Johnson v. MacAdo*	Plaintiffs claimed cotton tax revenue as unpaid wages (dismissed).
1974	*Pollard v. United States*	Plaintiffs were victims of the Tuskegee syphilis experiment (settled).
1994	*Berry v. United States*	Plaintiff sought either title to 40 acres of U.S. government land in San Francisco or $3 million in damages (dismissed).
1995	*Cato v. United States*	Plaintiffs sought an apology and $100 million in compensation for kidnapping and slavery (dismissed at the federal level).
1997	*Pigford v. Glickman*	Plaintiffs (Black farmers) sued U.S. Agriculture Department over discrimination (settled).
2003	*Alexander v. Governor of State of Oklahoma*	Plaintiffs were victims of Tulsa race riot (dismissed).
Cases against a private entity		
2002	*Farmer-Paellmann v. FleetBoston Financial Corporation, Aetna, Inc., CSX, C.A*	Plaintiffs claimed that corporation profited from holding contracts on slaves.
2002	*Barber v. New York Life Insurance Co.*	Plaintiff claimed that corporation profited from holding contracts on slaves.
2003	*Johnson v. Aetna Life Insurance Co.*	Plaintiff claimed that corporation profited from holding contracts on slaves.
2003	*Hurdle v. FleetBoston Financial Corp.*	Plaintiff (state of California) claimed that corporation profited from holding contracts on slaves.

Sources: Roy L. Brooks, *Atonement and Forgiveness* (Berkeley: University of California Press, 2004); and Charles J. Ogletree Jr., "Repairing the Past," 38 *Harv. C.R.–C.L.L. Rev.* 279 (2003).

corporations was filed in California under the California Business and Protection Code, section 17200, which permits suing for any type of fraudulent business practice, apparently including slavery. The third type of lawsuit does not involve slavery. In Oklahoma, the Reparations Coordinating Committee and local counsel in Tulsa were the plaintiffs in a suit against the state and local government as defendants. The statute of limitations remains an obstacle, however. According to Ogletree, the plaintiffs estimated that the harm done to African Americans amounts to trillions of dollars. If successful, these lawsuits would use any money awarded to create a community trust fund for those people who have suffered most.[36]

The reparations issue has used a variety of forms, such as contract law, trust law, restitution law, and tort law. For example, cases involving contract law focus on the unpaid labor of slaves or the underpayment of Black labor in a segregated labor force. In a claim using trust law, the descendants of slave masters become the trustees of a constructive trust composed of slaves' withheld wages. The slaves' descendants are the beneficiaries. In accordance with the law of restitution, the beneficiaries of goods and services may not be unjustly enriched at the expense of another person's disadvantage. Finally, tort law permits claims based on a cultural assault denying the humanity of Blacks and, for many, leading to an inferiority complex.[37]

All proponents of legal claims to racial reparations face formidable doctrinal hurdles. All jurisdictions use the statute of limitations in order to discourage stale claims and ensure that credible evidence still exists to allow the proper determination of a conflict. For the most serious wrongs, such as murder and crimes against humanity, there are exceptions. In addition, the doctrine of tolling the statute of limitations, also known as the continuing wrong theory, enables plaintiffs to sue despite the passage of time if they were prevented from suing earlier or if an earlier suit would have been futile. Also under the continuing wrong theory, the clock does not start running on the statute of limitations until the wrong culminates in an act of finality. Fraudulently concealing the availability of or grounds for an action is another standard exception to the statute of limitations.[38]

Suits against governments confront the doctrine of sovereign immunity, which prohibits lawsuits unless the government consents. For example, in the case of the 1921 Tulsa race "riot," sovereign immunity was a major barrier to those claiming that the city and state governments were responsible for their loss of property. The U.S. Supreme Court recently cited the Eleventh Amendment as protecting the states from being sued in federal courts. It is doubtful that Congress would be willing to challenge the states' immunity based on its power under the Thirteenth and Fourteenth Amendments.

Standing, or the legal right to initiate a lawsuit, is a third doctrinal hurdle for reparations advocates seeking legal redress. To bring a suit, the plaintiff (the victim) must have been injured; the defendant (the perpetrator) must have caused the injury; and the injury must be subject to redress (compensation). Racial reparations claims based on slavery are third-party claims, which makes it difficult to identify the perpetrators and victims. According to the theory of continuing group damage engendered by past wrongs, current victims are tied to past victims, and linking past perpetrators to those currently benefiting from the wrong is complicated, as is determining the damages owed.[39] In the 1995 case of *Cato v. United States*, the Ninth Circuit Court of Appeals dismissed the slave reparations claim for an apology and $100 million, stating that it could find no legally cognizable basis for advancing the case. The court asserted that the government had not given permission to the plaintiffs to sue and that the case was being filed too long after slavery had ended.[40]

In the *Cato* case, the court recognized the fundamental problem: we do not have a legal theory that can deal conceptually with group reparations claims. Because the paradigm for American law is individualistic, transactional, and oriented to the present, it assumes that injury is individual and that the harm is material/transactional and current. In general, the law does not acknowledge past group claims,[41] a procedural bias that leads to a substantive bias.

Activist lawyer and professor Mari Matsuda argues that this lack of legal redress for racist acts is often a more serious injury than the acts themselves because it signifies the victims' political nonpersonhood.[42] In her 1987 article, "Looking to the Bottom," Matsuda goes beyond the traditional paradigm by contending that reparations claims should be considered claims by a group of victims against a group of perpetrators, instead of by individual victims against individual perpetrators. This approach enables her to offer an alternative test for gauging the relationship between past wrong and present claim. Matsuda believes that a racial group's victim status should continue as long as the victims, as a class, continue to be in a stigmatized position enhanced or promoted by the wrongful act in question. In short, she substitutes racial identity for victim identity.[43]

In her essay "If the Shoe Fits, Wear It," legal scholar Vicene Verdun borrowed Matsuda's group or community focus but shifted from legal grounds to political grounds to build a case for reparations for slavery. Verdun advocates reparations for both economic and emotional injury, that is, the failure to pay for slaves' labor and "the presumption of inferiority, devaluation of self-esteem, and other emotional injuries, pain, and suffering, that resulted from the institution of slavery."[44]

In her essay "The Master's Tools, from the Bottom Up," another legal scholar, Rhonda Magee, sees reparations as yet a third way between separation and integration. She portrays reparations as a way to achieve a multicultural balance that she calls *cultural equity*. Education and political participation are important parts of Magee's remedy.[45]

In perhaps the most widely cited article on reparations, Robert Westley's "Many Billions Gone" builds a case for legislative reparations through a historical analysis of government discrimination against Blacks since slavery. Westley links this discrimination to current gaps between Blacks and Whites in wealth and education. The reparations movement, he maintains, is a response to the demise of affirmative action and should be seen as an entitlement rather than a need.[46]

These recent innovative legal approaches differ significantly from Boris Bittker's traditional civil rights approach. In his 1973 *The Case for Reparations*, he avoids the question of standing by focusing on segregated institutions' harm to living victims. His work dismisses slavery as weakening the legal claim and instead concentrates on the harm caused by segregated schools. The legal basis for his reparations claim is the U.S. Code, title 42, section 1983. Enacted more than a century ago as section 1 of the Ku Klux Klan Act, it provides that

> every person who, under color of any statute . . . of any State or Territory, subjects . . . any citizen of the United States . . . to the deprivation of any rights . . . secured by the Constitution and laws, shall be liable to the party injured in an action at law, suit in equity, or other proper proceeding for redress.[47]

Bittker's call for class action in the courts never materialized, however, and today he seems to favor congressional legislation.[48] Although legal action for redress in the case of segregated schools has not developed as Bittker hoped, political action seems to be producing some results.

In 1959 in response to the *Brown* decision, officials in Prince Edward County, Virginia, chained the doors of the public schools doors rather than allowing Black children to sit beside White children in the classrooms. Five decades later, the Virginia legislature, with the financial help of billionaire John Kluge, acknowledged its history of discrimination by offering reparations in the form of scholarships. The state provides up to $5,500 a year in college assistance for any state resident who was denied a proper education when the public schools were shut down. Several thousand students are eligible, and so far more than eighty applicants have been accepted.[49]

Another group of legal scholars have framed the issue as a matter for international law. This is perhaps best exemplified by Anthony Gifford, who makes the following seven assertions related to international law:

1. The enslavement of Africans was a crime against humanity as defined by the charter of the Nuremberg Tribunal.
2. International law recognizes that those who commit crimes against humanity must make reparations as defined by the Permanent Court of International Justice in 1928.
3. There is no legal barrier preventing the claim for reparations given payments to descendants and even states that did not exist at the time of the crimes such as Israel.
4. The claim would be brought on behalf of all Africans, in Africa and in the Diaspora through a representative body.
5. Claims would be brought against the governments of those countries that promoted and were enriched by the slave trade and the institution of slavery.
6. The claim amount should be assessed by experts in each aspect of life and in each region affected by the institution of slavery.
7. The claim, if not settled by agreement, would ultimately be determined by a special International Tribunal recognized by all parties.[50]

Gifford's argument is bolstered by legal scholars' contention that slave labor is a violation of human rights so serious that it is one of those violations viewed as *jus cogens*, or peremptory norms of international law from which no derogation is permitted.[51] Human rights groups like Human Rights Watch have proposed the establishment of national and international panels that would, in effect, serve as truth commissions and would be guided by international human rights law in making recommendations for reparations.[52]

Adopting an international law framework can be seen as a way of circumventing the doctrinal obstacles in U.S. law. International law offers several provisions for the redress of group harm. The Articles on State Responsibility of the International Law Commission, for example, provide that full reparation for the injury caused by the internationally wrongful act shall take the form of restitution, compensation, and satisfaction, either singly or in combination. But those same articles also acknowledge that a state is not in violation of an international obligation unless it is bound by the obligation in question at the time the act occurs: the doctrine of intertemporal law. This guarantee against the retrospective application of international law in matters of state responsibility also is found in article 11 (2) of the Universal Declaration of Human Rights, article 7 (1) of the European Convention for the Protection of Human Rights and Fundamental Freedoms, and article 15 (1) of the International Covenant on Civil and Political Rights.[53]

Of course, proponents of African American reparations face the same basic problem at the international level as at the national level. The same liberal individualism that characterizes the American legal process also prevents the United States from ratifying many international human rights instruments. Most recently, the United States not only refused to become a party to the new International Criminal Court but also is actively trying, through bilateral agreements, to undermine the participation of others in the court.[54] When the United States has ratified international human rights treaties, it has been with the condition that the treaty is non-self-executing; that is, it requires national legislation in order to be enforced.

From the Courts to the Legislature

The common thread running through most of these legal approaches—both traditional and novel—is the shift from the courts to the legislature for redress. By shifting from the legal to the political, a wider range of remedies has become available. Litigation is based on a confrontational model that tends to replicate the traditional individualistic structure of rights arguments. African Americans assert a claim right to certain property and White (and other) Americans assert a liberty right not to have their property seized.

Eric Miller, a legal scholar, offers a conversational model viewing reparations as a means of engaging in a national dialogue about race that is not limited to "preaching to the choir" but attempts to examine the complexity of modern race relations. Reparations in the form of a reckoning depend on the injury inflicted. Since the injury was not of one type or degree, no one "reckoning" or remedy is possible. A conversational approach, therefore, would open the discourse to a wide variety of political, moral, educational, and economic solutions.[55]

Roy Brooks, another legal scholar, also wants to shift the debate away from the confrontational model. He contends that the premises of a litigation approach to slave redress include compensation for the victims and punishment or White guilt for the perpetrators. The typical settlement agreement in civil litigation contains an exculpatory clause in which the defendant expressly denies any liability. Thus, redress received under the tort model is not true "reparation," and the compensation does nothing to mend the broken relationship between victim and perpetrator.[56]

Brooks offers an atonement model in which the government has a moral obligation to atone for its past atrocities. Because the United States has not atoned for slavery or Jim Crow, it has a moral obligation to do so. Because this is a matter of morality rather than legality, the duty to apologize remains as long as the perpetrator or its successor-in-interest is alive. Brooks adds that it would be a cruel irony if the perpetrators could absolve themselves of the moral duty to apologize simply by removing all their victims. Likewise, the perpetrators should not be denied an opportunity for redemption if, for example, the victims still living decided not to come forward and make their presence known. According to the atonement model, then, apology benefits the perpetrator as much as it does the victim.[57]

Brooks hopes that ultimately the government and the slaves' descendants can reconcile through moral reflection rather than political confrontation. He sees White opposition to slave redress as having two sources. One is those Whites who fear that they or their children would be racially disadvantaged if Blacks were given a genuine or measurable equality of opportunity. A second source of opposition is those Whites whose unbending belief in individualism leads them to oppose government benefits for "special interests."[58]

Even though the conversational model and the atonement model move the reparations discourse away from the obstacles and limitations of the litigation model, they are not without problems. The recognition that reparations is really a political and a moral problem rather than a strictly legal issue opens the discourse to a wider range of approaches and, hence, solutions. But given White opposition and Brooks's belief that racism often is cognitive rather than motivational, it is difficult to see how moral reflection rather than political confrontation will lead to reparations. Nothing in the history of race relations in the United States suggests that "moral reflection" can take place without political confrontation.

The Problem of American Exceptionalism

The issue of African American reparations is ultimately a question of how to guarantee the rights of a minority despite the opposition of a democratic majority. Reparations, including an apology for slavery, challenge the notion of American democracy and, implicitly, the very foundation of "American exceptionalism." Because our image of ourselves as American citizens and our role in the world rest on the belief in our status as a "chosen people," any challenge to that image falls outside the confines of public discourse. It is this national identity that enables the U.S. government to support reparations claims against European governments but to reject the claims against it from its own citizens.

From our "founding fathers" to our present-day political leaders of the major parties, all embrace the idea of American exceptionalism. Thomas Paine, an idealist, argued we had the power to remake the world, whereas George Washington, a realist, warned, in his second inaugural address, of entangling foreign alliances. John Adams always considered "the settlement of America with reverence and wonder, as the opening of a grand scheme and design in Providence for the illumination and emancipation of the slavish part of mankind all over the earth."[59] But as vice president in 1795, he said he had never given much thought to the problem of Negro slavery. When campaigning for the presidency, George W. Bush criticized the Clinton administration for acting like the world's policeman. Indeed, President Clinton's secretary of state, Madeline Albright, declared the United States to be the "one essential nation." But when he assumed office, Bush, the realist, initially demonstrated American exceptionalism by withdrawing from bilateral agreements with the Russians and then from such multilateral agreements as the Kyoto Protocol.[60] The week before the events of September 11, 2001, Bush refused to send Secretary of State Colin Powell or any other high-level official to the UN World Conference against Racism. After the attacks, the president, now an idealist, pursued a different kind of exceptionalism, declaring to the nations of the world that you are either "for us or against us" in the United States' self-proclaimed "war against terrorism." In his second inaugural address, Bush revealed his administration's intention to take democracy and freedom to every corner of the globe.

Its proponents in the academy have matched the long and prominent history of American exceptionalism in politics. The distinguished social scientist Daniel Bell differentiates between "uniqueness," which every nation can claim, and "exceptionalism," in the sense of being exemplary—"a light unto the nations, immune from the social ills and decadence that have beset all other republics in the past, a nation exempt from the 'social laws' of development that all nations eventually follow."[61] He also notes that the founders of the United States believed that the country would be morally superior and that the institutional foundation they provided had given its citizens a degree of social stability unmatched in history. The United States is perhaps the only complete civil society in political history, he continues, "an open society [in which] each man was free to 'make himself' and to make his fortune."[62] Bell's discussion never mentions the institution of slavery.

Seymour Martin Lipset, another distinguished social scientist, is even less restrained in his praise:

> However one comes to this debate, there can be little question that the hand of providence has been on a nation which finds a Washington, a Lincoln, or a Roosevelt when it needs him. When I write the above sentence, I believe that I draw scholarly conclusions, although I will confess that I write also as a proud American.[63]

Unlike Bell, however, Lipset does not ignore the status of African Americans but believes that their situation has been "qualitatively different" from that of any other racial or ethnic minority in the United States. It was the potentially complementary egalitarian and individualistic elements in the American creed that enabled the civil rights movement to succeed, says Lipset. The more recent focus of the civil rights movement on substantive equality and preferential treatment conflicts with the creed's individualistic achievement–oriented element. Accordingly, Lipset attributes the opposition to the government's enforcement of a group rights for Blacks to general principle rather than racism.[64]

The resurgent American exceptionalism vigorously promoted by the Bush administration has found its supporters in the academic community as well. Liberal proponents of the case for American empire, like Michael Ignatieff and Sebastian Mallaby, support American intervention to promote human rights and restore order to failed states. The more numerous conservative advocates of American empire, such as Max Boot, William Kristol, and James Kurth, are unapologetic supporters of not only American military power but also American rule. Indeed, Boot even suggested the creation of a new colonial office to better administer our new possessions in the Middle East and Asia.

Placing himself somewhere between the right and left (always a safe choice), Niall Ferguson argues in his *Colossus: The Rise and Fall of the American Empire* for a benevolent American imperialism. But his critique of the way that Bush has pursued foreign policy comes from the right, not the center. Ferguson regards both defense spending and American military casualties as being relatively low. In fact, he fears that Bush and the Republican Party will be defeated by the cost of the war in Iraq and pull out American troops too soon. He notes as well that substantial numbers of American troops have been stationed in both Germany and Japan since World War II and in Korea since the Korean War, in addition to the more than seven hundred U.S. military installations worldwide. Even so, Americans live in a state of imperial denial, which has led to three problems. The first is the huge economic deficit, which Ferguson recommends shrinking by reducing domestic spending on entitlement programs like Medicare. The second problem is the attention deficit, which Ferguson says militates against the farsighted leadership necessary for proper nation building. The third problem, the manpower deficit, limits the number of combat-ready troops necessary to defend the empire (even a benevolent one). Here his solution is telling: "If one adds together the illegal immigrants, the jobless and the convicts, there is surely ample raw material for a larger American army." Moreover, "reviving the draft would not necessarily be unpopular, so long as it was *appropriately targeted*."[65] Ferguson recalls that Britain solved its manpower shortage during wartime by using colonial troops, which made up roughly a third of the military in World I and almost half in World War II.

Nowhere in his discussion of benevolent American imperialism does Ferguson directly confront the issue of race. His index has one entry for African Americans and one entry for racism in the United

States. Africa's current problems he attributes to corrupt and ineffi-
cient rulers and not to the continent's colonial past. Although he
chides Americans for denying their imperial past and present, he ig-
nores the fact that much of this denial is rooted in a history of a now-
discredited, overt, and extreme racism.

Why Reparations, Why Now?

The discourse on reparations is a reminder of our history, which was
not benevolent. It also is a reminder of who bears the burden of empire and who benefits from it. It creates an opposing public space to
confront the proponents of American empire and to promote an alternative vision of the future. With this in mind, I try to answer two
central questions here: After at least two decades of relative obscu-
rity, why have racial reparations become a primary issue in the African American community? And why is the larger political community—in an "age of apology"—so opposed to even discussing racial
reparations?

Reparations is a divisive issue precisely because it is impossible to
avoid directly talking about race and race privilege. Slavery has become a focal point in this discussion because there were no White
slaves in the United States. Finally, even though there are no surviving
slaves now, there are many survivors of the legalized apartheid that
existed nationally until 1954 and in some state constitutions through
2000.

The removal of legal apartheid or the formal barriers of racial segregation led to a transitional period of what the political scientist and
Nobel laureate Ralph Bunche called the social construction of race.[66]
Both Black and White opponents of reparations argue that we currently live in a color-blind society in which race is irrelevant and the
past is past. From another perspective, those people with a mixed racial heritage contend that all their ancestral roots should be acknowledged and celebrated. Racial reparations therefore both challenge and
complicate issues of racial identification. Most leaders of the reparations movement in the United States reflect an earlier tradition that
saw the "one drop" rule or custom[67] as imposing an external unity.
The politics of reparations thus has forced an internal racial discussion
among Blacks over issues of racial identity.

One of the great political accomplishments of the Reagan revolution was to succeed in labeling civil rights interests as special interests. The fact that so many White Americans accepted this designation and supported Reagan's racial policies is indicative of the failure of American society to see the civil rights movement as a positive development for all Americans. This illiberal tradition in American politics[68] recently reached new extremes after September 11 with attacks on civil liberties and civil rights.

As an issue, reparations permit Blacks to assume the higher moral ground that was lost in the post–civil rights movement period. Unlike affirmative action, welfare, and other social programs, reparations discourse avoids counterarguments of merit or behavior. Reparations demands also tend to be redistributive rather than individual and incremental. Finally, reparations attempt to reclaim the sense of identity created during the civil rights and Black power movements. From Phyllis Wheatly to Gunnar Myrdal's exaggerated American to today's color blindness, Blacks could become modern political subjects only by giving up their Black identity. To become modern political subjects, that is, citizens, they would have to be remade and, in the remaking, would no longer be Black. Building on the ideas of the activists and scholars of the 1960s, reparations demand both citizenship and Black identity.

2

From Forty Acres to "We Must Have Our Money"

Reparations from Antebellum to Civil Rights America

We have turned, or are about to turn, loose four million slaves without a hut to shelter them or a cent in their pockets. The infernal laws of slavery have prevented them from acquiring an education, understanding the commonest laws of contract, or of managing the ordinary business of life. The congress is bound to provide for them until they can take care of themselves. If we do not furnish them with homesteads, and hedge them around with protective laws; if we leave them to the legislation of their late master, we had better have left them in bondage.

—Representative Thad Stevens, from W. E. B. DuBois,
Black Reconstruction in America 1860–1880

What's de use of being free if you don't own land enough to be buried in? Might juss as well stay slave all you days.

—Sixty-year-old ex-slave, from Roger L. Ransom and
Richard Sutch, *One Kind of Freedom: The Economic
Consequences of Emancipation*

We come not here for to ask an alm,
We must have our money or never shall yield,
But demand a debt from Uncle Sam,
We must have our money or never shall yield.

—Ex-slave pension song from A. Scales and J. W. Anderson
Committee, Record Group 15, Ex-Slave Pension
Movement, box 1, envelope 5

Fugitive Slave Laws and the Legal Invisibility of Blacks

Sometime in September 1850, a group of slaves escaped from Maryland and were known to be "lurking" near the village of Christiana in

Lancaster County, Pennsylvania. Their owner, Edward Gorsuch, a citizen of Maryland, came to Philadelphia to obtain, from a commissioner of the court, warrants for their arrest. These warrants were given to Harvey Kline, an officer of the court, to carry out.

On the morning of September 11, Kline, accompanied by Gorsuch, his son, nephew, cousins, and two other Maryland citizens proceeded to the house of a man, Parker, in Christiana. They then saw one of the fugitive slaves leaving the house, who on seeing them, retreated into the house and upstairs. Gorsuch pursued him and, on entering the house, found a group of armed Negroes resisting the fugitives' capture. While one of them fired a gun at Gorsuch, others threw objects from the upper windows. Kline fired a warning shot, displayed his warrant, and the two parties began to negotiate. As time passed, Castner Haney, who was White, and a large crowd of Blacks armed with various weapons gathered outside. Seeing the reinforcements, the Negroes in the house yelled in defiance, and the group of approximately one hundred Blacks attacked the slave hunters. Gorsuch was murdered and his son was shot, but the others escaped with their lives.

The Negroes were arrested and charged with murder, and Hanway, the White defendant, also was charged with "treason against the United States." In his instructions to the jury, Circuit Justice Grier noted that although an accessory to a murder must be present in order to be held liable as a principal, in treason all are principals whether or not they are present. The bill charged Hanway with "wickedly and traitorously intending to levy war against the United States."[1] The U.S. Constitution defines treason specifically and only as "levying war against the government."

The judge framed the case for the jury by reciting a brief history of the Fugitive Slave Act of 1793, which, he stated was essential to the formation of the Union. But, Grier added, this act was liable to very great abuse, since it did not distinguish the arrest of a master from the seizure of the vile kidnapper and man stealer. The new fugitive slave legislation contained in the Compromise of 1850 remedied this evil by giving the arrested party a hearing and thus protecting the free colored man. Opposition to the law, Grier stated, stems not from any danger to freemen of color but "because it is an act which can be executed, and the constitutional rights of the master in some measure preserved." "The real objection," Grier noted, "is to the constitution itself, which is supposed to be void in this particular from the effect of some 'higher law,' whose potential influence can equally annul all human and all divine law."[2] Despite his distaste for abolitionists whom "the blood taints with even deeper dye the skirts of those who promulgate doctrines subversive of all morality and all government" and who have sown the natural fruit of this murderous tragedy, he did not believe that Hanway was guilty of treason. Grier argued that there was no proof of previous conspiracy to make a general and public resistance to any law of the United States and that there was no evidence that any person concerned in the transaction knew there were such acts of Congress or had any intention other than to protect one another from what they termed *kidnappers*. Accordingly the jury found for the defendant.

This remarkable case contains two themes of particular relevance to this history of reparations. The first is the government's active opposition to abolitionist activity. Far from being neutral or detached from the institution of slavery, in this instance the government viewed an attack on slavery as an attempt to overthrow the government itself. That a local and seemingly spontaneous incident would be blown up into a case of treason speaks volumes about the fear of Black freedom either felt or promoted by Whites in order to maintain the institution of slavery.

Second, the fact that only Haney, a White man, was charged with treason illustrates the antebellum invisibility of Blacks. The judge contended that the new fugitive slave provisions were intended to protect free Blacks but nonetheless ignored their active resistance to the law's implementation. Once again it appears that only Whites have the capacity to "conspire" against the government. Thus the judge framed the law as in the best interest of Blacks—a theme repeated by President Andrew Johnson after the Civil War and by government officials investigating ex-slave pension societies in the twentieth century. If some Blacks and Whites did not see the benefits of this law, the government would repress their efforts to mobilize against it. In short, the government actively opposed the abolitionist movement.

The Revolutionary War presented political opportunities to African Americans, with their appeals for justice framed by the founding fathers' Enlightenment liberalism. But without citizenship rights, African Americans found it difficult to mobilize for action, as the following illustrates:

We beseech your impartial attention to our hard condition, not only
with respect to our personal sufferings, as freemen, but as a class of
that people who, distinguished by color, are therefore with a degrad-
ing partiality, considered by many, even of those in eminent stations,
as unentitled to that public justice and protection which is the great
object of Government.[3]

Absalom Jones wrote this statement as part of his petition to Congress
on behalf of four Black men who had been manumitted in North Carolina in 1797 but were now in danger of being re-enslaved. Jones
pointed out a "governmental defect" that allowed freemen to be seized
and sold into slavery and asked Congress to find a remedy. But Congress refused to accept the petition, as it did all other slave petitions for
many decades. Other Blacks saw their status as more than a defect in
the U.S. Constitution and were profoundly alienated by it. According
to Mark Brandon, this alienation accounts for Blacks' reluctance either
to legitimize the Constitution by appealing though its categories and
institutions or to confirm their political identities by referring to it.[4]

Perhaps it was this practice by Congress that led historian Donald
Robinson to say that with the exception of foreigner Toussaint L'Ouverture, "in national politics, black people were almost entirely mute,
politically passive."[5] Even if the Black voice in national politics were
silenced, the issue of racial slavery would remain central to the national political discourse, which offers three themes that are relevant
to reparations: the slave as property, the unconflicted view of Whiteness, and colonization.

Slavery was important to every North American colony. In fact, in
one form or another, Brandon asserts, slavery was at stake in almost
every significant debate in American national politics.[6] The rise of capitalism turned the desire to prosper into a constant of human behavior. According to sociologist Orlando Patterson, what made America
unique was that for aristocrats, property flowed from power and privilege but that for the new bourgeoisie, power and privilege flowed
from property.[7] Put another way, if property rights were the foundation of liberal theories of political order, property-in-oneself would be
the basis for conceptualizing republican government and political democracy. Self-ownership, in turn, was a cornerstone of both the market contract and the social contract.[8] Thus the role of slaves as property assumed great importance during the Revolutionary era.

Slavery developed, says Robinson, through a series of "unthinking decisions" made in various circumstances by men of various temperaments and predispositions. Despite its varied locations, the institution acquired the same characteristics: it was perpetual and heritable; it was confined to Blacks; unlike other forms of servitude in America, it typically resulted in the total deprivation of civil, political, and social rights; and unlike previous kinds of slavery in human history, its victims were denied any opportunity to improve themselves and were thus stigmatized by virtually indelible "badges of inferiority" that pursued them even after they were emancipated.[9]

The first "three-fifths" debate took place not in regard to representation in Congress but in regard to property. Alexander Hamilton and James Madison insisted that in order to create an effective government, Congress needed an independent source of revenue. In 1783, therefore, a congressional committee suggested that the Articles of Confederation be amended to base the distribution of the tax burden on a census of the population rather than on land values. It was at this point that the so-called federal ratio of calculating the value of a slave at three-fifths the value of a free man was first established in American law.[10] This "federal ratio" subsequently became the basis for enumerating the slave population for the census that would determine the states' representation in the House of Representatives.

Apart from issues of taxation and representation, slavery as a legal institution treated slaves as property that could be transferred, assigned, inherited, or posted as collateral. Since Whites could not be enslaved or held as slaves, the racial line between Black and White was critical. According to legal scholar Cheryl Harris, it became a line of demarcation from the potential threat of commodification, and it determined the allocation of the benefits and burdens of this form of property. The franchise may have been extended to White men without property at the same time that free Blacks were specifically disenfranchised to shift the property required for voting from land to Whiteness.[11]

Even though the designation *white* does not appear in the U.S. Constitution or the Declaration of Independence, it was widely used in American political discourse and in an immense body of statutory law. *White* appears in the Articles of Confederation, and in the colonies it determined who could marry whom, who could join the militia, and who could vote or hold office; and the word was used in laws governing contracts, indenture, and enslavement. "Although there were some exceptions," historian Matthew Frye Jacobson pointed out, "most laws of this kind delineated the populace along lines of color, and the word 'white' was commonly used in conferring rights, never in abridging them (with the single exception of proscribing whom 'whites' could marry)."[12]

Politically restrictive uses of the word *white* appeared in the constitutions of Missouri (1812), Mississippi (1817), Connecticut (1818), California (1849, 1879), and Minnesota Territory (1849). Conversely, Jacobson noted, eighteen state constitutions specifically classed Blacks as "dependents," thereby giving them the same political status as White women and children of all colors. In fact, to include Blacks as citizens would have been contradictory, since a citizen was, at bottom, "someone who could help put down a slave rebellion or participate in Indian wars."[13] Thus with the nation's first naturalization law in 1790, which limited naturalized citizenship to "free white persons," the government presented an unconflicted view of the presumed character and unambiguous boundaries of Whiteness.[14]

Political philosopher Hannah Arendt famously declared that the French Revolution was a social revolution and that the American Revolution was a political revolution. Although true in many ways, this does not mean that the American Revolution had no social consequences. Indeed, voluntary manumissions reached their peak during the Revolutionary era, with an estimated ten thousand Blacks freed in Virginia in the 1780s. Although Massachusetts failed to pass an abolition bill in 1777, the state's supreme court abolished slavery in 1783. Finally, Pennsylvania became the first state to pass a law of abolition in 1780, providing for gradual emancipation.

Moreover, the British were more interested in preserving the political status quo than the social status quo. Early in the war, the American strategy in the South had been hampered by the efforts of slave owners to protect their property. The British were certainly aware of the loyalists who owned slaves, and in November 1775 Lord Dunmore, governor of Virginia, promised freedom to those slaves who joined the British in fighting against the rebels. Although Dunmore's act applied only to slaves held by rebels, however, it did more than any other event to open the breach between planters and the Crown.[15]

Dunmore's "Ethiopian Regiment" produced much debate about Blacks with guns, both free and otherwise. General Washington permitted free Blacks who were already serving to remain in the army. Rhode Island alone, perhaps because of the presence of British troops in two-thirds of the colony, mustered a Black battalion of slaves who were immediately granted their freedom. Over the five years of the war, they fought in many battles, and their masters were compensated $400 for their loss.[16] Colonel John Laurens of South Carolina raised a company of three thousand Black troops from South Carolina and Georgia. Although he succeeded in securing congressional funds to compensate masters for the loss of slaves, the legislatures of Georgia and South Carolina were unwilling to endorse the proposal. In 1777, after Congress began to impose quotas on the states, slaves were frequently accepted as substitutes for masters.[17]

A particularly difficult point in the Treaty of Paris (article VII), ending the war, involved the return of slaves. The South was alienated by the actions of British commander Sir Guy Carleton and the treaty compromise worked out by John Jay. As a result, Virginia lost 30,000 slaves and South Carolina, 25,000.

At no point during the Revolutionary era was compensation for newly freed slaves discussed. When Massachusetts abolished slavery, a bill to provide support for destitute Blacks passed the assembly but died in the senate. Lauren's failed proposal for Georgia and South Carolina promised each Black soldier freedom and fifty dollars at the end of the war. Occasionally, though, emancipated slaves, like indentured servants, were given some assistance in starting their new lives. During the war, for example, Captain Samuel Smedley of Fairfield, Connecticut, not only freed Boston (his slave) but, before doing so, taught him a trade, gave him a workshop, established him in business as a shoemaker, and also stipulated that his executors should give him a thousand dollars. Boston's father was granted thirty dollars a year for the remainder of his life.[18]

The real problems facing mass abolition were, first, the value of the slaves, which made compensation financially impossible if their masters were to be compensated. It was nearly impossible to find anyone in the colonies who did not support compensating the masters. Second, any plan for mass abolition had to call for the physical removal of Blacks from the United States. Once again, the costs of colonization were prohibitive. Indeed, from Jefferson through Tocqueville to Lincoln, the disappearance of Blacks from the body politics was a prerequisite to a discussion of freedom. No one contemplated the integration of African Americans into American society on an equal basis. Thus the basic issue was not slavery but the relations between the races.

Silenced at the national level, Blacks began to form a counterpublic at the local level. In 1787, Prince Hall led a committee of his African Lodge in petitioning the legislature in Massachusetts for assistance to those wishing to emigrate to Africa. Two years later, the Union Society of Africans in Newport considered the issue of emigration. Perhaps the most ambitious of the emigrationists was Paul Cuffee. Starting as a sailor on a whaling vessel in 1776, Cuffee became wealthy as a shipowner and merchant. In 1808 he won support for colonization from the African Institution, a British humanitarian organization associated with Sierra Leone. Three years later, Cuffee visited Sierra Leone and, on his return, established the Friendly Society of Sierra Leone. Narrowly failing to win congressional support for his colonization plan, in 1815 Cuffee financed the return to Sierra Leone of about forty African Americans in family groups. Cuffee, a devoted Quaker, then returned to the United States and gave the benefit of his experience to White liberals who founded the American Colonization Society (ACS) in 1816.[19]

Some people regard Cuffee as the "father of Black Nationalism." But he did not stay in Africa and saw emigration as a way to end the Atlantic slave trade, spread Christianity, create a refuge for free Black people, and turn a profit. Similarly, Prince Hall did not emigrate to Africa, choosing instead to establish parallel and separate Black fraternal organizations in the United States. Other influential free Blacks like Daniel Coker, James Forten, Richard Allen, and Absolam Jones also considered colonization as a viable alternative for African Americans.[20]

The establishment of the American Colonization Society (ACS) and its colony of Liberia energized Black opposition to colonization. Although Cuffee and Hall may have seen emigration as one of several alternatives for disillusioned free Blacks, it became clear that White elites saw colonization as the only solution for the anomaly of free Blacks in a White nation. Most of the early-eighteenth-century White leaders supported the ACS's efforts, and from its founding up to the Civil War, the ACS transported some thirteen thousand free Blacks to West Africa. Anticolonization thus became an issue around which a national Black counterpublic began to form, beginning in 1831 with the National Black Convention movement.

Reconstruction marks the entrance of reparations into mainstream political discourse,[21] but they did not move to center stage until various colonization schemes were finally put to rest. Abraham Lincoln had campaigned for the presidency on a platform that called for colonization, stating that his first act would be to free all the slaves and send them to Liberia. During the war, negotiations were begun with foreign countries that owned West Indian colonies and with South American countries, in hopes of working out a colonization plan. As late as April 1865, Lincoln asked General Benjamin Butler to examine the question of colonization, stating, "I can hardly believe that the South and North can live in peace unless we get rid of the Negroes."[22] Butler reported that even using all available naval vessels and merchant marine ships sailing to the nearest site in the West Indies, they could only transport half as many Negroes as the number of Negro children who would be born here.

When the District of Columbia abolished slavery in April 1862, Congress appropriated a total of $600,000 to assist voluntary Black emigrants, at $100 each. Later, in July 1862, the president was authorized to colonize Blacks made free by the confiscation acts using proceeds from confiscated property to replace monies appropriated for colonization. By December 1863, the secretary of the interior reported that Blacks were no longer willing to leave the United States and that they were needed in the army.

Land Reform

Confiscated rebel land solved one problem for General William Tecumseh Sherman in early 1865. Plagued by the plight of thousands of impoverished Blacks following his army through Georgia and South Carolina, Sherman issued special field order no. 15, setting aside the Sea Islands and a portion of the low-country rice coast south of Charleston, extending thirty miles inland, exclusively for Black settlement. Under this order, each Black family would receive forty acres of land, and Sherman later provided that the army could assist with a *loan* of mules. Although the land provisions were meant to be temporary (until the end of the war), by June some 40,000 freedmen had been settled on 400,000 acres of "Sherman land."[23]

Apart from the union generals dealing with the immediate pressure of Black welfare, another governmental institution—the Bureau of Refugees, Freedmen, and Abandoned Lands—took on the issue of land reform. The Freedmen's Bureau, as it was popularly called, grew out of a commission created by the War Department in 1863. When it was finally established in March 1865, the bureau was authorized to divide abandoned and confiscated land in forty-acre plots for rental to freedmen and loyal refugees and the eventual sale with "such title as the United States can convey" (language suggesting the legal ambiguity concerning the government's hold on Southern land). Reflecting the government's concern that it might be seen as giving preferential treatment to Blacks, the bureau was authorized for one year only, given no budget, and broadened to include Southern White refugees as well as freedmen.[24] After overcoming two presidential vetoes, the Freedman's Bureau eventually was extended to 1870 and spent some $13 million on its war relief efforts. The modified legislation allowed the lands of former Confederates to be returned to them, but holders of valid Sherman titles on these lands could lease twenty-acre plots elsewhere, with a six-year option to purchase them.[25]

The 1866 Southern Homestead Act offered free Blacks eighty-acre plots on federal lands in Alabama, Arkansas, Florida, Louisiana, and Mississippi. Unfortunately, these lands were generally unfit for agriculture, and many Blacks lacked the subsistence and means needed to plant their first crop. As a result, freedmen were able to establish only about three thousand homesteads.[26]

Radical Republicans sought to reshape Southern society in the image of the North's small-scale competitive capitalism. Their two major obstacles to such reform were the "land monopolies" of the planter aristocracy and the "landless" ex-slaves. In September 1865, Representative Thaddeus Stevens (R-PA) called for the seizure of the 400 million acres belonging to the wealthiest 10 percent of Southerners. Forty acres would be granted to each adult freedman, and the reminder (90 percent of the total) sold to the highest bidder in plots not to exceed five hundred acres. With the proceeds, the federal government would finance pensions for Civil War veterans, compensate loyal men who had suffered losses during the war, and retire the bulk of the national debt.[27] Stevens asked whether the U.S. government would do less than the czar of Russia, who, when he freed 22 million serfs, compelled their masters to give them homesteads on the very soil that they had tilled.[28] Apparently, the U.S. government would do less, as even radical Republicans were reluctant to attack the sanctity of property. After nearly two years of debate, Stevens and his Senate colleague Charles Sumner (R-MA) were unable to force confiscation into the Reconstruction Acts of 1867.

The debate over land reform specifically and the Freedmen's Bureau generally reveal public attitudes toward Blacks that became staples of public policy debates in the future. In vetoing the second Freedmen's Bureau bill, President Andrew Johnson raised the specter of a huge federal bureaucracy interfering with citizen's rights. Moreover, by insisting that the ex-slaves help themselves rather than depend on the federal government, the president believed he was doing the best thing for the Blacks themselves. But Johnson's paternalism became more overtly racist in his message vetoing the civil rights bill. He argued that giving Blacks the privileges of citizenship discriminated against Whites: "The distinction of race and color is by the bill made to operate in favor of the colored and against the white race." Adding insult to injury, Johnson contended that immigrants from abroad were more deserving of citizenship than Blacks were because they knew more about "the nature and character of our institutions." Finally, the specter of racial intermarriage was suggested as the logical consequence of congressional policy.[29] Although Johnson's veto was overridden, the great opportunity to advance racial progress through land reform was lost. Indeed, in Georgia where Blacks made up 40 percent of the population, for example, Black landownership rose from 1.0 percent in 1864 to only 1.6 percent in 1880.[30]

Political scientist Linda Williams sees the legacy of the Freedmen's Bureau as still very much alive. First, it demonstrated severe limitations in the federal government's willingness to pursue a course of social rights for Blacks or any other poor population. Second, it established the precedent that the real job of welfare agencies was to put themselves out of business as rapidly as possible. Third, it refined the themes and ugly rhetorical flourishes that encouraged opposition to altruistic social policy in the United States and ratcheted up the power of Whiteness.[31] Williams also contrasts the assured federal appropriations for Civil War veterans to the temporary nature of Freedmen's Bureau funding. It is the origin of the two-tier system of social welfare that developed in the twentieth century and distinguished between those "deserving" and "undeserving" of federal assistance.

President Johnson's opposition to Black citizenship reflected the view implicit in law that recognizes that Whites' settled expectations, built on the privileges and benefits produced by White supremacy, acknowledge and reinforce a property interest in Whiteness that reproduces Black subordination. The abolition of slavery reinforced the need to protect the property interest in Whiteness because

> the abolition of slavery called into question the existence of the white race as a social formation, for if the main underpinning of the distinction between the "white" worker and the black worker was erased, what could remain to motivate poor "whites" to hug to their breasts a class of landowners who had led them into one of the most terrible wars in history? And if class replaced "race" interest in their hearts, who could say where it might end.[32]

Not only were class differences more exposed, but also Whiteness itself was fragmenting.

Matthew Jacobson contends that the Irish immigration of the 1840s marked the first fracturing of Whiteness into a hierarchy of plural and scientifically determined White races. The fall of slavery exacerbated this trend, and not all "Whites" were seen as fit for American citizenship. In 1877, the same year marking the end of Reconstruction, the first major act of overt anti-Semitism in American history was recorded in Saratoga Springs, New York. Joseph Seligman, a Bavarian Jewish immigrant, was barred from the (Hilton) Grand Union Hotel despite his prominence in American banking. During the same summer the *New York Tribune* reported on the trial of several members of the Irish Molly Maguires for murder in Pennsylvania, stating: "The Mollies belong to a race with more wholesome and probably unreasonable terror of law than any other . . . if Pennsylvanians intend to civilize them by terror, it will need other and more wholesome slaughters than that of last week to do it."[33] At the same time, the anti-Chinese movement was cresting in California and complicating the historical Black–White racial dichotomy.

No event better illustrates the rising property interest in "Whiteness" than the 1896 *Plessy v. Ferguson* case in which the U.S. Supreme Court spelled out its "separate but equal" doctrine. As Cheryl Harris points out, the right to exclude has been central to the concept of "Whiteness," which has been defined not so much by an inherent unifying characteristic as by the right to exclude others deemed to be "not White." Homer Plessy, who was one-eighth Black, was arrested after attempting to board a railway coach reserved for Whites. Plessy not only claimed protection under the equal protection clause of the Fourteenth Amendment but also charged that the refusal to seat him on the White passenger car deprived him of property. His lawyer, Albion Tourgee, argued that the property value in being White was self-evident:

> How much would it be *worth* to a young man entering upon the practice of law, to be regarded as a *white* man rather than a colored one? Six-sevenths of the population are white. Nineteen-twentieths of the property of the country is owned by white people. Ninety-nine hundredths of the business opportunities are in the control of white people. . . . Probably most white persons if given a choice, would prefer death to life in the United States as *colored persons*. Under these conditions, is it possible to conclude that *the reputation of being white* is not property? Indeed, is it not the most valuable sort of property, being the master-key that unlocks the golden door of opportunity?[34]

The Court ruled against him, observing that a White man assigned to a colored coach may have action for damages against the company for being deprived of his so-called property but that a colored man so assigned has been deprived of no property, since he is not lawfully entitled to the reputation of being a White man.[35]

Reconstruction also began the fragmentation of Black unity. Although newly enfranchised Black male voters helped elect twenty Black representatives and two Black senators to Congress in the latter third of the nineteenth century, they failed in land reform. Historian Tom Holt reports that in South Carolina, the state where Blacks were most politically powerful after the Civil War, intraracial differences helped prevent land reform. When the issue of land confiscation came before the state legislature, mulattoes, who had been free before the war, were the most conservative, and Blacks who had been slaves or free were the most liberal. Occupying the center were mulatto ex-slaves. Consequently, given White opposition and Black disunity, land reform was unsuccessful in South Carolina.[36] The political differences emerging among Blacks in South Carolina also surfaced nationwide. Black conservatives now vied for attention with Black nationalists, disillusioned liberals, and radical egalitarians in post–Civil War America. The onset of racial apartheid accelerated the movement toward Black nationalism that had lain dormant since the *Dred Scott*

decision, in which Scott, a slave whose master had died after taking Scott to a free territory, sued for, but was ultimately denied, his
freedom.

African Americans sought to escape Southern poverty and racism
by migrating West or to Africa. The "exoduster movement" created
Black towns in the West, while Bishop Henry McNeil Turner revived
the call of a return to Africa and also demanded $40 billion in "finan-
cial indemnity" for all ex-slaves. But it was a White businessman, Walter R. Vaughan, from Selma, Alabama, who established the first ex-
slave pension-and-bounty organization and lobbied Congress for economic relief.

The Freedmen's Pension Bill

The switch from a demand for land—either here or abroad—to
"financial indemnity," income in the form of pensions, marks the second stage of the reparations movement. Perhaps the end of "radical
Reconstruction" and the rise of "Jim Crow" led Blacks to believe that
demands for a land base were unrealistic. The only way the dominance of the planter class might have been overcome would have been
through a sweeping redistribution of land to the freedmen, and that
did not happen. By 1880, for example, Blacks owned only 1.6 percent
of all arable land in Georgia. Whites simply denied Blacks the opportunity of becoming a landowning class by refusing to sell them property even when they had the resources to purchase it. Consequently,
Whites at the same wealth level as Blacks owned seven times as much
land.[37]

Perhaps the aging ex-slave population was simply getting too old
to work any land that might come their way and so tried to take advantage of the popular sentiment behind pensions for Civil War veterans. In any case, Vaughan, a Democrat, was able to convince his congressman, William J. Connell, a Republican, to introduce an ex-slave
pension bill in 1890.

Vaughan was a Southerner whose father had owned slaves. Born
in Petersburg, Virginia, in 1848 and raised in North Carolina and Alabama, young Vaughan had appealed to his father to give his slaves all
or part of Saturday for their own time. After the war, he received a
business education in Philadelphia and soon opened his own business college in Council Bluffs, Iowa. In 1881 he was elected mayor, but
after serving two terms, he moved to Omaha, Nebraska. In Omaha,

Vaughan took over management of the *Omaha Daily Democrat* and revived an earlier project of his concerning pensions for ex-slaves. As early as 1870, Vaughan had written letters to politicians giving examples of the plight of ex-slaves and suggesting that they receive pensions. In responding to one such letter in 1883, Republican U.S. Senator Preston B. Plumb of Kansas stated that the "first duty of government is to disabled soldiers and that if governments are held responsible for all damages resulting from laws it passes it would soon go broke."[38] Vaughan countered that the soldiers had been taken care of and that laws supporting slavery could not compare with personal injury claims. Even in the latter case, Vaughan continued, there commonly is a means of redress.

The bill introduced by Congressman Connell in 1890 provided federal pensions to ex-slaves based on a scale. Those ex-slaves seventy years and older were to receive an initial payment of $500 and $15 a month, and ex-slaves between sixty and seventy years would receive $300 and $12 a month. Ex-slaves fifty to sixty years of age would get $100 and $8 a month, and those under fifty years old would receive $4 a month pension but no initial payment. Between 1890 and 1903, Vaughan secured the introduction of nine bills, none of which became law. Although various members of Congress sponsored them, the bills were identical, with the last introduced by Mark Hanna in 1903.[39]

Historian Mary F. Berry notes that the temporary Republican interest in Black voters—and thus ex-slave pensions—coincided with Republican support of increased pensions for veterans and the maintenance of high protective tariff levels. Starting with the debate on the tariff revision bill in April 1888, Republican supporters of a high tariff saw higher pensions as one way of satisfying a constituency while at the same time disposing of an embarrassing surplus.[40] Congress therefore could not claim that the country could not afford pensions for ex-slaves.

While refusing to pass the ex-slave pension bill, Congress did pass the Dependent Pension Act of 1890. This new legislation provided a pension to Civil War veterans whether or not their disability was attributable to Civil War service. In effect, this meant that veterans who were developing medical problems as they aged—much as were the ex-slaves—would now be given old age assistance. Consequently, the number of veterans on federal assistance rose dramatically from 126,722, or 2 percent of Union veterans in 1866, to a high of 999,446, or

83 percent in 1902. By 1915, the percentage of Union veterans on the pension rolls stood at 93.5. The average Civil War pensioner received nearly 40 percent of an earner's wage, and the benefits were not conditioned (needs-based) on destitution.[41]

In addition to the veterans, their dependents were entitled to benefits as well. By 1883, widows accounted for one in six on the pension rolls, and more than half had children under sixteen. The 1890 Dependent Pension Act made eligible for benefits those women who had married Union veterans up to *twenty-five years after* the war ended.[42] Thus the pension system for Civil War veterans and their families served as an early example of a social security system disproportionally benefiting Whites.

Perhaps sensing that moral appeals alone would not result in the passage of his ex-slave pension bill, despite the sentiment for veterans' pensions, Vaughan applied new tactics. In 1891, he published *Vaughan's Freedmen's Pension Bill: A Plea for American Freedmen and a Rational Proposition to Grant Pensions to Persons of Color Emancipated from Slavery*. This small book with the long title is remarkable in its historical scope, ranging from the accomplishments of Blacks in Africa, including Egypt, to contemporary biographical portraits of successful Black "men of merit" who had been slaves. Vaughan even tells the story of a successful former slave who supported his old mistress with $150 a month. Couched in Vaughan's appeal for "human rights" is a new emphasis. He points out that Union pensions do not benefit those who fought for the South. Nonetheless, Southern taxpayers are forced to support the Union pensions as well as provide relief for ex-slaves. As a result, the prosperity of the South lagged behind the North.

> The passage of a measure that would place former slaves upon the pension rolls would not only be the performance of a delayed act of justice, to a once enslaved race, but it would occasion an expenditure of treasure throughout the entire southern region that would visibly enhance the material prosperity of all classes of people within that section.[43]

Future iterations of the ex-slave pension bill paid as much if not more attention to fairness for the White Southern taxpayer as to redress for the ex-slave. In a statement in his own newspaper, the *U.S. Department*

News Eagle, Vaughan provided data showing the tax injustice to Southern states: "Michigan gets about $12 million pension money annually distributed in the various branches of business while Mississippi gets nothing in comparison. Pennsylvania gets $10 million, while Louisiana is practically neglected." According to Vaughan, "the taxpayers of Michigan and other Northern and Western states are schooling about one-tenth as many children and their poor fund is about one fifth compared with the Southern states."[44] In fact, the bill also became known as the "southern taxpayers revision bill."[45]

The second tactic that Vaughan used to promote his bill was the formation of a national organization with chapters run by Negroes to lobby for passage of the bill. He argued for the establishment of freedmen's pension clubs by quoting George Cable on the need for Negroes to form organizations to fight for their civil rights.[46] The revised constitution of the Ex-Slave Pension Association limited membership to "ex-slaves and their friends belonging to the race" and asked for an initiation fee of ten cents and five cents per month.[47] The primary objective of the clubs or lodges was to lobby for passage of the bill, and the secondary objectives were to provide for the care of disabled ex-slaves and travel to support the organization. The following ex-slave pension song by A. Scales and J. W. Anderson captures their spirit of determination:

Ex-Slave Pension Song

Why whisper now that all may hear,
We must have our money or never shall yield,
Go speak it out both far and near,
We must have our money or never shall yield.

Chorus:
Why stay in the field,
Camp on the grounds of the enemy,
Stay in the field,
We must have our money or never shall yield.

We come not here for to ask an alm,
We must have our money or never shall yield,
But demand a debt from Uncle Sam,
We must have our money or never shall yield.

We were sent to the fields at an early dawn.
We must have our money or never shall yield,
And kept out there till the sun went down,
We must have our money or never shall yield.

Dem'o, Pops, Repubs, fare you well,
We must have our money or never shall yield,
At Washington the tale we'll tell,
We must have our money or never shall yield.

You speak for gold and silver, too,
We must have our money or never shall yield,
If paid in paper that will do,
We must have our money or never shall yield.

The McKinley law and the Mills Bill,
We must have our money or never shall yield,
Why justice now, our pockets fill,
We must have our money or never shall yield.

Stay the railroad shops and planning mills,
We must have our money or never shall yield,
But lend us a hand to the Thurston Bill,
We must have our money or never shall yield.

(*Spoken*) Mr. President, your cause is a grand one, and we add almost
divine, so we say to the Populists, Democrats and Republicans, now
fellow citizens fall in line.

Now push on boys from shore to shore,
We must have our money or never shall yield,
And make your talk at the white house door,
We must have our money or never shall yield.

We know we are right and shan't keep still,
We must have our money or never shall yield,
Until they pass that Thurston Bill,
We must have our money or never shall yield.[48]

Pension Scams

Complicating the analysis of the pension movement is the secret nature of Vaughan's organization. "Vaughan's ex-slave pension

clubs," as they were popularly known, were organized along the lines of secret fraternities or lodges. The clubs received instructions from the parent lodge in Chicago and, for a fee of approximately $25, obtained the "secret work," grip, password, and masks. Vaughan controlled the Chicago lodge, and an explicit exception to the Negro-only rule was made for Vaughan and his family.[49]

Perhaps because of the secret nature of the organization and Vaughan's role in it, many Black leaders either opposed or were neutral to the clubs' existence. Support for the pension bills was more mixed. Eventually three Negro newspapers did support the bill. Most important, Frederick Douglass was persuaded to support the legislation. In an exchange of letters with Vaughan he wrote,

> I was somewhat amazed and startled by the apparent impracticality of the Bill but the more I thought of it the more practical it seemed and I saw that what the nation ought to do, that, the nation can do the nation, as a nation, has issued against the negro. It robbed him of the rewards of his labor during more than two hundred years, and its repentance will not be genuine and complete till, according to the measure of its ability, it shall have made restitution. It can never fully atone for the wrong done to the millions who have lived and died under the galling yoke of bondage, but it can, if it will, do justice and mercy to the living.[50]

Apparently reparations, in the form of pensions, was an idea whose time had come.

By 1915, there were at least seven pension associations, claiming up to five million members. Most notable were the National Ex-Slave Mutual Relief, Bounty and Pension Association (M.R.B.P.A.); the Ex-Slave Petitioner's Assembly; the Western Division Association; the Great National Ex-Slave Union; the Congressional, Legislative, and Pension Association of U.S.A.; the Ex-Slave Pension Association of Texas; and the Ex-Slave Pension Association of Kansas. While Vaughan's figure of five million may be exaggerated, government reports confirm the mass nature of the movement. As a 1902 Bureau of Pensions report stated, "This Bureau has had knowledge of ninety organizations at work simultaneously in a single Southern state."[51] Each of these organizations was required to have a minimal membership of twenty-five, and a Senate report in 1900 shows the "tremendous growth in membership" from 1,367 membership certificates issued in 1897 to 35,710 such certificates in 1899. It estimates that the membership had doubled again over the past year and that "an amount aggregating $100,000 has been taken from the poor and deluded victims of this nefarious scheme."[52]

Were these pension clubs legitimate lobbying groups, as their leaders claimed, or were they swindles, as the government charged? The evidence is mixed. It is clear that most of the societies lobbied for the passage of a pension bill for ex-slaves. One petition drive even collected some 600,000 signatures from ex-slaves and sent them to Congress.[53] It also is true that Vaughan's organization spawned a number of competitors. Rev. D. D. McNairy, president of M.R.B.P.A. in 1899, acknowledged that "there are many Ex-Slave organizations striving to secure the enactment of the Vaughan Bill (popularly known as the Mason bill), but they are each working through different channels and in different ways."[54] McNairy believed that this tended to confuse their work and retard their progress, and he called for unity of action as well as purpose. It is clear, too, that the national, state, and local organizers of the pension clubs either supported themselves or supplemented their incomes through organizing activities. Each organizer, Black or White, received a commission for each new member.

The most celebrated cases of fraudulent activity were those of Rev. Isaiah H. Dickerson and Mrs. Callie D. House. Dickerson was the general manager of the M.R.B.P.A., and House was the national secretary. Although their relationship with Vaughan is not clear, that they were in conflict with the founder of the movement by the late 1890s is clear. By 1897, Vaughan was issuing a caution to southern papers, warning them that Dickerson, among others, were "*unauthorized* to act for me or my bill, hence money paid them to aid the passage of the bill, is *improperly and wrongfully placed.*"[55] When Dickerson was charged with fraud in 1899, Vaughan applauded the action and warned ex-slaves about fraudulent clubs.[56]

Despite the warning, it seems that Dickerson and Vaughan had been connected in the past. A letter from the Bureau of Pensions in 1902 states that Dickerson had organized a political party in Washington, D.C., called Vaughan's Justice Party.[57] Dickerson had also issued a call for a national ex-slave congress under the auspices of the executive committee of Vaughan's Justice Party.[58] The most direct piece of evidence linking the two organizers is Robert A. L. Dick, who had been Vaughan's law partner until their Washington, D.C., firm was dissolved for unknown reasons. Dick then served as Dickerson's attorney.[59]

On September 21, 1899, the Post Office Department issued a fraud order against Dickerson, Callie House, and two other officers of the M.R.B.P.A. A newspaper account of the charges describes it: "The Post Office Department does not in any respect invade the right of any class of citizens to associate themselves together to petition for or otherwise influence the passage by Congress of legislation in behalf of their own interests."[60] According to the report, the only purpose of the government's action was "to protect ex-slaves and their descendants from the rapacity principally of unscrupulous members of their own race."[61]

Apparently there was insufficient evidence to convict the other officers of the association, but in March 1901, Dickerson was convicted of obtaining money under false pretenses and sentenced in Atlanta, Georgia, to pay a fine of $1,000 or serve twelve months with a chain gang.[62] Even though he was charged with running a nationwide scheme, only one witness testified for the prosecution. Scilla Smith claimed that she paid her membership dues based on Dickerson's promise that the money would be sent to Vaughan in Washington. When the Atlanta pension club sent Smith to Washington to meet with Vaughan, he told her that he had received no money from Dickerson. On her return, she confronted him and he admitted that he had sent Vaughan no money but claimed it had been used to bury the dead and care for the sick. Even though House was implicated in the scheme, she was not charged.[63]

The charges by the Bureau of Pensions led to the conviction of at least twelve other pension club organizers, including two Whites.[64] At least one city passed a "cheating and swindling" statute aimed at pension club organizers, and other cities were urged to follow suit.[65] In 1905, Dickerson was again the subject of an investigation by the Bureau of Pensions. The complaint states that Dickerson claimed to be an agent of the U.S. government who was authorized to collect one dollar from the complainant to process his pension. The investigative report also states, however, that

> I. H. Dickerson, late of Washington, D.C., who is a taller man than the party described by the complainant, has been actively instrumental in the ex-slave pension movement, and who is an extremely

smooth talker, well aware of the provisions of the act of April 18, 1884, has succeeded in avoiding a technical case against him under that act.[66]

The report also describes Callie House as "a thin-faced mulatto, who writes a fairly plain hand, and is an excellent talker."[67] With Dickerson under intense scrutiny, it seems reasonable to assume that House came to play an increasingly central role in the association. Then on May 10, 1916, House was indicted by a grand jury in Nashville, Tennessee, and charged with conspiracy and using the mails to defraud. She was arrested at her home on August 3, and bond was set at $3,000, which she made. Specifically, the indictment charged that in November and December 1914, House conspired with thirteen other individuals to defraud certain (unknown) parties by placing in the U.S. mail "certain circulars to be sent and delivered by the Post Office."[68]

A newspaper report of the indictment and arrest condemns House but states that she was so skillful the government had trouble finding complainants:

> The government's desire to protect the old Negroes from the alleged swindlers was sometimes misunderstood by those whose money was paid in, and it was with difficulty that the evidence was collected. Some of those who should have been willing witnesses protected the schemers, believing them to be working for the interest of their race.[69]

Apparently the government's case against House was weaker than the newspaper reported.

A Bureau of Pensions letter indicates that House entered a guilty plea on the understanding that she would receive a sentence of one year and one day in a penitentiary. Yet when called for sentencing, she denied any moral turpitude and claimed that she was ignorant and really thought the legislation pertaining to ex-slaves had been passed and that she was rendering a service to Negroes to enable them to secure the money Congress had appropriated. Hearing this, the Court declined to accept her plea of guilty and ordered her placed on trial.[70] Ultimately, House was convicted and sentenced to one year and one day in the penitentiary in Jefferson City, Missouri, in October 1917.

The government also proceeded with an indictment against Rev. Augustus Clark, who had replaced I. H. Dickerson as the male leader of the organization.[71] Although the case against Clark was unsuccessful, the association that he and House headed did not survive.

The ex-slave pension clubs are remarkable in that they represent the largest mass political movement by Blacks before the Garvey movement, which followed immediately on its heels. Significantly, the ex-slave pension movement was organized and directed without the support of the established Black leadership. Although not openly hostile to the pension clubs, most Black leaders kept their distance. Like Garvey, however, the leaders of the pension club movement were subject to extraordinary government scrutiny and, ultimately, prosecution.

Undoubtedly, the pension movement included a number of charlatans and swindlers, but three facts stand out in relation to the government's interest in the movement. First, despite the prominence of Vaughan as the founder of the movement, the secrecy of his pension clubs, and his acknowledged role in selling club paraphernalia, the government seemed to have little interest in investigating or prosecuting him or his family. When Rev. Dickerson and House organized the M.R.B.P.A. in 1894 in Nashville, Blacks assume a leading role in the movement. But many of the complaints that began to flow into Washington came not from Blacks who felt defrauded but from Whites upset with Blacks active in political organization in their city or state. Over at least a ten-year period, investigators from the Bureau of Pension could not find any evidence of federal law violations. As Berry reported, these "Professors or Preachers" were not violating federal law, but many town authorities had simply "run them out of town" when they first came to organize.[72] Vaughan was apparently so concerned about Dickerson's and House's success in the South that he moved his own organizational headquarters to Nashville to compete with them.[73]

Second, the extraordinary steps taken by the federal government to prevent ex-slaves from being cheated and defrauded contrast strikingly with the lack of federal concern about other human rights violations in the South. At the peak of Jim Crow, with race riots in Atlanta and Springfield, Illinois; hundreds of lynchings; massive fraud committed by landowners against sharecroppers; and the disenfranchisement of Blacks across the South; the federal government singled out pension club organizers for prosecution! An unusually negative report from the Senate Committee on Pensions opposed the pension bill for ex-slaves because "the introduction of these bills has given an opportunity for dishonest people to impose upon the ignorant and credulous freedmen and their children of the South in a way that will surprise the people of this country when they know the facts."[74] Thus Congress urged citizens not to petition their government for redress because this might encourage dishonest people to take advantage of them!

Of course, one solution to this problem would have been to pass the pension bill providing material assistance to the "ignorant" and "poor" ex-slaves. Vaughan, however, cited bitter opposition to the pension bill, mainly focusing on the cost of the legislation. Newspapers such as the *Chicago Herald, Nashville American,* and *Cleveland Leader* published attacks. Some argued that it would cost $200 billion over the next thirty years, but Vaughan estimated that if all five million slaves who were freed in 1865 were still alive and given $1,000 each, the total would be only $5 billion.[75]

Third, the prosecution of Callie House coincided with the class action suit against the United States filed in federal court in the District of Columbia on July 13, 1915. Four Black plaintiffs claimed that the Treasury Department owed Blacks some $68,073,388.99, which was collected as taxes on cotton between 1862 and 1868. The plaintiffs asked that the court declare a lien against these taxes for the unpaid labor in the production of the cotton from which the taxes were realized. House and her associates were rumored to be behind the suit. Having determined that the Senate report made it impossible to find sponsors to introduce their pension bill, the pension movement organizers switched tactics and now were organizing around the legal case.[76] House's indictment was handed down within a year after the legal suit was filed.

Writing to defend her reputation following the adverse Senate committee report in 1900, Callie House stated the motivation for her efforts:

> The M.R.B.&P.A. is to take care of the sick, Burry [*sic*] the dead & petition Congress for the passage of some measure to pension the Old Ex-slaves for this Government owes the Ex-slaves an indemity [*sic*] for the Labor they was Rob [*sic*] of after the Adoption of the Declara-

tion of independence that declared all men born Equal the negro was work and tax [sic] as Chattels under the Flag that you all claim to all nations to wave over the land of the free and home of the Brave. Now since we have been freed and made citizen we can read for our selves that we ought to have been free nearly 100 years before we was. We the officers & members of the M.R.B.&P.A. are working by the Laws that the white man north & south made we are citizen [sic] made so by our white friends . . . the Constitution of the United States grants it [sic] citizen the priviledge [sic] to petition Congress for a redress of Greviance [sic] therefore I can't see where we have violated any law what ever.[77]

Ultimately, House and the Bureau of Pensions could agree on only one thing: that the pension movement would "be followed by inevitable disappointment, and probably distrust of the dominant race and of the government.[78]

From Civil Rights to Economic Rights

On August 11, 1965, the Watts area of Los Angeles exploded in the worst urban violence in nearly fifty years. Less than a week after the historic Voting Rights Act of 1965 was signed, the civil rights movement was dead. The nation's attention shifted to the north where rioters rejected the soothing words of civil rights leaders and instead shouted, "Burn, Baby Burn" and "Get Whitey." The immediate cost was thirty-four dead, more than one thousand injured, four thousand arrested, and an estimated $200 million in property damage.[79]

Martin Luther King Jr., as well as the other leaders of the civil rights movement, were shocked by the rage, violence, and loss of life. In the two years between the March on Washington and the Watts riot, King saw his "dream turn into a nightmare," and he conceded that the dream of a "beloved community" based on interracial brotherhood was "shattered when the riots developed in Watts."[80]

According to the leader of the Southern Christian Leadership Conference (SCLC), the civil rights movement had entered a new phase, expanding its focus from one region—the South—to the entire nation. Moreover, it expanded its scope from civil rights to human rights. While speaking to a meeting of the Illinois AFL-CIO shortly after the Watts riot, King stated,

It is a constitutional right for a man to be able to vote but the human right to a decent house is as categorically imperative and morally absolute as was that constitutional right. It is not a constitutional right that men have jobs, but it is a human right.[81]

King's promotion of economic rights was not new, but it now assumed center stage.

As early as 1960 King used a version of the "dream" metaphor that included economic rights. The dream encompassed "equality of opportunity, of privilege and prosperity widely distributed; a dream of a land where men will not take necessities from the many to give luxuries to the few."[82] Indeed, the slogan of the 1963 March on Washington was "jobs and freedom." After the Watts riot, King was saying that freedom was not free and was meaningless without the economic means to pursue it. As Ella Baker put it, "The movement was bigger than a hamburger."[83]

In the early 1960s, King's economic strategy largely revolved around more welfare services and more job opportunities directed primarily toward the Black community. The SCLC launched its major economic thrust—Operation Breadbasket—in Atlanta in 1962. The idea behind Operation Breadbasket, which reached its full potential in Chicago under Rev. Jesse Jackson, was to use "selective patronage" to force retailers to stock products manufactured by Black businesses and to hire Black employees in ghetto stores. Rev. Leon Sullivan of Philadelphia was the inspiration for the program, and he came to Atlanta for its inauguration. King explained that it was the next step toward desegregation in Atlanta.[84]

In mid-1963, the Urban League's Whitney Young proposed "an immediate, dramatic and tangible domestic Marshall Plan" that would enable Blacks to begin the social race at the same starting line. Carefully distinguishing between "a special effort" and special privileges, he called for massive compensatory action over ten years by government, business, and foundations to generate employment; to improve education, housing, and health; and to "reverse economic and social deterioration of urban families and communities."[85]

Although King supported Young's proposal, his colleague Professor L. D. Reddick directly challenged the program's race-based nature. Moreover, foreshadowing the debate over affirmative action, Reddick cautioned that Young's slogan, a "Marshall Plan for the Negro," should be discarded completely and that the word *maximum* should replace *preferential*.[86]

For Reddick, the use of the word *preferential* was both politically unsound and violated the movement's principle of equality. In *Why We Can't Wait*, King cites Reddick's opposition to the Indian government's special treatment of untouchables. King disagreed with Reddick and argued that compensatory measures were necessary and had been used to benefit other groups.[87] However, when King announced his own program for economic and social advancement that same year, he was careful to call it a "bill of rights for the disadvantaged." Putting a price tag of $50 billion over ten years on his proposal, King called for the development of a federal program of public works, retraining, and jobs for all, "so that none, white or black, will have cause to feel threatened."[88] Stressing that his principal goal was jobs, not relief, King was careful to point out that economic insecurity caused by automation was a problem for Whites as well as Blacks and challenged President Lyndon Johnson's rosy economic forecasts.

Neither Young's "Marshall plan" nor King's "bill of rights" received serious legislative or media attention. It seemed clear that King and Johnson were moving in different directions, with King looking for economic programs that would empower the poor and Johnson promoting welfare policies that would keep them quiet. But the Watts riot proved that they could not be kept quiet.

When King visited Watts and asked the participants in the riot what they had gained, he was struck by their answer: "They paid attention to us." King decided that the need was real even if the form in which it was expressed, rioting, was counterproductive. After visiting several northern cities and over the objection of Bayard Rustin and the SCLC staff, he decided to focus his efforts on Chicago.

The story of King's lack of success in Chicago is well known.[89] In fact, King admitted that many of the problems he demanded that Mayor Richard Daley solve would take at least ten years to make a good start. In addition, he oversimplified the primary issue as economic exploitation in order to avoid confronting Daley politically. Nonetheless, the experience in Chicago was profoundly instructive for several reasons. First, actually living in a Chicago tenement and dealing with the daily frustrations of ghetto residents deepened his identification with the poor. King learned that if he were to truly speak for the poor, as well as gang members, his voice must be more urgent, more demanding, and less utopian. Second, the refusal of the Chicago Democratic machine, the national Democratic Party, and the unions to concretely support the goals of his Chicago campaign drove a wedge between King and his former allies that was never overcome. Because White union members had participated in the mobs attacking King in Chicago neighborhoods and Cicero, he began to identify less with this liberal coalition and more directly with the poor. Third, Daley's use of Black middle-class leaders in Chicago to blunt King's attacks led King to challenge the Black middle-class leadership itself: "The fact is that the civil rights movement has too often been middle-class oriented, and that it has not moved to the grass-roots levels of our communities."[90] Finally, King realized that the massive problems faced by Chicago's poor could not be solved in Chicago alone, that the battle must be expanded to include the entire country and, in particular, the nation's capital.

By 1966, King had moved from a conception of poverty as something caused by the deficiencies of the poor that the broader community could compensate to a conception of poverty as the inevitable outcome of steps taken by the privileged classes to sustain their privileges. In his new rhetoric he urged the public to see poverty as systemic rather than personal. The piecemeal approach to poverty that offered welfare and job training had to be replaced by a comprehensive and redistributive policy of full employment and a guaranteed income adjusted for inflation and at higher than subsistence levels. The very definition of work needed a "radical redefinition" to include such services as health care and child rearing. Most important, King joined Kenneth Clark and Michael Harrington in arguing for the democratic participation of the poor in devising solutions to the problems that face them. King no doubt recalled the words of the president of the Woodlawn Organization (TWO), who testified before a congressional committee that everyone in Chicago benefited from the war on poverty except the poor. It had become another source of patronage for Mayor Richard Daley's political machine, which TWO presidents had termed the "maximum feasible participation of the rich." Privately, King criticized capitalism and its materialism.[91]

King's conception took concrete form in the 1966 "Freedom Budget for All Americans" put forth by Bayard Rustin and A. Philip Randolph. The Freedom Budget grew out of a June 1966 White House conference[92] that President Johnson convened to address increasing urban unrest and racial hostility. Randolph and Rustin called for outlays of $185 billion over ten years, including guaranteed jobs and income. The eighty-four-page proposal followed the precedent set by the full employment bill of 1946 and was in part Randolph's response to the self-help programs advocated by Black nationalists. He believed that the proposal would make possible the unity of the White and Black working class because it left "no room for discrimination in any form [and] because its programs are addressed to all who need more opportunity and improved incomes and living standards—not just to some of them."[93] The Freedom Budget itself was drawn up by a team of Black and White economists and intellectuals, including Leon Keyserling, Vivian Henderson, Tom Kahn, Nathaniel Goldfinger, and Michael Harrington. "No matter what you think of the war, whether you favor or opposite the administration's policies," Randolph testified in the Senate, "if the war goes on, and if the country makes the Black and White poor pay for it, this will have the most disastrous consequences on our democratic way of life."[94] Johnson never seriously considered the "Freedom Budget" that emerged from his own White House conference, and when Randolph and other civil rights leaders attacked him for budget cuts in the war on poverty, he told an aide to call "and tell them to cut this stuff out."[95]

King, too, had become increasingly concerned about the Vietnam War and about Johnson's decreasing concern with the War on Poverty. As early as October 1966, he had called for protests regarding a guaranteed income in northern cities, including Washington, D.C. But it was not until a conversation with the director of the Mississippi NAACP-LDF, Marian Wright (later Edelman), that he decided on a "poor people's" march on Washington. Wright had testified before the Senate Labor Committee's Subcommittee on Poverty in March 1967. Following her testimony, Senator Robert Kennedy (D-NY), who sat on the subcommittee, accompanied her to Cleveland, Mississippi, where he personally saw the huge personal price the poor paid for their efforts to register to vote. Kennedy told her to bring the poor to Washington as part of "some national visible push," and she relayed that suggestion to King. According to Wright, "King instinctively felt that that was right and treated me as if I was an emissary of grace. . . . Out of that, the Poor People's Campaign was born."[96]

Wright's initial suggestion that King and other religious leaders join her and a few disposed Mississippi Delta farmers was transformed into a massive, long-range campaign of civil disobedience comparable to the "Bonus army" of World War II. King was responding to something even more urgent than the plight of rural Blacks in Mississippi, and that was the violence sweeping across the nation's urban centers in 1966 and 1967. Testifying before the National Advisory Commission on Civil Disorders (Kerner Commission) in October 1967, King explained that the real cause of the uprising was "the greater crimes of white society"—the White backlash, heavy Black unemployment, racial discrimination, and the effects of the Vietnam War. Speaking to reporters after his testimony, he said that the SCLC planned on "escalating non-violence to the level of civil disobedience" by bringing thousands of needy citizens to Washington to "just camp here and stay to await meaningful federal action." "The city will not function," he warned, until Congress approved "a massive program on the part of the federal government that will make jobs or income a reality for every American citizen."[97] In its report, the Kerner Commission eventually endorsed a jobs programs and a guaranteed income.

Already depressed about the growing violence at home and in Vietnam and the greatly increased hostility of the Johnson administration since his public attacks on the president's Vietnam policy, King grew despondent as his staff and friends tried to shoot down the proposed campaign. Almost no one on his staff thought poverty was the best issue around which to carry the struggle forward, and many thought that the civil disobedience campaign would doom the organization if not the movement. Ironically, two of King's most radical mentors and allies led the charge.

Bayard Rustin, who with Randolph had promoted economic programs while King was a school boy, preferred a program that used the new Voting Rights Act to put Democrats in Congress. Although Rustin was eventually brought around to supporting the goals of the campaign, he was categorically opposed to any disruptive civil disobedience. He and Michael Harrington urged King to formulate goals that were achievable in order to reverse the movement's demoralization. When King refused to moderate his plans, Rustin stunned King by going public with his opposition.[98]

At least Rustin did agree with King that the movement had entered a new "revolutionary" phase which, in Rustin's words, required a "qualitative transformation of fundamental institutions" in order to realize "full employment, the abolition of slums, the reconstruction of our educational system and new definitions of work and leisure." Stanley Levison, King's close friend and ex-Communist, strongly disagreed with the radical emphasis. In opposing the Alabama boycott that King had called for after the 1965 Selma protest march, Levison contended that the civil rights coalition of liberals was "militant only against shocking violence and gross injustice and that in the North the movement could aspire only to reform but not revolution.

> The American people are not inclined to change their society in order to free the Negro. They are ready to undertake some, and perhaps major reforms but not to make a revolution. It is unwise to put that question in that alternative form particularly when it may well be wrong.[99]

Old-timers like Rustin and Levison were not the only ones to oppose the Poor People's Campaign (PPC).

James Bevel and Jesse Jackson each strongly opposed the project for different reasons. Bevel had become absorbed in efforts to end the Vietnam War and thought the PPC detracted from that effort. Jackson wanted to stay in Chicago with Operation Breadbasket, which King thought was too limited in its approach to bring about structural change. According to Andy Young, King was quite rough on Jesse because he believed that jobs would finally have to be provided by the public sector and that Breadbasket was essentially a private-sector program.[100]

Of course, King was assassinated before the PPC sank in the mud, internal violence, bad press, and external repression of Resurrection City. King accepted Rev. James Lawson's appeal to come to Memphis to speak precisely because the strike of sanitation workers emphasized the PPC's very goals. The sanitation workers' low wages and lack of health care highlighted the class issues in the antipoverty struggle. At the same time, all of the more than one thousand sanitation workers were Black and were fighting for union recognition from an all-White city government. Moreover, the youthful violence that marred King's visit and brought him back for one tragic last effort was symbolic of the forces that he was trying to harness in the late 1960s and direct toward positive change.

It seems uncertain, at best, that King—had he lived—could have forced the federal government to pass the economic bill of rights that his campaign demanded.[101] King cited a 1967 Harris poll showing that "a clear majority in America are asking for the very things which we will demand in Washington."[102] Less than a year later, though, a Harris and Gallup poll revealed that only 3 percent of Americans would list "poverty" as a key issue for the nation. While much of this fall from the national agenda is attributed to White backlash against increasing urban violence, the drop in public support for government action predated the worst urban violence. The American National Election Study, which polled Americans on the question of government responsibility between 1952 and 1986, reported in 1964 a dramatic 28 percent drop among respondents who believed that it was the government's responsibility to ensure the availability of a job and a good standard of living.[103] The drop came at the peak of the civil rights movement but coincided with beginnings of racial polarization between the two major political parties, driven by Barry Goldwater's "southern strategy," which shifted the presidential campaign focus to issues of "states rights" and "law and order" and helped the Republican Party win electoral votes in the South.[104]

As King's popularity in the general community and the Black community declined, the status of groups such as the Nation of Islam and the Black Panthers rose. Both groups, representing different tendencies in Black nationalism, made demands for land in the their organization's ten-point programs.[105] A host of smaller nationalist formations, like the Republic of New Africa and the Revolutionary Action Movement, also included land as a central goal of their political activity. Ironically, it was King's death that led to the best-known incident regarding reparations.

In the aftermath of King's assassination, religious organizations pledged almost $50 million for social action and racial justice. But very little money was actually distributed. With the failure of the Poor People's Campaign and the declining support for social programs by a new Republican administration, the prospects for the economic development of urban America were not bright. After first presenting the Black Manifesto at the National Black Economic Development Conference, on May 4, 1969, the leader of the Student Non-violent Coordinating Committee (SNCC), James Forman, dramatically interrupted services at New York's Riverside Church to voice the manifesto's demand for reparations. Forman's demand for $500 million produced relatively few dollars but created a great deal of conflict between Black and White clergy.[106] With Forman's appeal, the path of reparations in the civil rights era moved from a broad Marshall plan–like program for all disadvantaged Americans financed by the federal government to a Black-only program to be funded by the nation's churches.

What does this history of reparations activity in the United States tell us about contemporary efforts to obtain reparations? Could the current activity have been predicted? Can we learn anything from previous failures?

At least four legal scholars regard reparations as a movement divided into five to six historical periods or stages. The general reasons for this periodization are ambiguous but seem to be meant to demonstrate a continuous movement for reparations by Blacks since before the Civil War and to document a continuing series of grievances on which to claim reparations. The historical categories do little, however, to further our understanding of reparations as an issue or the paths of various reparations organizations and leaders. Neither do they contribute to our understanding of events today or to any social theory or legal theory that might explain current developments.

Vincene Verdun appears to have initiated this method of historical categorization by delineating five periods of reparations activity. The first period was Reconstruction, which was inspired by the political opportunity of restructuring Southern politics. While Blacks benefited from this restructuring by achieving unprecedented access to the political arena, they were unsuccessful in their attempts at land redistribution. The second wave or period of reparations has no definite time line but seems to extend from the end of Reconstruction to World War I. Verdun contends that this new wave of reparations activity, such as the formation of ex-slave pension associations, was inspired by the harsh racial oppression under Jim Crow at the turn of the last century. The third wave of reparations is represented solely by Democratic U.S. Senator (MS) Theodore Bilbo's World War II efforts to repatriate Black Americans back to Africa and is thus reminiscent of pre–Civil War repatriation plans. The civil rights movement, including such Black power elements as James Foreman's "Black Manifesto," constitute Verdun's fourth stage. Verdun's current and fifth period of reparations activity was initiated by passage of the Civil Liberties Act of 1988.[107]

Verdun's periodization has influenced other writers, although some have changed or added stages. Citing Verdun, the *Southern Law Review* added a precolonial stage of African rebellions extending back to the sixteenth century. It also substituted the Garvey movement for Bilbo's efforts at repatriation as a stage of reparations activity.[108] Irma Jacqueline Ozer excluded the precolonial African period but accepted the Garvey movement as a stage replacing Bilbo. Finally, Tuneen Chisolm used the same five stages or periods as Ozer's.[109]

Perhaps because the historical information has so few details, there has been no attempt to explain similarities or differences either within or between each stage. The periods themselves are assumed to be separate, but there has been no explicit effort to justify periodization. Given the cursory treatment of these historical efforts, it is not surprising that the authors offer no theory of legal redress or theory of social movement.

In fact, what little theory of redress we have comes from the comparison of a few well-known cases: Holocaust claims, Japanese American claims, and Native American claims. For example, legal scholar Roy Brooks offered the following theory of redress:

1. The demands or claims for redress must be placed in the hands of legislators rather than judges.
2. Political pressure must be applied.
3. Strong internal support must be generated.
4. It must be a meritorious claim.[110]

Mari Masuda elaborated on this theory by establishing prerequisites for a meritorious claim:

1. A human injustice must have been committed.
2. It must be well-documented.
3. The victims must be identifiable as a distinct group.
4. current members of the group must continue to suffer harm.
5. Such harm must be causally connected to a past injustice.[111]

Saul Levmore supplemented the meritorious claims prerequisite by emphasizing the importance of survivors. Yet, he maintained, it is the number of survivors that is important. It must be large enough to be visible, but enough time must have elapsed to lessen the guilt or defensiveness of the current generation. Moreover, the survivors should be few enough in number that compensation would be seen as bringing an end to their claim.[112]

John Torpey chose a different approach. Starting with the outcomes, he mapped out the types of claims being made from symbolic to material and from cultural to legal. The likelihood of a claim being redressed, then, depends on the nature of the claim. For example, memorials are more likely to be achieved than apologies, and apologies are more common than reparations. From this perspective, the nature of the claim triggers the path or arena leading to claim adjudication.[113]

Neither Verdun's five stages or periods of reparations activity nor Brooks's theory of redress help us explain why reparations have become an important political issue for current Black political elites and Black public opinion. Nor do they shed light on the hostility of White political elites and general public opinion on the issue of racial reparations.

In summary, what these elaborated theories of redress do is extract from a number of historical cases the characteristics thought to be essential to the success of the reparations claim. These characteristics are not bound by time or place, and the cases are not seen as influencing succeeding cases. That is, the cases from which the theory is drawn are viewed as equivalent and independent. In addition, success is measured by the outcome of the claim and not by any qualities or by-products of the process itself. Torpey's approach, which looks at the type of claim being made as the most significant factor in predicting success, is useful in distinguishing among reparations cycles. We have seen that the period after the Civil War was dominated by land claims by ex-slaves and their Reconstruction allies. The next cycle, beginning in the late nineteenth century and extending to World War I, marked a shift from land claims to individual demands for pensions for ex-slaves. The broad expansion of pensions for Civil War veterans and their families stimulated this movement. The next cycle we identified occurred during the civil rights movement. Without any direct victims of slavery, reparations demands are implicitly contained in the group-centered demands for economic rights by major civil rights leaders such as Young, King, Rustin, and Randolph. Moreover, King's, Rustin's, and Randolph's economic programs expand the recipients to include disadvantaged Whites as well. With King's death, the demands of the "Black Manifesto" represent a shift from the public arena to private institutions and a narrowing to Black victims. However, Forman's effort gained little political momentum and thus does not represent a different cycle.

As we will see, with the passage of the Civil Liberties Act of 1988, we entered a new cycle of heightened claims for racial reparations. It was the passage of this legislation that inspired the most successful action for racial reparations to date, the case of Rosewood, Florida. Yet a similar claim from Tulsa, Oklahoma, met a very different response. Thus, Torpey's focus on the nature of the claim does not completely answer the question of what type of claim is likely to succeed.

3

A Winning Case

Comparing the Rosewood and Greenwood
Reparations Claims

> Once the majority has irrevocably decided a question, it is no longer
> discussed. This is because the majority is a power that does not re-
> spond well to criticism.
>> —Alexis de Tocqueville, quoted in "Tulsa Race Riot: A Report by
>> the Oklahoma Commission to Study the
>> Tulsa Race Riot of 1921"

> If you burn the house you cannot hide the smoke.
>> —Ugandan proverb, quoted by Tim Wise in Raymond A.
>> Winbush, ed., *Should America Pay? Slavery and the*
>> *Raging Debate on Reparations*

> People who imagine that history flatters them (as it does, indeed,
> since they wrote it) are impaled on their history like a butterfly on a
> pin and become incapable of seeing or changing themselves or the
> world. . . . This is the place in which it seems to me most white Amer-
> icans find themselves. Impaled. They are dimly, or vividly, aware
> that the history they have fed themselves is mainly a lie, but they do
> not know how to release themselves from it, and they suffer enor-
> mously from the resulting personal incoherence.
>> —James Baldwin, from Scott L. Malcolmson, *One Drop of Blood:*
>> *The American Misadventure of Race*

The two best-known claims for African American reparations involve
well-established Black communities in the South (Rosewood, Florida)
and the Southwest (the Greenwood section of Tulsa, Oklahoma). The
two communities were destroyed by neighboring Whites at roughly

the same time, between 1921 and 1923, and both events were largely erased from the historical record—though not from Black memory—until recent times. The similarities in the destruction of the two communities and the subsequent rejection of Black claims for redress are striking. The final outcome of these historic cases also contains important differences relating to how the claims were framed and how the resources were mobilized.

The Rosewood Case

In 1923, Rosewood, Florida, was a prosperous, nearly all-Black town of 150 in western Florida. It contained three churches, a general store, a Masonic lodge, a school, a baseball diamond, and, three miles down the road in Sumner, a sawmill. The occupants of the nearly thirty homes in Rosewood made their living by felling the trees that gave the town its name or by trapping mink, otter, and raccoon for furs they could sell up in Gainesville or down in Cedar Key. Some people worked distilling turpentine or for the railroad. Many Black women, like Sarah Carrier, worked as domestics for Whites in neighboring towns.

Rosewood's history stretched back to 1847. A rail line was opened in 1861 and a depot was established at Rosewood. As the neighboring Cedar Key became the most important Gulf Coast port in Florida in the 1870s, the unincorporated village grew. Its name came from the pale rose hew of the cedar that the town cut and shipped to Cedar Key. Census records from 1885 place the White population of Rosewood at 140 and the Black residents at 84. But by 1920, a decline in the timber business had led to the departure of most Whites, and Blacks had become the majority, with 355 residents. while Whites numbered 345.[1]

Florida had a history of violence toward Blacks. When two Black men tried to vote in Ocoee in 1920, the Ku Klux Klan retaliated by killing at least six Blacks and burning down the entire community of twenty-five homes. In the same year, four Blacks were taken from a jail in McClenny and lynched. In December 1922, less than a month before the Rosewood massacre, a Black man accused of murder in Perry, Florida, was burned at the stake. Two others were hanged as well, and the town's Black church, school, and Masonic lodge were set on fire and destroyed. On New Year's Eve 1922, a massive Klan rally in Gainesville demonstrated the popularity of White supremacy and vigilante justice.[2]

The trouble started in Sumner in the early morning of New Year's Day 1922 when Fannie Taylor stumbled out of her house bleeding and battered. As a crowd of neighbors gathered around her, the weeping and hysterical White housewife claimed that a "nigger" had attacked her.[3] By the time Fannie's husband James arrived back home from his job of oiling machinery at the sawmill, county sheriff Rob Walker was already there, and a posse was forming. Sheriff Walker believed the likely culprit was a Black convict, Jesse Hunter, who had escaped from a county road gang the day before.

Quickly the hounds, followed by the posse, shot off in the direction of Rosewood. The dogs stopped at the house of a Black WWI veteran, Aaron Carrier. Storming into Carrier's house, the mob pulled him out of a sick bed, tied his wrists to the bumper of a car, and dragged him up a hard dirt road. Carrier pleaded that he had done nothing wrong and said that Sam Carter had taken in the convict, Hunter. Some of the mob of now nearly fifty men stayed with Carrier while the others tore through Rosewood looking for Carter. It wasn't until dusk that Carter's wagon rolled into town. Carter, a forty-seven-year-old blacksmith, was immediately seized by the mob. He admitted to helping Hunter but refused to tell the mob where he had hidden him. Enraged, the Whites strung Carter from a tree while others in the crowd used knives to carve souvenirs from his body. Nearly dead, Carter agreed to take them to the hiding place. By the time they reached the spot in the swamp where Carter said he left Hunter, he was gone. A man stepped from the mob, pointed a gun in Carter's face and pulled the trigger. Members of the crowd took additional body parts for keepsakes, and one grabbed Carter's pocket watch. For years afterward it would show up in a bar or barbershop in the region, and someone would laugh and say, "Let's see what time it is by old Sam Carter."[4]

With Carter dead and Carrier rescued by W. H. Pillsbury, the White superintendent of the sawmill, the mob went home. But the air was full of tension, and some Rosewood men sent their families away. Sylvester Carrier, Aaron's cousin and a man whom Whites viewed as arrogant and disrespectful, decided to bring all of his extended family to his parents' home. When word reached Sumner that nearly twenty people had gathered at Sarah Carrier's place, another mob formed on the night of January 4 and, fortified by moonshine whiskey, headed to Rosewood. They suspected that the Carrier family was stockpiling arms and planning an attack.

In reality, only two men, Sylvester and his disabled uncle, James, were at Sarah Carrier's house—the rest were women and children. When the mob arrived, Sarah went to the window and shouted for them all to "go on home." Someone in the crowd responded by shooting her through the head. The shot unleashed a torrent of buckshot from the posse into the Carrier home. Miraculously, only Sylvester was hit. As the mob came through the door, Sylvester shot and killed its leader, Poly Wilkerson, a former "private" sheriff at the sawmill, and another mill supervisor, Henry Andrews. Another member of the mob tried climbing through an upstairs window and was wounded in the head. Two more Whites were wounded, and at 4 A.M. the gang retreated to wait for dawn and reinforcements.

As word of the siege spread, White reinforcements brought the mob number to 250, and they surged forward again, finding only an empty house containing the bodies of Sylvester Carrier and his mother, Sarah. Nonetheless, the mob continued to grow, with cars pulling into Rosewood from as far away as Jacksonville and even across the state line from Georgia. After torching the Carrier home, they proceeded to set fire to other homes and then to the Methodist church. Those Blacks too old or sick to flee into the swamp were at the mercy of the crowd. Lexie Gordon, a fifty-five-year-old widow, was ill with typhoid fever. When her home started to burn, she pulled herself out of bed and attempted to flee through the rear door. She was gunned down in a hail of bullets. On the morning of January 5, Florida's governor, Cary Hardee, offered to send the National Guard to Levy County, but Sheriff Walker declined the offer, saying that he "feared no further disorder."[5]

One Black man, Mingo Williams, living some twenty miles east of Rosewood, was killed by a car filled with White men as he was chopping down a tree. Another group of Whites pulled disabled James Carrier from one of the few unburned homes and shot him after making him dig his own grave with his one good arm. John and William Bryce, two White railroad conductors, managed to rescue a number of Blacks by slowly running some railcars through the swamp three days after the start of the violence. Others hid in homes of Whites for whom they worked in Sumner. John Wright, who ran Rosewood's largest store and was the only White living in Rosewood proper, sheltered a number of Blacks. As the mob torched buildings all over Rosewood, they deliberately passed over Wright's grand home. By Sunday afternoon, when sheriffs and deputies began to arrive from Bronson and Alachua counties, there was nothing left to protect. Rosewood and its inhabitants were gone, never to return.[6]

Word of the burning of Rosewood spread as far north as Washington and Chicago. The *Chicago Tribune* termed it a "race war," and the *Washington Post* accused a "negro desperado" who had the nerve to defend his home of having sparked the conflict. The Carrier home was described by the *St. Louis Post-Dispatch* as a "barricaded hut" inhabited by a "band of heavily armed Negroes." In New York, the burning of Rosewood was a front-page story in the *New York Times* and quoted Sylvester Carrier as saying the rape of Mrs. Taylor was "proof of what Negroes could do without interference."[7] Unsubstantiated statements like this provided a catalyst for an attack on the town. Although the *Tampa Times* labeled the attack a foul and lasting blot on the people of Levy County, the more general feeling of Whites was expressed by the *Gainesville Sun,* that Rosewood was no "Southern Lynching Outrage" but the proper avenging of a "crime against innocent womanhood."[8]

The Black newspapers' coverage was decidedly different. Baltimore's *Afro-American* cited a much higher death toll and praised the residents of Rosewood as heroes for defending their homes. The military experience of the Black veterans was noted, as was the call of Negro leaders urging colored residents across Florida to sell their property and move northward. The *New York Amsterdam News* compared the defense of Rosewood with "the bravest feats on Flanders Field," and the *Pittsburgh American* declared that Negroes everywhere should "feel proud and take renewed hope."[9]

A month later an all-White grand jury meeting in Bronson heard testimony from more than thirteen witnesses and pronounced the evidence "insufficient" for indictments. No charges were ever brought against any person for the assault on Frances Taylor, for the killing of Sam Carter, for the deaths at the Carrier home, or for the deaths of Lexie Gordon, James Carrier, and Mingo Williams. Jesse Hunter, the alleged rapist, was never found, and the case was closed.

Some sixty years after the destruction of Rosewood, Gary Moore, a reporter from the *St. Petersburg Times,* was working on a travel story.

While driving along the Gulf Coast, he stopped in the small fishing town of Cedar Key. Moore was curious about the total absence of Blacks in a town that at the turn of the century had been one-third Black. Now the old Black school and all the Black churches were gone. Even a place the locals called "Nigger Hill" had no Black residents. After repeated inquiries, Moore finally found a woman who mentioned "the massacre." He then began to hear the pieces of a horrific tale that might have been dismissed as legend were it not for the severed body parts stored in Mason jars and still pulled out with pride on special occasions.

Despite its national prominence as a news story in 1923, the "race war" in Rosewood had been effectively eliminated from history books. But even though it has been erased from Florida's official history, it certainly had not been forgotten by those with a direct knowledge of the events. Moore's story about Rosewood came out in the summer of 1982. Some Blacks with knowledge of the events had refused to talk to him, reluctant to reopen old wounds, and the story provoked little reaction until the television program *60 Minutes* decided to feature it. The broadcast in December 1983 revived memories that could not be suppressed.

Rosewood family reunions, prompted by the *60 Minutes* broadcast, began in 1985. For the first time, the long-held secret of many of the massacre survivors was now in the open. One person willing to talk was Lee Ruth Davis. The person who tracked her down in Miami was Michael O'McCarthy, a Hollywood deal maker and promoter of social causes. O'McCarthy had become enthralled with Moore's Rosewood story after coming across it in 1991 on a tip from a Hollywood friend. He decided that a reparations case against the state of Florida would make a great movie story and that Lee Ruth Davis would be its star.[10]

Arnett Doctor, the son of Rosewood survivor Philomena Goins Doctor, had been trying for months to get someone interested in the Rosewood case. Although his interest in the history of Rosewood was long-standing, his motivation to obtain redress was spurred at the 1991 Rosewood reunion when one of his relatives told him about the "Japanese American Reparations Act." Throughout 1992, he called, wrote, and visited Black attorneys across the state of Florida, and he met with social justice organizations like the state NAACP. Doctor

could not believe that his people had no interest in seeking racial justice for the survivors of Rosewood.[11]

O'McCarthy had better luck. He convinced Steve Hanlon, of the
high-profile Florida law firm of Holland and Knight, to talk with Lee
Ruth Davis. After talking with Davis and her cousin, Rosewood survivor Minnie Lee Driver (Langley), Hanlon agreed to take on the case
and made the key decision to take the Rosewood story to the state legislature rather than a state court. He also decided that a claims bill for
the two survivors—Davis and Driver—could not pass as an exclusively African American issue. To broaden the base of support to include moderate Democrats and even Republicans, Hanlon sought
Cuban American support by citing the injustice of the dispossession of
Rosewood citizens run out of their homes and off their land. With this
powerful message, he found empathy and a sponsor for the bill in
Miguel De Grandy, a Republican and chairman of the Cuban American caucus in Florida's House of Representatives. De Grandy also suggested appointing Al Lawson, the chair of the Black caucus, as a cosponsor.[12]

Hanlon's decision to seek support from De Grandy and the Cuban
American caucus diverged from Florida's political history, which had
been one of conflict between Cuban Americans and African Americans. Since the failed Bay of Pigs invasion under the Kennedy administration, Cuban Americans had strongly identified with the Republican Party, and perhaps more significantly, Cuban Americans saw
themselves as Whites, not people of color. Outside the Miami–Dade
County area, however, White Floridians regarded Cuban Americans
as another minority group.[13]

Class was another major divide between African Americans and
Cuban Americans. The number of Cubans immigrating to the United
States between 1959 and 1980 was more than 800,000, consisting
mainly of middle- and upper-class Cubans who quickly established
themselves economically and politically in south Florida. African
Americans resented their success and the approximately $2 billion
that the U.S. government spent to help them resettle.[14]

But with the arrival of the first Marielitos—Cuban refugees
brought to the United States via the Mariel boatlift in 1980—the class
and color status of Cuban Americans began to change. The approximately 125,000 Marielitos who fled Cuba in 1980 had a lower socio-

economic status, and 40 percent of them were Black.[15] This influx of Cuban immigrants to the Miami community further strained relations between African Americans and Cuban Americans, ultimately leading to three major riots between 1980 and 1992.

At the state level, the conflict between the two groups was manifested politically on the issues of redistricting and establishing a third state law school. In the state legislature, the two sponsors of the Rosewood claims bill wound up on opposite sides of these two issues. The greatest rupture between these two communities, however, was sparked by Nelson Mandela's visit to Miami in 1990. Black plans to honor Mandela were shattered when the South African leader publicly expressed his appreciation for the support of Fidel Castro, who had stood behind the African National Congress in its struggle against apartheid. In Dade County, five Cuban American mayors publicly denounced Mandela, and to the dismay of Black Miami residents, Miami withheld any civic recognition of Mandela.[16]

How could these two antagonistic forces be brought together in the state legislature? The primary focus of the Rosewood claims bill was dispossession. The citizens of Rosewood had been rightful owners of their own homes and land and had been forced to flee without receiving any form of compensation. Because the idea of loss was central to the identity of the Cuban American community, it was able to overcome the racial and class differences that had divided the communities. Thus the Cuban exiles could identity with the Rosewood exiles through the frame of lost property, lost home, and lost hope.[17]

The first major obstacle facing the claims bill was the survivors' disunity. Davis and Driver had proceeded without the consent of the other survivors, and some news stories portrayed them as the only survivors. In January 1993 therefore, Arnett Doctor arranged for Hanlon to meet the remaining survivors. Seven additional survivors (two were physically unable to attend) met Hanlon and agreed to support the claims bill. Their testimony became crucial to the legislation's success.

Introduced late in the session, the first claims bill, containing only the names of Davis and Driver, quickly died. Al Lawson then proposed establishing a state-funded study commission, which won the support of Governor Lawton Chiles and Bo Johnson, the speaker of the Florida house.

The state's board of regents selected a study team of five prominent historians, three Whites and two Blacks. Many of the doors that had been closed to Arnett Doctor were now open to the study commission members. Not surprisingly, White residents of the region around Rosewood were now openly hostile to all the negative attention the story brought them. Even the Ku Klux Klan began to lobby against a claims bill. In the meantime, however, the study team found Ernest Parham, a detached and disinterested White witness to the events surrounding Rosewood. Now retired from the laundry business, Parham recalled the jealousy of some poor Whites of those Black Rosewood residents who were better off than they were. Moreover, others resented Sylvester Carrier's "aloof" and "distant" attitude. Most important though, Parham had been an eyewitness to the murder of Sam Carter.[18]

Claims bills against the state of Florida are sent to a "special master" whose job is to provide an initial assessment of the claim. At that time, Richard Hixson was the "special master" who reviewed the roughly two dozen claims bills filed each year in the Florida legislature, and his award recommendations were almost always seconded by the legislature. It thus was Hixson who asked the questions that Hanlon and Doctor had been avoiding for the sake of unity. Who should be compensated, and how much should they get? Significantly, the Rosewood bill sought *compensation,* not *reparation.*

Arnett Doctor reported that they had identified twenty-six Rosewood families surviving from the time of the massacre and thought that $1 million per family, or a total of $26 million, would be fair. A stunned De Grandy countered that $1 million or possibly $2 million in all was the most they could hope for. After a good deal of discussion on both sides, De Grandy and Lawson agreed to support a claims bill for $7 million.

Hixson began the hearings on the Rosewood bill in February 1994. Special security was needed because of the threats against Doctor and Lawson. Hanlon testified that the Japanese American Reparations Act was the basic model for the bill, but opponents thought that the bill would open the door for a slave compensation claim. Others argued that Blacks had ambushed Whites in Rosewood.

The state of Florida took the position that the claims presented in the Rosewood bill were without legal basis and were barred by the statute of limitations and that bringing the claims at this time prevented a reasonable defense, since the officials charged had died.

Moreover, the state added that at least since 1983 there had been no justifiable impediment to bringing these claims to the legislature. Hixson acknowledged the legal problems but insisted that the Rosewood claim was not a legal proceeding. His report stated: "In an equitable claim bill proceeding, however, these legal principles do not, as a matter of law, restrict the legislature's consideration of these claims."[19] Hixson distinguished between a legal proceeding and a claims bill on the basis of the "moral obligations of the state," which are within the legislature's prerogative.

Hixson cited the actions of Congress in the case of Japanese American claims and noted that there was no question that government officers were aware of the violent situation that existed during the entire week of January 1923. Furthermore, although they had helped evacuate the Rosewood residents, they had not secured the area. Hixson therefore contended that the Rosewood families should be compensated. The amount he offered was based on the equitable claim bills redressing the "moral obligations" that the legislature had earlier enacted, especially for the case of *Gamble v. Wells,* in which the legislature awarded $150,000 to a child who was physically and emotionally damaged because of the state's failure to provide adequate foster care. Ultimately, Hixson supported a claim for $2.1 million, including a $500,000 property compensation fund, college scholarships for needy students with preference to children of Rosewood descendants, and $150,000 for each survivor.[20]

Unlike most cases in the past, the state legislature did not automatically go along with Hixson's recommendation. Debate on the claims bill consumed the legislature and many of the state's media. But the bill survived an attempt to strip out its monetary provisions and make it a symbolic proclamation of regret. Perhaps the key to its final passage was belated pressure on the governor from the legislature's Black caucus,[21] and on May 5, 1994, the governor signed into law the Rosewood Compensation Act.

The Tulsa Case

After viewing the destruction in Tulsa's Black neighborhood of Greenwood, the NAACP's Walter White exclaimed: "I am able to state that the Tulsa riot, in sheer brutality and willful destruction of life and property, stands without parallel in America.[22] The destruction was all the more ironic for a state that once was seen as the Black "promised land." After the great land rush of 1889, Black leaders planned to put Black citizens in each of the Oklahoma Territories' districts, with the goal of making Oklahoma a majority Black state when it joined the Union. Edward P. McCabe, often called the father of the all-Black town movement, traveled to Washington, D.C., to lobby President Benjamin Harrison to admit Oklahoma as a "Black state." As a result, Oklahoma had more all-Black towns (fifty-eight) than any other region in the country. But when it became a state in 1907, Blacks were already being expelled from some areas, and the first act of the new state legislature was to segregate the state between Whites, broadly defined to include Indians and Mexicans, and Blacks, those with African blood.[23] Oklahoma's first governor, William H. "Alfalfa Bill" Murray, longed for the old days: "I appreciate the old-time ex-slave, the old darky, and they are the salt of their race—who comes to me talking softly in that humble spirit which should characterize their actions and dealings with white men."[24]

Only two years after its incorporation in 1898, Tulsa was a raw frontier town of 1,300 residents, but with the discovery of "the biggest small [oil] field in the world" by two Tulsa wildcatters in 1905, it soon grew in population and sophistication. By 1907 ninety-seven oil companies were working the field, and Tulsa's population soared to 7,298. Three years later it had more than doubled and by 1920 stood at 72,075.[25]

Tulsa's Black population also surged, increasing from 1,959 in 1910 to 8,873 in 1920. Most of this population voluntarily segregated themselves in a four-square-mile area of north Tulsa known as Greenwood (after Greenwood, Mississippi), which was annexed by the city in 1909. As Greenwood's population grew, it supported clothing shops, banks, restaurants, movie houses, ice-cream parlors, drug stores, and J. B. Stradford's hotel, the largest Black-owned hotel in America. Greenwood also was home to thirteen churches, two newspapers, a hospital, two schools, and a Black public library.[26]

Although Greenwood's business district had earned the title of "the Black Wall Street," this moniker masked a harsher reality. By 1920 only six blocks of Greenwood were paved, and sewage connections were rare as indoor plumbing. Many residents were housed in weather-beaten shacks or sheds, and cows and chickens roamed freely along the dirt roads.[27] What affluence Greenwood enjoyed came only indirectly from the oil business, which excluded Blacks. In addition, a 1930 employment survey found that nearly 40 percent of all Black male employees and 93 percent of all Black female employees—62 percent of all Black workers—were domestics.[28]

Tulsa's history of vigilante activity extends back to at least 1894 when a White man known as "Dutch John" was lynched as a suspected cattle rustler. In 1904, a lynch mob was prevented by the city marshal, mayor, and a local banker from taking an African American prisoner. During 1917 the local White press praised the tarring and feathering of more than a dozen local members of the Industrial Workers of the World, who were then driven from town. Blacks also had been "driven" from the Oklahoma towns of Norman and Dewey in the years preceding the Tulsa race riot.[29]

The lynching of Roy Belton in the summer of 1920 was an important precursor of things to come. Belton, who was White, had participated in the robbery of a taxi in which the driver was shot and later died. Belton was caught, and on news of the taxi driver's death, a lynch mob snatched Belton from the courthouse and hanged him outside town. The sheriff and police chief did little to stop the mob and afterward seemed to endorse the action by claiming it would deter further crime, to which the White press agreed.[30]

On May 30, 1921, Dick Rowland, a bootblack, took the elevator to the "colored" restroom in the office building near the shine parlor where he worked. As he got on the elevator, he apparently tripped and grabbed the arm of seventeen-year-old Sarah Page, the White elevator operator, to balance himself. Page screamed, and as Rowland hurried away, a clothing store clerk spotted him. The clerk called the police and claimed that Rowland had attempted to rape Page, although there is no record of what Page said to the police.[31]

Police arrested Rowland the next morning at his adopted mother's home, and Tulsa's afternoon paper, the *Tulsa Tribune*, ran a front-page story entitled "Nab Negro for Attacking Girl in Elevator." Some Tulsa residents of the time also recall an editorial entitled "To Lynch a Negro Tonight."[32] After the paper came out, talk of a possible lynching spread like wildfire in both Tulsa's White and Black communities.

Remembering the fate of Roy Belton, who had been imprisoned in the same jail cell as Rowland was, a group of approximately twenty-five African American men, many World War I veterans, some in uniform, drove from Greenwood to the courthouse around 9 P.M. Armed with rifles and shotguns they offered their services to shocked authorities. Police assured the group that Rowland would be protected, and the men departed.

Word of the arrival of armed Blacks had an electrifying effect on Whites, some of whom had already begun to gather near the courthouse. Some tried to break into the armory to obtain guns while the crowd at the courthouse grew to nearly two thousand. At no time did the police make a show of force to break up the mob. Possibly hearing that the mob was attacking the courthouse, a second contingent of seventy-five armed Blacks returned to the scene, offering once again to protect Rowland. Their offer also was refused again, but on departing a White man tried to disarm an African American veteran. In the ensuing struggle, the White man was shot, and America's worst race riot began.[33]

As the violence flared, perhaps as many as five hundred White men and boys were sworn in by police officers as "special deputies." According to one special deputy, a police officer bluntly instructed him to "get a gun and get a nigger."[34] Sporadic fighting and looting broke out across the downtown area. The National Guard was called in around 11 P.M. and deployed downtown to stop what it termed as a "Negro uprising." By 1 A.M., Whites were setting fires in Black neighborhoods. Rather than protecting Black homes, however, the National Guard set up a "skirmish line" facing the African American district.

Many Black Tulsans began to stream out of the city while at the same time others armed themselves and prepared for confrontation. Rumors spread among Whites that five hundred armed Blacks were arriving by train from Muskogee, and Whites accompanied by a National Guard patrol hurried to the station to meet the phantom train. For a while it looked as though Greenwood's residents might hold off the White mobs, estimated to number between five thousand and ten thousand. At one point, several residents reported explosives being dropped on Greenwood from an airplane. Other witnesses stated that an unusual whistle or siren sounded at dawn, signaling a massive assault.

As Blacks were driven from their homes and businesses into the street, they were rounded up at gunpoint and led to internment centers. Those who resisted were shot, as were any Black men with firearms. Next, Whites looted the Blacks' homes and businesses, setting fire to them as they left. Witnesses reported seeing Tulsa police officers participating in the rioting and looting along with the special deputies. Rather than disarming and arresting White rioters, the Tulsa police and local National Guard units focused on arresting and imprisoning Greenwood's citizens, leaving their property unprotected. For example, Captain John W. McCuen of the National Guard reported:

> At the northeast corner of the Negro settlement 10 or more Negroes barricaded themselves in a concrete store and dwelling and a stiff fight ensued between these Negroes on one side and guardsmen and civilians on the other. Several whites and blacks were wounded and killed at this point. We captured, arrested and disarmed a great many Negro men in this settlement and then sent them under guard to the convention hall and other points where they were being concentrated.[35]

The internment camps eventually held four thousand to six thousand Blacks, who were required to carry identity or "green cards" and were held for up to three days.

Even when martial law was declared and state troopers belatedly arrived, they were sent to protect downtown businesses rather than to Greenwood, where homes were still being torched. By 8 P.M. on June 1, the riot was over. Thirty-five blocks of Greenwood lay in ruin, with property damage placed at $1.8 million. Estimates of the death toll range from 39 to more than 250. Of the 39 death certificates issued, 26 were for Blacks. A number of Blacks died because they did not receive medical attention. In addition, most of the Blacks killed were older residents of Greenwood, whereas most of the dead Whites were young, single oil workers from outside Tulsa. None of the recorded deaths was investigated, and many were never recorded.[36]

Many of the Greenwood residents released from the various internment centers found that their homes had been destroyed. Others had missed the burial of loved ones, and some could not even find the burial sites. In the immediate aftermath of the riot, some Tulsans talked of the city's moral duty to help rebuild Greenwood. The Public Welfare Board even announced plans to assist in the rebuilding, and both White newspapers backed the effort. By mid-June, however, Mayor T. D. Evans had replaced the private board with an official city board, the Reconstruction Committee.

Leaders of the new and misleadingly named Reconstruction Committee shifted the focus from rebuilding Greenwood to immediate relief projects like "old furniture day" and the provision of washing
basins to Greenwood domestics so that they might continue doing
White families' laundry. At the same time, the Tulsa Real Estate Exchange, a board established by the Chamber of Commerce, proposed
relocating Greenwood farther north and converting the burned district into an industrial area. The city zoning board encouraged this
plan by adopting an ordinance that made rebuilding residences in the
area prohibitively expensive.[37]

Greenwood's residents naturally suspected a plot to displace them.
Some began rebuilding in defiance of the ordinance, while others went
to court for a restraining order against it. Finally, in late September,
they won a permanent injunction against the ordinance as a violation
of property rights.[38]

Black and White Tulsans filed claims against the city, totaling ap-
proximately $5 million, but only one claim, for $2,000, was paid to the
White owner of a hardware store looted at the beginning of the riot.
The county and city did, however, spend $100,000 on relief efforts.

By June 1923, more than one hundred legal suits had been filed,
but only two went to trial. One case did not reach the jury. But the case
of William Redfearn, a Native American who lost a theater and a hotel
in Greenwood, did go all the way to the Oklahoma Supreme Court.
Redfearn had sued both the city and his insurance company, which
had refused to pay his claim based on a riot exclusion clause in his
policy. The suit against the city was dropped largely on grounds of
the city's immunity from liability, but the insurance case hinged on
whether the loss was caused by police or the special deputies. Although the court's decision acknowledged the role of the deputies
in the destruction, it questioned whether the men wearing "police
badges or sheriff's badges were in fact such officers or acting in an official capacity."[39] Thus, Redfearn's claim was denied.

In September 1921, the case against Dick Rowland was dismissed
when Sarah Page failed to appear as the complaining witness. A grand
jury issued several dozen indictments, mostly for Blacks, and Tulsa
prosecutors sought to extradite Greenwood leaders A. J. Smitherman
from Boston and J. B. Stradford from Chicago to try them for inciting
the riot. Both had urged Blacks to protect Rowland from the lynch
mob. In its final report, the grand jury cited two, more remote, causes

of the riot: the "agitation among Negroes of social equality" and the breakdown of law enforcement. Regarding the former, the grand jury stated that "all of [this agitation] was accumulative in the minds of the negro which led them as a people to believe in equal rights, social equality, and their ability to demand the same."[40] On the latter point, it was not the special deputies at fault but the weakness of law enforcement in Greenwood that had led to the "indiscriminate mingling of white and colored people in dance halls and other places of amusement."[41] The riot had at least solved this problem, since those places no longer existed. In this context, it is not surprising that the Tulsa race riot provided a tremendous boost in membership for the Klan in Tulsa and in Oklahoma more generally.

The Tulsa race riot is not mentioned in Oklahoma's history books when discussing the 1920s and 1930s. Angie Debo's popular 1943 book entitled *Tulsa: From Creek Town to Oil Capital*, which takes Oklahomans to task for stealing Indian land, barely mentions the riot. The quarterly journal of the Oklahoma Historical Society, the *Chronicle of Oklahoma*, never published a single story on the riot. Key documents, including the front-page *Tribune* story and editorial accused of inciting the riot, disappeared from the archives. Even police and state militia records associated with the riot vanished. Daniel Boorstin, one of the nation's most distinguished historians and a Librarian of Congress, grew up in Tulsa and was six years old at the time of the riot. But this Pulitzer Prize–winning scholar of the "American experience" never wrote a word about the Tulsa race riot.

Don Ross, who grew up in Greenwood in the 1950s, became the central figure in rescuing the race riot from the dustbins of history. As a high school student, Ross had been stunned when he heard the story of the riot from W. D. Williams, a high school history teacher. Initially disbelieving, Ross began his own investigation of the riot, confirming Williams's account. After leaving high school and the air force, Ross began writing articles for the weekly *Oklahoma Eagle,* and in 1968 he wrote three consecutive columns on the Tulsa race riot. The other brief pieces in academic journals in the early 1970s did not attract the attention of White Tulsa.[42]

Instead, White Tulsa's awakening was left to Ed Wheeler, a conservative Republican from Oklahoma who became a brigadier general in the U.S. Army. Wheeler, a gifted storyteller, was asked to write a piece for *Tulsa* magazine commemorating the fiftieth anniversary of the riot. Wheeler accepted and interviewed sixty survivors, both Black and White. But as he continued his research, he began to receive threatening telephone calls, and the magazine rejected the story he submitted. Wheeler then took it to a friend at the *Tulsa World*, who praised it and then rejected it, saying that "the *World* won't touch it with an eleven-foot pole."[43] Finally, a new Black magazine, edited by Don Ross, published the piece in 1971. Also remembering the anniversary was the *Tulsa Tribune*, whose own stories had played such a central role in sparking the violence. Ignoring its own role, the *Tribune* cited only one hero, its editor Richard Lloyd Jones, who, the *Tribune* asserted, "did much to calm the stricken city."[44]

The first full-scale scholarly investigation of the Tulsa race riot was the publication in 1982 of Scott Ellsworth's *Death in a Promised Land*. Ellsworth was a native of Tulsa, and the book grew out of a college thesis project in the mid-1970s. Perhaps his best sources were a late 1920s book by a young Black riot survivor, Mary E. Jones Parrish, and a 1946 master's thesis at the University of Tulsa by Loren Gill.

Don Ross became a state legislator in 1982, the same year that Ellsworth's book was published. Ross wanted to commemorate the seventy-fifth anniversary of the riot, so he asked Ellsworth and a young Jewish lawyer, Ken Levit, for assistance. The result was the "Black Wall Street Memorial" dedicated on June 1, 1996, in a ceremony covered by the *New York Times, Washington Post,* NPR, and the *Today* show. Judge Cornelius E. Toole of Chicago, great-grandson of J. B. Stradford, watched the *Today* show broadcast. Having long resented the destruction of the Stradford Hotel and his great-grandfather's indictment, Toole contacted Tulsa officials. Through the efforts by Toole and the Tulsa district attorney, the charges against Stradford were dismissed. In a ceremony attended by four generations of the Stradford clan at the Greenwood cultural center, Oklahoma Governor Frank Keating presented Stradford's family with an honorary executive pardon.[45]

In 1994, the state of Florida passed legislation compensating the survivors of the Rosewood massacre, and Don Ross believed the Tulsa survivors were entitled to no less. In January 1997, he submitted a joint resolution to the Oklahoma legislature calling for $6 million in compensation for the survivors of the riot, for the descendants of the riot victims, and for children's programs in north Tulsa.

Although Ross's bill generated publicity—some negative—it failed to pass. He then proposed a fact-finding commission to investigate the Tulsa race riot. The legislature agreed, and an eleven-member commission was established, which included two state officials and other members appointed by the governor and mayor of Tulsa. Six of the eleven commission members were Black, and eight of the commissioners favored payments to survivors. The commission hired Scott Ellsworth as its chief investigator and asked him to draft a report.

After two years of work but no report, the commission tried to replace Ellsworth, as his lack of political skills and the strong divisions among commission members had made him unpopular. In addition, both Don Ross and Ellsworth resented the attention the other had received for rescuing the story of the Tulsa riot. Only intervention from the distinguished historian John Hope Franklin, a commission consultant who had grown up in Tulsa, saved Ellsworth's job.[46]

Neither Ellsworth nor Franklin, however, could bridge the growing racial divide on the commission. Verbal confrontations between Black and White commissioners grew personal. At commission meetings, the audience and commissioners began voluntarily to segregate themselves. Don Ross had the commission change its stationery letterhead from the official Oklahoma state seal to the Black nationalist colors of red, black, and green.

In this charged atmosphere, it is remarkable that all but one commissioner—the Republican state senator Robert Milacek—signed the final report. This document recommended making direct payments to the riot survivors and their descendants; a scholarship fund available to students affected by the riot; the establishment of an economic development enterprise zone in Greenwood; and a memorial for the riot victims.[47]

The racial conflict in the commission was reflected in public opinion. A poll taken in December 1999 found that only 12 percent of Oklahomans favored spending tax dollars for reparations, and only 26 percent of the respondents favored reparations if no tax dollars were used (i.e., only private funding).[48]

More surprising was Don Ross's failure to endorse the commission report (whose introduction he had written). Perhaps reading the polling data and listening to the objections of his fellow legislators convinced Ross a reparations bill could not succeed. For whatever reason, he proposed a largely symbolic bill that called for low-income student scholarships in Tulsa, an economic development authority for Greenwood, and a memorial. Even Ross called the bill, which allocated no funding, "at best, an opportunity; at worst, smoke and mirrors."[49] Even this symbolic act passed only narrowly and was signed into law by Governor Keating on June 1, 2001, exactly eighty years after the riot. In a final symbolic gesture, the state legislature passed a joint resolution authorizing the awarding of medals to the 118 known living survivors of the destruction of Greenwood.

Although the Rosewood and Greenwood cases have remarkable similarities, the outcomes of their reparations struggles were different. On at least seven factors, the two communities were similar: time, place, resistance, prosperity and its loss, the role of the press, the failure of legal redress, and the erasure from history.

First, both incidents occurred roughly within a year and a half of each other. The period following World War I was marked by a shift in American race relations from the paternalism of the antebellum South and the rural, agricultural economy of the post–Civil War era to the more competitive urban and industrial relationships of the twentieth century. Pushed from their southern homes by the institutionalization of Jim Crow (i.e., apartheid) and pulled to cities in the North and West by the new economic opportunities produced by World War I, nearly 400,000 African Americans started their first great internal migration to more cosmopolitan destinations. But the growth of the Black population, especially in Tulsa, alarmed Whites, who feared they might lose control over the Black community.

Second, some of the worst racial riots in American history and a dramatic increase in lynching took place in the period after World War I. Spurred by the enormously popular film *Birth of a Nation* in 1915, the Klan enjoyed a rebirth. Thirty-nine Blacks and nine Whites died in a race riot in East St. Louis in 1917, the worst of several urban conflicts in that year. During the "red summer" of 1919, racial violence broke out in twenty-five cities across the country, the worst being in Chicago where the homes of new Black residents had regularly been bombed since 1917 and where fifteen Whites and twenty-three Blacks died in the 1919 riot.[50] Greenwood and Rosewood, as well, were in areas experiencing a rise in racial violence.

Third, after World War I, many Black ex-servicemen were determined not to accept the same second-class citizenship they had endured before the war. Having fought to make "the world safe for democracy" and having experienced relative racial equality in countries such as France, the Black veterans demanded respect at home. Moreover, they now had the military training to back up their demands. Veterans in both Rosewood and Tulsa led Black resistance to the White mobs, and undoubtedly this resistance that inflicted casualties on Whites incited them to new levels of fear and brutality.

Fourth, Rosewood and Greenwood were relatively prosperous Black communities. Although the passage of time may have romanticized that image to some extent, especially because of Tulsa's "Black Wall Street" label, both communities contained Black residents who were doing better economically than some of their White neighbors. Blacks in both communities owned land and established civil institutions such as churches, lodges, and schools. Today, however, Rosewood no longer exists as a Black community, and Greenwood still displays deep scars from its past. After the Blacks were chased out of Rosewood, Whites—especially John Wright—were able to buy their land at bargain prices from the state of Florida, which had confiscated it because the property taxes had not been paid. Even though the Black residents of Greenwood were able to prevent real estate developers from turning the town into an industrial area, they were never able to reestablish its former glory. The final blow came in the 1950s when urban renewal projects resulted in a freeway through the heart of the old Greenwood community.

Fifth, the legal process failed to bring justice to the many claims for redress brought by Black residents. In Rosewood, the removal of Blacks was so thorough that no property claims were filed in the immediate aftermath of the riot, even though all the Black-owned homes, three churches, a school, and even a baseball diamond had been destroyed. Some evidence shows that Whites feared Blacks would return to reclaim their land. Tulsa, in contrast, was flooded with more than a hundred claims, all denied by the courts. No Whites were convicted in the racial deaths and destruction of the two communities. Ironically, the incidents that sparked both riots also ended with no convictions.

Sixth, the irresponsible actions of the White press were crucial to both cases. In Tulsa, the *Tulsa Tribune*'s reporting of the initial incident between Dick Rowland and Sarah Page is clearly linked to the outbreak of violence. It inflamed Whites' opinion by raising the specter of interracial sexual assault and increased Blacks' fear that Rowland would be lynched. The disappearance of archival evidence from the newspaper only contributes to the suspicion of the press's lack of accountability. Although Florida's newspapers played no direct role in the initial incident in Rosewood, the White press tended to frame the violence as started by Blacks, with Whites simply retaliating. Certainly the *New York Times* story that reported the challenging comments from Sylvester Carrier was provocative. On the other side was the Black press presenting an image of a besieged Black community defending itself.

Seventh, given the extensive local and national media coverage of each event, it is remarkable that both events could have been erased from historical memory. Indeed, some of the survivors themselves were too ashamed or too afraid or too bitter to help recover this lost history. Thus, from official state histories to school classrooms, the incidents in Rosewood and Greenwood never happened. Only in the context of the post–1960s civil rights movement and a new interest in Black history and community were these stories able to emerge. And only after the successful effort of Japanese Americans to obtain some measure of redress in 1988 could the survivors of these two communities and their supporters hope for some recognition of the injustice inflicted on them.

The outcomes of the redress efforts in Tulsa and Rosewood were quite different. The Rosewood survivors received monetary compensation; a property fund was set up to settle land claims; and a college scholarship fund was created for their descendants. Rosewood also was the subject of a major Hollywood motion picture. In Tulsa, the financial compensation endorsed by the Tulsa Race Riot Commission was rejected by the legislature. Nonetheless, a "Black Wall Street" memorial was erected, and the survivors received medals.

The two cases' different outcomes may be attributed to several factors. Florida is a more cosmopolitan state than Oklahoma. Blacks have significantly more political power in Florida's state politics, and the governor at the time of the Rosewood bill was a Democrat well aware of Black voting power. Rosewood also had fewer survivors, and so the financial compensation recommended by the "special master" in Florida was considerably smaller ($2.1 million) than that proposed in Oklahoma ($33 million).

Equally if not more important was how the reparations process unfolded. The study commission created for Rosewood was primarily a group of scholars who set out to determine the facts. Although not without disagreements, they eventually produced a report that was generally viewed as credible. That report then went to a "special master" who was seen as an impartial arbiter of claims against the state. Even though the legislators' reaction to his recommendation was anything but typical, it was difficult for opponents to single out the Rosewood claims bill for special and negative treatment. Finally, and perhaps most significant, the claims bill was presented as a property issue rather than a racial justice issue. Both Steve Hanlon and Al Lawson tried to downplay the case's social and racial aspects, maintaining that Rosewood residents won "compensation" from the state for the loss of their property, not "racial reparations."

From the outset, however, the reparations process in Tulsa was framed as a racial issue. When Don Ross submitted his first reparations bill in 1997, he lacked the support of the governor, many key legislators, the major newspapers, and the most influential law firms. He told the *Tulsa World* that "money is a magnificent healer . . . you know [Whites] mean forgiveness when they are willing to pay," adding, "I don't need white people to make a speech about how sorry they are. That's almost an insult."[51] The reaction of Whites was instantaneous and almost all negative. Following the defeat of Ross's bill, the study commission that was created by the state legislature was a much different group from the Rosewood study commission. In contrast, the Tulsa Race Riot Commission was composed of politicians and/or political activists rather than scholars. Their meetings quickly took on an adversarial character, and their final recommendations were lambasted by both Black and White commissioners as either too little or too much. Ironically, Ross, who had done much to frame the issue in racial terms, backed away from the final recommendations and submitted a bill focused on "reconciliation" rather than "racial justice."

The final irony is that Tulsa's Black residents may have had a stronger claim than Rosewood's residents did. Law enforcement in Rosewood did not attempt to prevent the lynching of Sam Carter or the assault on the Carrier home. But there is no evidence that they actively participated in the murders or the destruction of the community, and Sheriff Walker was credited with saving Aaron Carrier's life by taking him into protective custody. But in Tulsa there is overwhelming evidence that some police and special deputies took part in the burning and looting. Moreover, the actions of the National Guard in rounding up Greenwood residents facilitated the burning and looting by eliminating any resistance to the rioters. The testimony and legal claims of Greenwood residents seeking redress for their losses also offer a paper trail. Although the charges against J. B. Stradford eventually were dropped, neither he nor his descendants received a penny for the loss of "the finest Black hotel in America."[52]

Conclusion

What do the examples of Rosewood and Tulsa tell us about theories of redress? Success through the political process in Florida would appear to justify Steve Hanlon's decision to take the Rosewood claim to the legislature rather than the courts. Neither Don Ross nor other supporters of the Tulsa claim seem to have seriously considered legal action. Perhaps the success of the Rosewood claim in Florida made the political route seem more viable, as the failure of the legal suits in the years immediately following the riot in Tulsa may have suggested to reparations supporters that the legal hurdles were too great.

Even though the advocates of reparations in Tulsa actively promoted their cause, they did not have the sophisticated, well-connected lobbying operation that Steve Hanlon and Martha Barnett launched in Florida. Black legislators in Oklahoma were not organized in a Black caucus, and although Don Ross was an experienced legislator, he did not forge an effective coalition to support the bill.

Even though more people survived the racial violence in Tulsa than that in Rosewood, they were not as closely united. No annual reunions of survivors were held in Tulsa, as they were in Rosewood, and they did not establish a survivors' association or leadership, as Arnett Doctor and the Rosewood Advisory Committee did. Thus, the presence of survivors appears to have been an essential but not necessarily a sufficient element to guarantee success.

Both moral claims seem to have been well grounded in fact and thus meritorious, but the White residents of Tulsa were better placed to express their opposition than were the relatively few Whites living in the region of Rosewood. That is, White Tulsans appear to have been more defensive about the events that occurred in their city many years ago, whereas White Floridians generally feel removed from Rosewood in both time and place. In addition, the size of the Tulsa claim increased the probability that Greenwood survivors would be presented with symbolic rather than material benefits. The Rosewood settlement seems to have brought some finality, whereas the reconciliation in Tulsa is far from complete. Most tragically, the historical record indicates that the destruction of Black communities like Rosewood and Greenwood were not anomalies.

Since September 11, 2001, fresh attention has been devoted to the victims of terrorist acts. In addition to the compensation fund established for the families of these victims, Congress passed the Job Creation and Worker Assistance Act of 2002 to stimulate the economy in lower Manhattan. In Oklahoma itself, five years after the homegrown terrorist bombing of the Alfred P. Murrah Building in downtown Oklahoma City, the state of Oklahoma allocated $28 million to erect the Oklahoma City National Memorial and Memorial Center Museum in honor of the 168 victims. Perhaps the destruction of communities such as Rosewood and Greenwood should be seen for the domestic terrorist acts they were, and appropriate tribute paid for the lives lost.

4

The Contemporary Debate

The Legacy of Slavery and the
Antireparations Movement

Wherever the real power in a Government lies, there is the danger of
oppression. In our Governments the real power lies in the majority of
the Community, and the invasion of private rights is chiefly to be ap-
prehended, not from acts of Government contrary to the sense of its
constituents, but from acts in which the Government is the mere instrument of the major number of the constituents.
>   —James Madison, from James MacGregor Burns and Stewart
>   Burns, *A People's Charter: The Pursuit of Rights in America*

There is nothing inherent in democracy that requires majority rule.
>   —Lani Guinier, *The Tyranny of the Majority*

An Age of Apology

We live in an age of apology. International apologies include Queen
Elizabeth's apology to and reparations for New Zealand's Maoris
for British-initiated nineteenth-century race wars, French President
Jacques Chirac's recognition of French complicity in the deportation of
76,000 Jews to Nazi concentration camps, the Catholic Church's apology for its assimilationist policy in Australia that contributed to the
Aborigines' spiritual and cultural destruction, and the apology by the
Evangelical Lutheran Church of America for founder Martin Luther's
damaging anti-Semitism.[1] More recently, in a speech before Parlia-
ment, British Prime Minister Tony Blair expressed "deep sorrow" for
the "crime against humanity" represented in Britain's role in the slave
trade, although he stopped short of an explicit apology.[2]

Of the numerous apologies in the United States are Congress's apology to Native Hawaiians in 1993 for the illegal United States–aided overthrow of the sovereign Hawaiian nation; the Southern Baptists' apology to African American church members for the denomination's endorsement of slavery; the Florida legislature's payment of $2 million to the survivors of racial violence in Rosewood, Florida; Rapper Ice Cube's apology to Korean American merchants for his rap "Black Korea" that threatened the burning of Korean American–owned stores; the apology by the president of Rutgers University for suggesting that Blacks lacked the "genetic background" to perform well on standardized tests; Senator Alfonse D'Amato (R-NY)'s pseudoapology for his linguistic mocking of Judge Lance Ito's Japanese ancestry; President Ronald Reagan's apology and granting of reparations to Japanese Americans for their internment during World War II; President Bill Clinton's apology to the survivors of the U.S. government–sponsored syphilis tests in Tuskegee, Alabama; Senate Majority Leader Trent Lott's (R-MS) apology for a statement supporting Senator Strom Thurmond's (R-SC) 1948 call for states' rights; the U.S. Agriculture Department's payment to Black farmers for discrimination in the administration of farm aid programs; and Congress's 1990 apology to uranium miners and others injured by nuclear testing.

Democratic Congressman Tony Hall of Ohio said that when he introduced a resolution providing a simple apology for slavery in 1997, he received more hate mail than any other time in his long political career. As noted earlier, President Clinton offered an apology to Africans for the slave trade but pointedly did not apologize to African Americans. What is it about African American reparations that raises such strong resistance?

In June 2005, 105 years after the first antilynching bill was proposed by a Black congressman, the U.S. Senate approved, by voice vote, S.R. 39, which called for the lawmakers to apologize to lynching victims, survivors, and their descendants, several of whom were watching from the gallery. In the past, seven presidents had lobbied Congress for antilynching legislation, and some two hundred bills had been introduced. Even a 1937 Gallup poll indicated that 72 percent of Americans, including 57 percent of southerners, supported such a law.[3] But despite popular and presidential support, the Senate failed to enact an antilynching law. Three times the House of Representatives approved such a bill only to have it blocked by filibusters in the Senate. Although some senators, such as Senate Majority Leader Richard Russell (D-GA)—for whom a Senate office building is named—claimed it was a states' rights issue, others like Senator James Thomas Heflin (D-AL) were more direct. According to Heflin, "Whenever a Negro crosses this dead line between the white and the Negro races and lays his black hand on a white woman, he deserves to die."[4] Although Heflin and many other apologists for lynching cited their desire to protect White women from sexual attacks by Black predators, many of the approximately five thousand *recorded* lynchings had nothing at all to do with interracial sex.

Doria Dee Johnson, the great-great-granddaughter of Anthony Crawford, was present to hear the Senate's apology. Anthony Crawford was lynched for arguing over the price of cotton. Crawford said he was willing to die if he were struck by a White man; instead, he died for merely arguing with one. As a result of the lynching, Johnson's great-great-granddaughter said that the family went bankrupt and was scattered. Most of the other Black families were driven out of Abbeville, South Carolina, by the lynch mob, which numbered between two hundred and four hundred persons.[5]

The descendants and the only known living survivor of a lynching, James Cameron, appeared grateful for the Senate's action, but some observers questioned the sincerity of the apology. Senator John Kerry (D-MA) noted the absence of twenty senators to cosponsor the resolution or sign a placard expressing support. Senators Thad Cochran (R) and Lott of Mississippi, the state with the most lynchings, questioned the wisdom of official apologies. Cochran admitted, "I don't think I'll get into the business of apologizing for acts that previous Senates took." Senator Lott asked, "Where do we end all of this? Are we going to apologize for not doing the right thing on Social Security?"[6]

Given his past support for Strom Thurmond and states' rights, Senator Lott's opposition might be expected. More surprising was the support of the Republican sponsor of the bill, Senator George Allen of Virginia. Allen has a noose hanging from a tree in his office, symbolizing, he says, his admiration for "frontier justice." Moreover, when Allen served as governor of Virginia, he called the NAACP an "extremist organization," proclaimed the month of April as Confederate History and Heritage Month, and kept a Confederate flag in his living room. Allen's critics suggest that his presidential ambitions were the reason for his sponsorship of the antilynching apology.[7] The nostrum that "politics makes strange bedfellows" was never more evident than in the passage of the most significant reparations and apology legislation of our time, the Civil Liberties Act of 1988.

The Japanese American Reparations Case

The passage of the Civil Liberties Act of 1988 was the catalyst for African American reparations advocates. Japanese Americans' success in gaining reparations for their internment during World War II provided a model for a badly demoralized community of Black political activists. Their case proved inspiring because Japanese Americans represented only a small, apparently prosperous, fraction of the American population (three-tenths of 1 percent) concentrated in a few West Coast states that had been relatively inactive as a political community. Moreover, they succeeded in an environment of near record federal deficits with a president elected for his conservatism. They won for several reasons.[8]

First, Japanese Americans had a well-documented grievance. As early as 1941, an internal report prepared by the State Department determined that Japanese Americans were exceptionally loyal to the United States and were no threat to America's security. Nonetheless, similar reports by the FBI and Naval Intelligence confirmed these findings were not made public until after World War II. In 1980 Congress created a study commission of well-respected figures to examine the facts and make recommendations. The commission's fact-finding report also was issued well in advance of its recommendations, thereby allowing it to serve as a public education tool and not get lost in a debate over compensation.

Second, there was little formal opposition. Japanese American activists feared a negative reaction from veterans' groups that would argue that everyone had sacrificed during World War II. But these groups remained largely neutral, with two even passing general resolutions of support in national meetings. These veterans' groups were heavily influenced by the war record of Japanese Americans fighting in the 100th Battalion (from Hawaii) After so many men in the 100th were killed, the rest were folded into the 442nd Regimental Combat Team. This unit was the most decorated group of its size in World War II. Although a small organization called the Americans for Historical Accuracy, led by Lillian Baker, did oppose the legislation in congressional hearings, Baker's opposition was largely seen as racist retribution for the loss of her husband in fighting in the Pacific during the war. Furthermore, starting in 1948, Congress passed three pieces of legislation dealing with Japanese American claims, so, given the lack of strong opposition, legislators could view their vote on this issue as a "throwaway" vote.

Third, the Japanese American Citizens League (JACL) first began addressing the issue of redress in 1970. Although such factions as the National Council for Japanese American Redress (NCJAR) also developed and pursued a class action lawsuit, The JACL was able to maintain its credibility as the oldest and largest Japanese American civic organization. The 1982 report and hearings of the study commission created by Congress opened an emotional floodgate of older Japanese Americans' pent-up feelings, generating new energy and commitment to the issue. Consequently, both major parties endorsed redress for Japanese Americans in their 1984 presidential platforms.

Fourth, internal changes in Congress following the 1986 elections put more favorable legislators in key positions. Among them was Representative Barney Frank (D-MA) replacing Representative Dan Glickman (R-KS) as chair of the subcommittee in which the legislation rested. A group of four well-respected senior Japanese American legislators then pushed hard for the bill's passage. In the Senate, Daniel Inouye (D-HI) took the early lead, with Spark Matsunaga (D-HI) doing the later lobbying. Norm Mineta (D-CA) and Robert Matsui (D-CA) led the fight in the House. To gain the support of Senator Ted Stevens (R-AK), redress for Aleutian Islanders was attached to the legislation.

Fifth, the redress issue was framed as a constitutional rather than a racial issue. That is, the internment of Japanese Americans was presented as governmental discrimination violating the rights of private citizens and denying them equal opportunity. Framed in this way, Republicans like Newt Gingrich, Alan Simpson, Jack Kemp, and Henry Hyde were able to support the bill.

Finally, a variety of external factors may have eased the bill's passage. Legal battles in the *coram nobis* cases of *Korematsu, Hirabayashi,* and *Yasui* as well as the NCJAR's class action suit made arguments in support of legislative redress more compelling. The media also gave generally favorable coverage to the Japanese Americans' efforts. Passage of the Civil Liberties Act of 1988 authorized a national apology, an education fund, and individual payments of $20,000 to each surviving internee.[9]

African Americans Follow Suit

The success of the Civil Liberties Act of 1988 led to a spate of race apologies and served as a catalyst for renewed interest in African American reparations. The following year, Representative John Conyers (D-MI) submitted H.R. 40 (for forty acres), the Commission to Study Reparations Proposals for African Americans Act. Modeled after the Japanese American study commission bill which preceded the Civil Liberties Act of 1988, Conyers's legislation would (1) acknowledge the fundamental injustice and inhumanity of slavery, (2) establish a commission to study slavery and its subsequent racial and economic discrimination against freed slaves, (3) study the impact of those forces on today's living African Americans, and (4) make recommendations to Congress for appropriate remedies to redress the harm inflicted on living African Americans.[10] The National Coalition of Blacks for Reparations (N'COBRA) also was formed in the late 1980s to develop a grassroots reparations movement. In fact, Black activist Ron Daniels made reparations a central issue in his independent bid for the presidency in 1992.

In Nigeria, President Ibrahim Babangia took the lead in establishing a reparations movement during his tenure as head of the Organization of African Unity (OAU). After the first meeting of the International Conference on Reparations in Lagos, Nigeria, in the winter of 1990, the OAU formed the Group of Eminent Persons, and in 1992 the OAU formally embraced and endorsed reparations as "the last stage in the decolonization process."[11] Later, Chief Moshood Abiola, a Nigerian businessman, played a leading role in the international reparations movement.

In 1994, the U.S. Internal Revenue Service (IRS) reported receiving about 20,000 bogus tax-reparation claims. Capitalizing on the publicity surrounding federal payments to Japanese Americans, con artists falsely informed Blacks that the federal government had passed such legislation for African Americans and offered, for a fee, to file their claims. Again in 2001, the Social Security Administration issued a special alert to senior citizens involving a reparations scam. An investigation by the agency found that the so-called Slave Reparation Act had duped more than 29,000 people.[12] The agency received nearly 80,000 returns claiming more than $2.7 billion in false reparation refunds.[13] Throughout the 1990s, a number of individual cities and states took action on reparations. Cities like Tulsa and Elaine, Arkansas, considered making payments to survivors of racist violence against their citizens. Other cities, such as Dallas, Atlanta, Nashville, Cleveland, Chicago, and Detroit, passed bills providing symbolic support for reparations. Finally, the state legislatures of New York and California passed bills dealing with some aspect of reparations.[14]

Comparing the Japanese American and African American Cases

Despite some success at the state and local levels, at the national level Conyers's bill has remained buried in a subcommittee. At this point, it might be instructive to compare the African American case for reparations with the successful Japanese American example. We will combine Roy L. Brooks's theory of redress with social movement theory to give us a better method of comparing the Japanese American and African American cases. Brooks's first condition for successful redress—that demands or claims for redress must be placed in the hands of legislators rather than judges—certainly speaks to the need for political opportunity. The second condition, requiring that public and private political pressure be exerted on the legislators, relates to the need for resource mobilization, as does the third condition of strong internal (group) support. The final condition, that the claim must be meritorious, refers to the need to frame the issue as one deserving of support.

Did the passage of the Civil Liberties Act of 1988 mark a window of political opportunity for proponents of African American reparations? Although Conyers had as many as forty cosponsors for his bill, the Republican control of Congress (until the 2006 election) made remote, at best, the prospect of getting the bill out of committee and onto the floor for a vote. During the Clinton administration, Vice President Al Gore was asked for his views on reparations, and he answered,

> I think that it is a question that needs to be dealt with respectfully and with great sensitivity to those who are interested in the idea, not really for the money it represents but rather for the symbolic atonement they associate with it. At the end of the day, most agree that it's not a politically feasible idea.[15]

When asked specifically about the Conyers bill calling for a study commission Gore added, "I'm for handling it sensitively without conveying a sense that it's ever likely to occur, because it's not."[16] Senator Patrick Leahy (D-VT) added, "I suspect there are a lot of things we could have reparations on. Is it a debate that benefits anyone— black or white? I don't know the answer to that question."[17] "I have never been a fan of reparations for anything," confessed Senator Rick Santorum (R-PA). "There have always been bad things that have happened to people. Slavery was awful. But I don't think there is anything to be gained by going backward to try to come up with some way to pay for something that you can't put a monetary price tag on."[18] Senator Olympia Snowe (R-ME) stated, "It's something I certainly would consider . . . has anybody held hearings on this issue?"[19] In the summer of 2000, the Democratic Party adopted a plank endorsing the idea of establishing a federal commission to study the lingering effects of slavery.[20]

Congressional views largely reflect public opinion on reparations. A Fox News–Opinion Dynamics poll conducted on March 28 and 29, 2001, of registered voters reported that 81 percent were opposed to reparations and 11 percent supported them. A national ABC News poll in June and July 2000 revealed that 77 percent of Whites believed that no Black people should be compensated, while 19 percent thought that only those whose ancestors were slaves should be compensated. The American Enterprise Institute reported that one poll conducted in 2000 found that 53 percent of Blacks, but only 3 percent of Whites, favored federal compensation for slavery. In New York City, 62 percent of Blacks supported reparations, but only 22 percent of Whites agreed.[21] In more conservative Chicago, a *Chicago Tribune* readers' poll was running three to one against reparations until U.S. Representative Bobby Rush (D-IL) urged Blacks to respond to the survey.[22] A CNN/USA Today/Gallup poll in February 2002 found that 90 percent of White respondents were opposed to cash reparations and 55 percent of Blacks supported them.[23] Nationwide, an ABC News poll in 2000 found that 53 percent of Whites opposed an apology by the federal government to Black Americans for slavery and that 66 percent of Blacks favored an apology.[24] Five years earlier, a survey by the *Washington Post*, Kaiser Foundation, and Harvard University produced almost identical results on the question of an apology.

Beginning in 1989, in its decisions in *Croson v. Richmond, Wards Cove v. Antonio,* and *Adarand v. Pena,* the U.S. Supreme Court attacked a number of affirmative action programs. Following eight years of active hostility to Black civil rights by the Reagan administration, this Court's action created a crisis environment in which the gains of the civil rights movement were put in jeopardy. Indeed, the Black counter-public saw those years as the end of the second Reconstruction.

Both symbolically and substantively, the 1980s were reminiscent of the rollback of Black progress that followed the first Reconstruction. The decade began with presidential candidate Ronald Reagan speaking to thousands of cheering Whites at the Neshoba County Fair in Mississippi. The county fairgrounds are just outside Philadelphia, Mississippi, the infamous site of the murder of three civil rights workers in 1964. After warming up the crowd with attacks on Washington bureaucrats, big government, and welfare, Reagan then shouted: "I believe in states' rights. I believe that we've distorted the balance of our government by giving powers that were never intended in the Constitution to the federal establishment."[25] Following in the footsteps of George Wallace and Richard Nixon, Reagan resurrected the codified reference to race—"states' rights"—to win white support without being labeled a racist.

Symbolically, the decade closed with President George H. W. Bush vetoing the 1990 civil rights bill. Bush's election as president was widely attributed to his using the escape of convicted Black murderer, William (Willie) Horton, as a "wedge" issue in his attack on the Massachusetts governor, Michael Dukakis, his Democratic opponent. Several years after the election, when voters were asked what they remembered about the 1988 campaign, they offered three names—Dukakis, Bush, and Horton.[26]

The Legacy of Slavery

An overwhelming amount of basic socioeconomic evidence points to a growing disparity between Blacks and Whites. Moreover, this evidence also demonstrates a widening disparity between the Black middle class and the Black poor. These post–civil rights movement trends continued from the Reagan and Bush administrations through the Clinton administration.

Andrew Hacker's widely read *Two Nations* was one of the first works to draw attention to this disparity. Other trends are highlighted in table 4.1.

Table 4.1

- In general, southern metropolitan areas appear to be converging to a level of Black–White segregation in the range of 65 to 70 percent, about ten points *below* their northern counterparts.[a]
- Forty percent of all urban schools are intensely (90% students of color) segregated.[b]
- The ratio of Black incomes to White incomes widened from 53 percent in 1967 to 58 percent in 1992, but in absolute terms, the discrepancy in income rose from $4,700 to $6,700.[c]
- The ratio of Black to White poverty has remained at 3 percent, and there are now about four million *fewer* poor Whites than thirty years ago, but 686,000 *more* poor Blacks.[d]
- The poorest fifth of African Americans *lost* almost as large a share of their income as the richest fifth *gained* of theirs.[e]
- The number of well-off Americans, both Blacks and Whites, who are the victims of violence is steadily *decreasing*, while the number of poor Americans who are victimized by violence is steadily *increasing.*[f]
- Between 1969 and 1999), federal funding for education decreased from 1.35 percent to 1.03 percent of the federal budget while money spent on prisons rose from 0.42 percent to 1.52 percent of the federal budget.[g]
- African Americans make up 12 percent of the population and 12 percent of U.S. drug users but are 38 percent of those arrested for drug-related offenses.[h]
- Thirty-one percent of all Black men in Alabama and Florida have been permanently disenfranchised as a result of felony convictions. Nationally, 1.4 million Black men have lost the right to vote.[i]
- Black life expectancy declined in the United States from 1984 through 1989. In 1993, only 66 percent of African American men reached age sixty, compared with 84 percent of White men.[j]
- At *all* age levels, African American males die disproportionately in accidents and violence.[k]
- African American men received fewer doctorates in 1995 than they did in 1977.[l]
- Within the Black population, one out of four men who reaches age twenty-five will have spent time in prison or on a suspended sentence, whereas three out of four of their White counterparts will have gone on to college.[m]
- At age twenty, 29.7 percent of African Americans have experienced poverty. By age forty, the figure is two-thirds, and by age sixty, 81.9 percent of Blacks have spent some period of time below the poverty line.[n]
- In 2002, 24 percent of all Blacks were poor, compared with 10 percent of Whites.[o]

Sources: [a] Douglass S. Massey and Nancy A. Denton, *American Apartheid: Segregation and the Making of the Underclass* (Cambridge, Mass.: Harvard University Press, 1993), p. 222.
   [b] Applied Research Center, "Still Separate, Still Unequal," May 2000, p. 6.
   [c] Jennifer L. Hochschild, *Facing Up to the American Dream: Race, Class and the Soul of America* (Princeton, N.J.: Princeton University Press, 1995), p. 44.
   [d] Ibid., p. 45.
   [e] Ibid., p. 49.
   [f] Ibid., p. 50.
   [g] Applied Research Center, p. 3.
   [h] Ronald H. Weich and Carlos T. Angulo, *Justice on Trial* (Washington, D.C.: Washington Leadership Conference on Civil Rights, 2000), p. iv.
   [i] Ibid.
   [j] K. D. Kochanek et al., "Why Black Life Expectancy Declined . . . ," Mortality Statistics Branch, National Center for Health Statistics, available online at www.pubmed.gov, 2/28/07.
   [k] Orlando Patterson, *Rituals of Blood: Consequences of Slavery in Two American Centuries* (New York: Basic Books, 1998), p. 14.
   [l] Ibid., p. 18.
   [m] Mark Robert Rank, *One Nation, Underprivileged: Why American Poverty Affects Us All* (New York: Oxford University Press, 2004), p. 159.
   [n] Ibid., p. 95.
   [o] Ibid., p. 31.

Even the Black middle class, to which roughly one-third of Black families now belong, has limited mobility. Blacks hold less than 4 percent of the 26,000 jobs in magazine and newspaper journalism and represent less than 2 percent of the lawyers working in the 250 largest law firms and less than 1 percent of the law partners. Only 37 of the 20,000 partners in major accounting firms are Black, and Black professionals and managers are almost twice as likely to be unemployed as are Whites in similar job categories. Even economic success does not lead out of the ghetto, as a Black earning more than $50,000 per year is as likely to live in a segregated neighborhood as is someone making $2,500 a year.[27]

The current prospects for reversing these trends seem remote. President George W. Bush assumed office after a contested election process in which Black voters in Florida were disproportionately disenfranchised.[28] More recently, the then Senate Majority Leader Trent Lott (R-MS), in a tribute to Senator Strom Thurmond (R-SC), confessed: "I want to say this about my state: When Strom Thurmond ran for president, we voted for him. We're proud of it. And if the rest of the country had followed our lead, we wouldn't have had all these problems over all these years."[29] Although Lott did not identify "all these problems," in 1948, Thurmond left the Democratic Party to form the Dixiecrat Party, which was dedicated to the preservation of racial segregation.

For his remarks, Lott was forced to resign as Majority Leader, although he still holds his seat in the Senate. But why don't these alarming statistics and remarks create more outrage in the general public? The most obvious answer is that a majority of Whites blame the dismal state of Black affairs on Blacks themselves. That is, they believe that Blacks should be held responsible for their socioeconomic status and therefore Whites should not be responsible for improving these conditions. Less obvious is the general belief that Whites have earned their superior position, that they have achieved their status through individual effort in an open and meritorious process. In short, Whites believe there are no structural barriers to Black advancement or structural advantages that benefit their interests.

To win White support, a reparations argument must demonstrate the legacy of slavery in terms of its current consequences. It must show that this legacy not only hurts Blacks but also benefits Whites.

Harvard sociologist Orlando Patterson contends that slavery had

three important consequences that relate to Blacks' current deprivation. First, throughout the New World, slave systems, Africans, and
their descendants refused to reject the strong valuation of kinship and
the fundamental West African social tendency to use kinship as the id-
iom for expressing all important relationships and rankings. Second,
the worst effect of slavery was its devastation of the roles of father and
husband. Third, throughout the Americas, because slaves were considered to be property, they were legally defined as persons either
bought as slaves or born to a slave mother.[30]

These three factors led to two distinctive features in the repro-
ductive strategies of African American men. First, they have as many
children as possible to ensure progeny, and they do so without regard
to their control over their resources. By 1880, 31 percent of all African American households were headed by a single person, and of
those, 25.3 percent were headed by women. Southern rural African
Americans who were tenant farmers had no need to postpone marriage or children until they acquired land and other resources. In fact,
male tenants needed their children's labor. Patterson contends that today African American men still have no economic incentive to marry
the women who bear their children.[31] This pattern, he maintains, is
unique among known societies.[32]

Whites nonetheless tend to focus on Black tenant farmers' immoral behavior rather than acknowledge it as a consequence of the
system. In regard to the institution of slavery, Southerners "seldom attributed the defeat of their cause to the sin of slavery, for as a whole
they did not believe ownership of slaves to be a sin."[33] Thus, it was the
slaves that were sinful, not slavery.

It is this emphasis on the sinfulness of the slaves and their progeny that enables White Americans to pass on their inherited wealth
without contradicting their stated belief in meritocracy. Patterson
states that

> as long as people are able to pass on to their children, however aver-
> age their native intelligence, most of their tangible wealth and power
> as well as their intangible assets—their *social* capital, or network of
> contacts, and their *cultural* capital, by which I mean those learned
> patterns of mutual trust, insider knowledge about how things really
> work, encounter rituals and social sensibilities that constitute the lan-

guage of power and success—America will remain what it has been since the turn of the last century—a plutocratic democracy.[34]

Political scientist Ira Katznelson calls this "plutocratic democracy" a form of "White affirmative action." Focusing on the most extensive and generous social legislation ever enacted by the federal government, the Social Security Act of 1935 and the Selective Service Readjustment Act of 1944 (GI Bill of Rights), Katznelson demonstrates that discrimination against Blacks actually widened the economic and educational gaps between the races. Even though the condition of Blacks improved, it did not improve as dramatically in housing, education, and welfare as it did for Whites. Furthermore, southern Democrats' control of key congressional committees held President Franklin D. Roosevelt's New Deal legislation hostage to White supremacy. Katznelson cites three mechanisms that made sure that federal funds would not upset the racial status quo. First, whenever the legislation permitted, African Americans were excluded. A good example is Social Security, which excluded from coverage the two employment areas in which Blacks were most overrepresented: agricultural labor and domestic service. Second, these programs, including assistance to the poor and support for veterans, had to be administered by local officials, who were deeply hostile to Black aspirations. Third, Congress was prevented from attaching any sort of antidiscrimination provisions to the wide array of social welfare programs that distributed funds to their members' regions.[35]

Some of the best evidence of the central role of the legacy of slavery in contemporary affairs is found in the area of wealth. Sociologist Dalton Conley discovered that at all income levels, White families hold significantly more assets than Black families do. In 1994, the median White family held assets worth seven times more than those of the median nonwhite family. The median African American family at the lower end of the income spectrum (less than $15,000 per year) has no assets, whereas the equivalent White family has equity worth $10,000. Whites at the upper income levels (greater than $75,000 per year) have a median net worth of $308,000, almost three times higher than the figure for upper-income African American families ($114,600).[36] Conley argues that these gaps in wealth are a much better indicator of the impact of slavery on the socioeconomic condition of

African Americans, since the accumulation of wealth depends heavily on intergenerational support issues such as gifts, informal loans, and inheritances. Wealth is much more stable within families and across generations than is income, occupation, or education. In short, says Conley, we are less likely to have earned it and more likely to have inherited it or received it as a gift.[37]

In 1865, African Americans owned 0.5 percent of the total worth of the United States, and by 1990, Black Americans owned only a meager 1 percent of the nation's total wealth. Even so, African Americans save at least as much as Whites do, 11 percent of their annual income, compared with 10 percent for Whites, with no significant difference in rates of self-employment.[38] When predicting the wealth levels of young adults, the single most important factor is their parents' net worth. The only other factor that mattered significantly was gender.[39]

Home ownership is the way that most Americans accumulate assets. Home equity accounts for roughly 44 percent of a person's total measured net worth, and home wealth accounts for 60 percent of the total wealth of America's middle class. A set of federal policies enacted in the 1930s has given the United States the world's highest rate of home ownership. The Federal Housing Administration, the Veterans Administration, and the GI Bill helped guarantee the long-term, low-interest mortgages that made the dream of home ownership possible for most families. In addition, the tax status of home mortgages and the tax treatment of profits from home sales have kept homes affordable and built wealth for home-owning families.

The well-documented discrimination against Blacks in these federal programs has contributed to a dramatic gap in home ownership between Blacks and Whites. In 2002, 74 percent of Whites owned their own home, compared with 48 percent of Blacks. This 26 percent gap is the legacy of residential segregation; federal housing, tax, and transportation policies; and discrimination in real estate and lending markets. Sociologist Thomas Shapiro contends that family inheritance and continuing racial discrimination are reversing the gains made in school and on the job and are making racial inequality worse. In turn, these inequalities deny Blacks the transformative assets that give families a head start in living in better communities and attending quality schools. Thus, Shapiro asserts, the same set of processes typically benefits Whites while hurting African Americans.[40]

In this hostile political environment, could Blacks mobilize enough resources to pass a reparations bill in Congress? Even with the stimulus of the Reagan/Bush retrenchment and the example of the Civil Liberties Act of 1988, Blacks needed a community of believers or a network of activists to bring the issue of reparations to the forefront. Black nationalist activists, who were better organized and focused than disillusioned Black liberals during this period, provided this network. Black nationalism has always been more popular in the African American community when the larger society has cut off or narrowed their access to the mainstream.[41] Another key to mobilizing resources was a shift in the Black middle class's attitudes. Newly affluent Blacks have become more frustrated and alienated over racial progress than lower-class Blacks are. Members of the Black middle class, such as Randall Robinson, an African American lawyer, activist, and author of *The Debt: What America Owes to Blacks,* bring greater credibility and clout to an issue that was marginalized during the twentieth century.

Supporters of reparations outside the Black nationalist community have probably never heard of Queen Mother Moore. Yet for most of the 1950s and 1960s, she was the best-known advocate of African American reparations. Operating out of Harlem and her organization, the Universal Association of Ethiopian Women, Moore actively promoted reparations from 1950 until her death in 1996. She was a Garveyite and then a Communist and spent much of her time pressing for reparations through the United Nations.[42]

A 1987 conference on the U.S. Constitution sponsored by the National Conference of Black Lawyers produced the National Coalition of Blacks for Reparations in America (N'COBRA). Kalonji T. Olusegun and Adjou Aiyetoro led the new organization, which is the largest national organization devoted solely to reparations. Besides supporting the Conyers bill, N'COBRA holds education campaigns designed to pressure state and local legislators to support reparations, and it also has been involved in legal action on reparations.[43] However, as historian Clarence Mumford pointed out, "The organization must break with nationalist sectarianism" if it is to develop a true mass base.[44] Another group working with N'COBRA is the Black Reparations Commission, headed by Dorothy Lewis and established in 1978. In addition, Silas Muhammad, of the Lost Found Nation of Islam, formed the National Commission for Reparations in 1991. Like Queen Mother Moore, this group concentrates on the UN to apply international laws within the framework of the international system. Yussef Naim Kly, head of the International Human Rights Association for American Minorities, has helped these groups use international law in the reparations debate.[45]

In its 1974 Black agenda, the National Black Political Assembly (NBPA) endorsed the concept of African American reparations, and members of the NBPA currently are active in the reparations movement. Ron Daniels, the executive director of the Center for Constitutional Rights (CRC), for example, established the Institute of the Black World, whose principal purpose is reparations.[46] Older nationalist organizations, such as the Black United Front, led by Conrad Worrill, and the Republic of New Africa, led by Imari Obadele, have been active supporters of the reparations movement as well. The African National Reparations Organization, linked to the African People's Socialist Party, has conducted tribunals on U.S. racism each year since 1982 and has demanded $4.1 trillion in reparations for stolen labor.[47]

Many of the meetings, conferences, and tribunals sponsored by these groups open with the pouring of traditional African libations and African drumming, but Black nationalists now are not alone in their demands. Perhaps no one more typifies the newfound respectability of the reparations movement than Randall Robinson. Robinson, a graduate of Harvard Law School and the founder and former president of TransAfrica, a U.S. lobby for Africa and the Caribbean. The brother of the late network news anchor Max Robinson, Randall Robinson is very much a member of the Black leadership class. His best-selling book, *The Debt: What American Owes to Blacks,* was, for many Americans of all races, their first exposure to the reparations debate. In the introduction to his book, Robinson expresses frustration with diversionary programs like affirmative action that ignore poor Blacks and offer no solutions to Black problems. Robinson's book also recounts a pointed critique of the Clinton administration by political scientist Ronald Walters and is surprised by Blacks' affection for Clinton:

> In his first term, Clinton's policies followed a distinct slant toward a
> more conservative and Republican course on social issues. He spon
> sored the most punitive crime bill in history, which passed in 1993;
> after suffering the defeat of his "economic stimulus package," which
> contained funds for urban development, he never put it back on the
> table. He signed the most punitive welfare reform bill in history, ef
> fecting a revolution in New Deal policy toward government support

for the poor; and thousands of people silently have been sifted out of federal government employment through the "reinventing government program." . . . When one examines the impact of the crime bill on the sharply increased criminalization of black youth in particular, the exposure of the poorest blacks to the labor market without sufficient training or family support, and the lack of investment in urban schools or communities, Clinton's positive initiatives may be viewed as largely symbolic.[48]

Robinson concludes that if Black claims are to have any chance of success here, "we must make it clear to America that we will not allow ourselves to be ignored."[49]

Robinson's frustration and anger reflect a widespread feeling among the Black middle class. As political scientist Jennifer Hochschild observed, "Not only has the idea of universal participation been denied to most Americans, but also the very fact of its denial has itself been denied in our national self-image."[50] The result of this denial is that Whites believe that race discrimination is declining, and Blacks believe the opposite. More precisely, poor African Americans now have more faith in the "American dream" than middle-class Blacks do. Hochschild noted that while both classes of African Americans were more optimistic about their race in the 1960s than in the 1980s, the optimism of affluent Blacks has plummeted when compared with that of poor Blacks.[51] Affluent Blacks more closely identify with their racial status than their class status than does any other racial/class group, which may explain why, unlike the upwardly mobile immigrants of all other groups, the new Black middle-class commitment to the American dream is declining, not rising.[52]

Michael Dawson's findings also reflect Blacks' waning support for liberalism. "Liberalism has become a weak force in shaping the politics of the black community," Dawson asserts, "even though a large percentage of blacks support the radical egalitarian program."[53] By 2000, 71 percent of African Americans believed that racial progress would not be achieved in their lifetime or maybe not at all.[54] Dawson also recognizes the multiple liberal traditions within the Black community, just as within the larger society. Overall, however, he believes that Black liberals' concern with the egalitarian aspects of liberalism has led them to seek a much stronger state than other American liberals are seeking. For example, public opinion polls in the 1960s and

1970s revealed that Blacks ranked equality at the top and liberty toward the bottom of their value scales, whereas Whites did the opposite. Over time, what moves Blacks from hope to despair, says Dawson, is "the evaluation of white willingness to 'accept' black equality, the evaluation of the nature of American society, and the assessment of prospects for gaining full democratic citizenship."[55]

Not all Black citizens are nationalists or liberals. The rise of the new Black middle class also produced a new Black neoconservatism. Linguist John McWhorter, for example, wrote an opinion piece for the *Los Angeles Times* entitled "Why I Don't Want Reparations for Slavery." McWhorter noted that "if all black Americans living below the poverty line were given a subsidy to move to the suburbs, free tuition for college and/or a small business loan, all indications are that, for most, in the long run it would make no difference in the overall condition of their lives."[56] Journalist Juan Williams, not generally considered a conservative, opposes reparations because he fears that they would spark a White backlash and result in the further segregation of poor Blacks. He also fears that reparations would mean an end to Americans' moral responsibility for racial oppression. Unlike Robinson, Williams prefers support for affirmative action and welfare. In fact, he even accuses affluent Blacks like Robinson of wanting to "take control of the massive budgets dedicated to social-welfare policy."[57] Despite their prominence in the media, Black conservatives enjoy less support in the Black community than do the adherents of any Black ideology with virtually no mass support.[58]

When compared with Japanese American support for reparations, the African American community appears unfocused and fragmented, even though reparations have a much longer history in the Black community, with organizations devoted to that single issue alone. The success of the Japanese American struggle helped bring the issue into the mainstream in the African American community. Consequently, with such mainstream organizations as the NAACP and the Urban League joining the reparations movement, the issue has gained new respectability. Academics and professionals have joined in sponsoring conferences at Columbia University, Fisk University, UCLA, the University of California at Berkeley law school, and the National Bar Association. As we have seen, many of the leaders of reparations organizations are lawyers or academics, and because Democratic politicians depend heavily on Black voters, they cannot summarily dismiss the issue as they could in the past. But neither can they endorse it, given the strong White opposition to reparations. Can reparations, therefore, be framed in a way that attracts broad political support, as did the Japanese American claim?

The Antireparations Movement

During Black history month (February) of 2001, the conservative author David Horowitz offered the campus newspapers of some fifty elite universities an advertisement entitled "Ten Reasons Why Reparations for Blacks Is a Bad Idea for Blacks—and Racist Too," which I quote later in this chapter. Most campus newspapers rejected the ad, including those at Harvard, Columbia, and the University of Virginia. Only seven newspapers ran the ad: those at Brown, the University of Wisconsin at Madison, Duke, the University of Chicago, the University of Arizona, and the Universities of California at Berkeley and at Davis.[59] The last two newspapers later apologized for running the ad.

A firestorm of criticism rose on each campus that chose to run the ad. At Brown, ad opponents trashed nearly the entire press run of four thousand copies, and students burned the newspapers on the Madison campus. Berkeley, the home of free speech, came under particular scrutiny. The *Daily Californian* ran the ad and, after vociferous protests, published an apology. The apology, in turn, received even more condemnation than the original ad had, for "caving in" to protesters.[60]

At the heart of the controversy was David Horowitz, the former editor of the radical magazine *Ramparts* and now head of the Center for the Study of Popular Culture, a conservative think tank. Horowitz offered a copy of his book *The Death of the Civil Rights Movement* to those readers who supported further placements of the ad with a contribution of $100 or more.

Ironically, those campus newspapers that did not run the ad were spared any criticism over press censorship, while the few that did print the ad found themselves in the middle of a debate over First Amendment rights. Newspapers that routinely reject ads, such as the *Washington Post* and the *Wall Street Journal*, ran editorials criticizing the Berkeley newspaper editor for his lack of support for freedom of speech. *U.S. News & World Report* condemned the emotional uproar by the ad opponents, calling their protests a language of feelings rather than a powerful case for suppressing the ad. The magazine also found Horowitz's text to be "a responsible, well-reasoned political argument that students should have been able to read without swooning,"[61] even suggesting that up to 90 percent of Americans supported Horowitz's opinion as expressed in the ad.

It is not hard to understand why Horowitz would run an inflammatory ad against reparations at some of the United States' most liberal universities during Black history month. Had the ad run at Bob Jones University, Horowitz would not have been able to claim the victim status that he denies Blacks in his ad. Nor would he have reaped the whirlwind of national publicity for his new book that the ad and his subsequent campus appearances generated.

The freedom of speech issue along with the destruction of some newspapers brought Horowitz the liberal defenders—the ACLU, the NAACP, and the *Progressive* magazine—that he loves to criticize. He could, and did, claim that he was being censored by a dictatorship of the left, even as his views were featured on every media outlet available.

Lost was any discussion of the almost minority-free staffs of many of the college newspapers he solicited. One college newspaper article attributed the absence of Black and Latino writers to the entrenched distrust of the press and the minority communities it covers. The Student Press Center reported that since 1993, of the 205 removals of campus newspapers that the center had recorded, 37, or approximately 18 percent, were related to race.[62] Most significantly, as Horowitz must have known, any serious discussion of reparations was lost in the outcry.

The ad reads as follows:

> Ten Reasons Why Reparations for Blacks Is a
> Bad Idea for Blacks—and Racist, Too!
>
> ONE
> *There Is No Single Group Clearly Responsible for the Crime of Slavery*
>   Black Africans and Arabs were responsible for enslaving the ancestors of African-Americans. There were 3,000 black slave-owners in the ante-bellum United States. Are reparations to be paid by their descendants too?

TWO

There Is No One Group That Benefited Exclusively from Its Fruits

The claim for reparations is premised on the false assumption that only whites have benefited from slavery. If slave labor created wealth for Americans, then obviously it has created wealth for black Americans as well, including the descendants of slaves. The GNP of black America is so large that it makes the African-American community the tenth most prosperous "nation" in the world. American blacks on average enjoy per capita incomes in the range of twenty to fifty times that of blacks living in any of the African nations form which they were kidnapped.

THREE

Only a Tiny Minority of Americans Ever Owned Slaves, and Others Gave Their Lives to Free Them

This is true even for those who lived in the ante-bellum South where only one white in five was a slaveholder. Why should their descendants owe a debt? What about the descendants of the 350,000 Union soldiers who died to free the slaves? They gave their lives. What possible moral principle would ask them to pay (through their descendants) again?

FOUR

America Today Is a Multi-Ethnic Nation and Most Americans Have No Connection (Direct or Indirect) to Slavery

The two great waves of American immigration occurred after 1880 and then after 1960. What rationale would require Vietnamese boat people, Russian refuseniks, Iranian refugees, and Armenian victims of the Turkish persecution, Jews, Mexicans, Greeks, or Polish, Hungarian, Cambodian and Korean victims of Communism, to pay reparations to American blacks?

FIVE

The Historical Precedents Used to Justify the Reparations Claim Do Not Apply, and the Claim Itself Is Based on Race Not Injury

The historical precedents generally invoked to justify the reparations claim are payments to Jewish survivors of the Holocaust, Japanese-Americans and African-American victims of racial experiments in Tuskegee, or racial outrages in Rosewood and Oklahoma City [sic]. But in each case, the recipients of reparations were the direct victims of the injustice or their immediate families. This would be the only case of reparations to people who were not immediately affected and whose sole qualification to receive reparations would be racial. As has already been pointed out, during the slavery era, many blacks were free men or slave-owners themselves, yet the reparations claimants make no distinction between the roles blacks actually played in the injustice itself. Randall Robinson's book on reparations, *The Debt*, which is the manifesto of the reparations movement is pointedly sub-titled "What America Owes to Blacks." If this is not racism, what is?

SIX

The Reparations Argument Is Based on the Unfounded Claim That All African-American Descendants of Slaves Suffer from the Economic Consequences of Slavery and Discrimination

No evidence-based attempt has been made to prove that living individuals have been adversely affected by a slave system that was ended over 150 years ago. But there is plenty of evidence the hardships that occurred were hardships that individuals could and did overcome. The black middle class in America is a prosperous community that is now larger in absolute terms than the black underclass. Does its existence not suggest that economic adversity is the result of failures of individual character rather than the lingering aftereffects of racial discrimination and a slave system that ceased to exist well over a century ago? West Indian blacks in America are also descended from slaves but their average incomes are equivalent to the average incomes of whites (and nearly 25% higher than the average incomes of American born blacks). How is it that slavery adversely affected one large group of descendants but not the other? How can government be expected to decide an issue that is so subjective—and yet so critical—to the case?

SEVEN

The Reparations Claim Is One More Attempt to Turn African-Americans into Victims. It Sends a Damaging Message to the African-American Community.

The renewed sense of grievance—which is what the claim for reparations will inevitably create—is neither a constructive nor a helpful message for black leaders to be sending to their communities and to others. To focus the social passions of African-Americans on what some Americans may have done to their ancestors fifty or a hundred and fifty years ago is to burden them with a crippling sense of victim-hood. How are the millions of refugees from tyranny and genocide who are now living in America going to receive these claims, moreover, except as demands for special treatment, an extravagant new handout that is only necessary because some blacks can't seem to locate the ladder of opportunity within reach of others—many less privileged than themselves?

EIGHT

Reparations to African Americans Have Already Been Paid

Since the passage of the Civil Rights Acts and the advent of the Great Society in 1965, trillions of dollars in transfer payments have been made to African-Americans in the form of welfare benefits and racial preferences (in contracts, job placements and educational admissions)—all under the rationale of redressing historic racial grievances. It is said that reparations are necessary to achieve a healing between African-Americans and other Americans. If trillion dollar restitutions and a wholesale rewriting of American law (in order to accommodate racial preferences) for African-Americans is not enough to achieve a "healing," what will?

NINE

What about the Debt Blacks Owe to America?

Slavery existed for thousands of years before the Atlantic slave trade was born, and in all societies. But in the thousand years of its existence, there never was an antislavery movement until white Christians—Englishmen and Americans—created one. If not for the antislavery attitudes and military power of white Englishmen and Americans, the slave trade would not have been brought to an end. If not for the sacrifices of white soldiers and a white American president who gave his life to sign the Emancipation Proclamation, blacks in America would still be slaves. If not for the dedication of Americans of all ethnicities and colors to a society based on the principle that all men are created equal, blacks in America would not enjoy the highest standard of living of blacks anywhere in the world, and indeed one of the highest standards of living of any people in the world. They would not enjoy the greatest freedoms and the most thoroughly protected individual rights anywhere. Where is the gratitude of black America and its leaders for those gifts?

TEN

The Reparations Claim Is a Separatist Idea That Sets African-Americans against the Nation That Gave Them Freedom

Blacks were here before the *Mayflower.* Who is more American than the descendants of African slaves? For the African-American community to isolate itself even further from America is to embark on a course whose implications are troubling. Yet the African-American community has had a long-running flirtation with separatists, nationalists and the political left, who want African-Americans to be no part of America's social contract. African Americans should reject this temptation.

For all America's faults, African-Americans have an enormous stake in their country and its heritage. It is this heritage that is really under attack by the reparations movement. The reparations claim is one more assault on America, conducted by racial separatists and the political left. It is an attack not only on white Americans, but on all Americans especially African-Americans.

America's African-American citizens are the richest and most privileged black people alive—a bounty that is a direct result of the heritage that is under assault. The American idea needs the support of its African-American citizens. But African-Americans also need the support of the American idea. For it is this idea that led to the principles and institutions that have set African-Americans—and all of us—free.[63]

This ad does indeed contain most of the objections offered by the opponents of reparations.[64] But many of the ad's opponents argue that on several points, it crosses the line from "reasoned" debate to provocation. For example, reason 9, which essentially argues that Blacks should be grateful for being "kidnapped" (Horowitz's term) from Africa is reminiscent of the positions of the Ku Klux Klan and other White supremacist groups. Moreover, Horowitz throws gasoline on the fire by praising Whites for ending the transatlantic slave trade that they started.

After the initial flare-up at the ad's appearance, a number of thoughtful responses appeared, although none of them received the wide coverage of the original ad. The editors of *The Black Scholar,* for example, produced a point-by-point response to the ad. Among them was that Horowitz's claim that all societies had slaves does not remove moral responsibility for slavery, and the journal cited a number of historical authorities on the central role of the slave economy in Europe and North America. Another historical claim from the ad that is easily refuted is that the major impetus for the Civil War was the desire to end slavery.[65] As many historians have pointed out, the Civil War was fought over economic issues, not an end to slavery for the slaves' sake.

More controversial points are the responsibility of today's citizens for slavery and the continuing consequences of slavery in the African American community. These points deserve careful examination, and it is surprising that they have not been the topic of extensive public discourse. Horowitz supplies the answer, however, in reasons 7 through 10. Opponents of reparations assume that there is no debt or that it has already been paid. In addition, they label Blacks who raise the issue as divisive and as playing the "victim" card.

Although Horowitz presents these points in a provocative way designed to inflame, they deserve serious attention because they are a good example of why the United States has never had a serious discussion about racial oppression and its consequences for the American community. Most recently, President Clinton's Commission on Race refused to discuss the issue of reparations precisely because Clinton deemed it too divisive.

The Horowitz ad is a masterful example of the historic tradition in American racial discourse. Those with power and resources are able to frame the issue of race in a way that either gives them an advantage or precludes serious discussion. This tradition has either individualized Black claims for justice or denied Whites' responsibility or made them the victims. This paternalistic tradition also holds that whatever action Whites take must be in the best interest of Blacks—even if Blacks argue otherwise.

We see these traditions reflected in the Horowitz ad. Beginning with its title, Horowitz presents himself as the benevolent albeit paternalistic protector of Black interests and makes Whites the victims of "Black extortionists." He then presents ten reasons why Blacks should oppose reparations and adds that those who promote reparations are not only wrong but racist as well! Thus anyone who supports reparations must be a racist and ultimately unpatriotic (see reason 10).

Almost all the ad's reasons explain why reparations are a bad idea for Whites and immigrants. Only the tenth reason appeals directly to

African Americans to support the principles and institutions of the "American idea," which Horowitz never spells out. This ad, then, articulates both the serious and the unfounded objections of many White Americans toward reparations, not as serving White or majoritarian interests, but as serving Black interests, which they consider to be not only anti-White but also anti-American.

Although Horowitz may represent an extreme position among reparations opponents, in the 2004 presidential campaign both the Republican president George W. Bush and his Democratic challenger, John Kerry, labeled the issue of reparations as divisive.[66] In a campaign that was already highly polarized along racial lines, as evidenced by the president's refusal to address the annual meeting of the NAACP, they did not say who viewed the issue as divisive: Whites, Blacks, or immigrants? Based on public opinion polls, we can assume that it was divisive for Whites, who preferred not to discuss it, and especially for Democratic candidates, who did not want to alienate their Black or White constituencies. We should remember the walkout of Democrats caused by Hubert Humphrey's invocation of human rights at the 1948 Democratic National Convention. The absence of discussion about the issue of reparations should thus be seen as part of a historic denial (censoring) of Black participation in the larger political community.

David Horowitz's ad "Ten Reasons Why Reparations for Blacks Is a Bad Idea for Blacks—and Racist Too" is a mode of discourse that has become increasingly popular in the public sphere. A horrible problem or event is identified, and a line is drawn. Those who favor the writer's position are good and those who oppose it are evil. The causes or origins of the issue in question are usually ignored or suppressed while participants engage in public rituals of sloganeering and embracing symbols. Such practices pass as public debate on complicated topics such as fundamentalism, immigration, and terrorism.

The paucity of discourse about race is not new. More than half a century ago James Baldwin published one of the best critiques, "Everybody's Protest Novel." Baldwin targeted literature that attempts social improvement by stirring its readers into moral outrage. Such works as *Uncle Tom's Cabin* and *Native Son*, Baldwin maintained, have almost the opposite effect on social change. Instead of provoking self-examination or radical criticism, they lead us to a kind of comfortable anger that affirms our own moral framework. This "medieval morality" is inadequate to confront the implications of slavery or the racial injustices that follow it.[67]

According to Baldwin, protest novels—and, by extension, racial discourse in general—refuses to acknowledge the fundamental difficulties of moral improvement. Martin Luther King Jr. was quick to add that our technological capabilities had far outstripped our moral capacity to control them. Or, as he stated the problem, we have "guided missiles in the hands of misguided men."[68] For Baldwin, however, the first question is finding a language that conveys a moral message without entirely sacrificing complexity to intelligibility. After all, he stated, American public discourse has no way to accommodate a story that so deeply undercuts its own assumptions.[69]

In the area of race discourse in general and reparations in particular, the task is daunting. Social theorists from Alexis de Tocqueville and Peter Hartz through John Rawls and Michael Walzer have tended to ignore it.[70] Only the most extraordinary works, *The Souls of Black Folk* by W. E. B. DuBois, for example, transcend the superficial and contribute to our understanding of racial dynamics. W. E. B. DuBois, writes Lawrie Balfour, found a language that challenged official memories of slavery, Reconstruction, and the disappointments that followed. In particular, DuBois addressed the economic requirements of a reconstructed democracy. He also supplemented the language of apology with the language of gratitude for the "gifts of Black folk."[71]

Using a very modest theoretical approach of reiterated problem solving, we have looked at the continuing problem of racial inequality. Specifically, our case studies examine contrasting cases of reparations both during and between particular time periods.

Still Baldwin pushes us beyond the simple problem of racial equality by asking us to define what we mean by equality. After all, inequality is a state of nature. None of us is equal in all or even one of our characteristics. Thus, we have to ask, unequal compared with whom or according to what standard? As Baldwin put it, "It is easy to proclaim all souls equal in the sight of God," as does Harriet Beecher Stowe, but "it is hard to make men equal on earth, in the sight of men."[72]

One of the reasons that the Horowitz ad was so infuriating to African American readers was its comparison of the status of Blacks in the United States with that of Blacks in Africa and its diaspora. Implicitly Horowitz is saying, be grateful that you are citizens of the United

States rather than citizens of the "Third World." Your aim is too high. You seek equality with White Americans when your true reference group should be Black non-Americans. Just as Daniel Patrick Moynihan urged in the late 1960s the "benign neglect" of African American demands on the state, Horowitz promotes a benign neglect of reparations demands now.

In the same ad in which Horowitz encourages African Americans to lower their sights compared with those of other Americans, he appeals to them as citizens: "The American idea needs the support of its African-American citizens."[73] To complicate matters further, he charges advocates of reparations of subscribing to a separatism that is part of "a long-running flirtation with separatists, nationalists and the political left, who want African-Americans to be no part of America's social contract."[74]

At the same time that Horowitz attacks African American separatists, he celebrates the America of today as a multiethnic nation composed of people who themselves have suffered human rights abuses in the land they fled. Horowitz insists that because the immigrants making up these great waves of post–Civil War immigration had no connection to slavery, they are permitted to keep their heritage of suffering (victimhood) but that Blacks are to be denied theirs. Most significantly, these immigrants are allowed to be full partners in the social contract sharing in its glories but are shielded from its darker side. Ironically, many of these same immigrants are beneficiaries of the struggle for human rights in the United States that has made this country a refuge for victims.

What are we to make of this mishmash of principles and history? It reflects both liberal and conservative views. It appeals to an "American idea" but absolves everyone from responsibility for America's shortcomings. It denies victimhood for African Americans but claims it for Whites who died in the Civil War and immigrants who were oppressed. And it lumps together nationalists and leftists as opponents of the "American idea."

Pluralist theory, the dominant theory in mainstream politics, would suggest that given Conyers's seniority, reparations legislation like the Conyers bill would receive a quick hearing in the subcommittee and even the full committee. With the support of the Congressional Black Caucus, the bill would likely be debated on the floor of Congress. After all, pluralism guarantees that in a system of multiple centers of power ensuring access to all organized interest groups, policy can proceed within established channels. allowing initial disagreements to dissolve into compromise solutions. Accordingly, no single set of interests gets all it wants, but every set of interests has its issues addressed. Although pluralism has detractors, no other single theory has replaced it in the American political canon.[75]

The problem, of course, is that Congressman Conyers's bill, H.R. 40, deals with the subject of reparations. It does not call for reparations but instead for a commission to study the economic effects of slavery on Black Americans and make recommendations. Therefore, it is very much like the legislation that was first put forward by Japanese American legislators and groups calling for a study of the impact of the World War II internment camps on Japanese Americans and then proposing solutions. Why did the Civil Liberties Act of 1988 make it through Congress to be signed by a conservative president, while H.R. 40 has languished in subcommittee for a decade and a half?

Rogers M. Smith provides one answer in his challenge to the notion of "American exceptionalism." First, he centers his work on the fact that for more than 80 percent of U.S. history, its laws declared most of the world's population to be ineligible for full American citizenship solely because of their race, origin, nationality, or gender. Moreover, for at least two-thirds of American history, the majority of the domestic adult population also was ineligible for full citizenship for the same reasons.[76] Second, he acknowledges the distinctive justifications that American intellectual and political elites devised for this exclusion, such as inegalitarian scriptural readings, the scientific racism of the "American school of ethnology," racial and sexual Darwinism, and the romantic cult of Anglo-Saxonism in American historiography. Third, Smith describes such political traditions as liberalism, republicanism, and ascriptive forms of Americanism. Thus Smith questions the contention of Alexis de Tocqueville through Gunnar Myrdal to Louis Hartz that the dominant American political tradition is the one encompassed in the American creed of liberty, equalitarianism, individualism, populism, and laissez-faire. Smith contends that the liberal and republican traditions contain elements that threaten the status of White males. Americans have therefore incorporated opposing beliefs in their institutions, and the resulting mix is as likely to lead to inequality and exclusion as to progress.[77]

These illiberal traditions help explain Horowitz's contradictory list of objections to reparations. Illiberal traditions also explain why periods of racial progress have been the exception rather than the rule in American history. Philip Klinkner, along with Smith, believes that there have been only three such periods: the Revolutionary War era, the Civil War era, and the World War II era. In each case, the war brought to the front the essential American values with which the majority of citizens identified. Because both Blacks and Whites fought for these values and rights, their denial to Blacks became impossible to sustain. In each case, however, progress for Blacks was only partial and was always followed by retrenchment and backlash. Wars that did not center on the nation's inclusive, egalitarian, and democratic traditions, such as World War I, produced relatively little racial progress.[78]

Legal scholar Derrick Bell offers a similar theory: "Black rights are recognized and protected when and only so long as policymakers perceive that such advances will further interests that are their primary concern."[79] Bell's "interest-convergence theory" offers three examples of the meshing of Black and White interests: the abolition of slavery in the Northern states, the Emancipation Proclamation, and the Civil War Amendments to the U.S. Constitution. Bell's examples roughly correspond to Klinkner's and Smith's Revolutionary War era and Civil War era. Another example that Bell offers—the U.S. Supreme Court's 1954 *Brown* decision—is seen as a product of World War II.[80] Thus Bell's theory supports Klinkner's and Smith's theories that only war produces racial progress in the United States.

Obviously, though, wars and crises are not conducive to political stability. *Federalist Paper* no. 10—the tenth of a series of papers in which James Madison argued in favor of ratifying the United States Constitution—suggests that the U.S. system of government works best when factions are shifting and temporary and that permanent divisions based along racial lines result in a tyranny of the majority.[81]

The current period of racial regression more closely resembles the period following the end of Reconstruction than the more optimistic era of Reconstruction or the period of the civil rights movement following World War II. The current lack of political opportunity is closer to that of the period of the ex-slave pension movement, and the inability to advance a reparations agenda in the United States has increased the importance of the international arena as a forum for reparations demands.

5

Reparations Go Global

Pan Africanism and the World Conference against Racism

> Any "Pan" concept is an exercise in self-definition by a people, aimed at establishing a broader re-definition of themselves than that which had so far been permitted by those in power. Invariably, however, the exercise is undertaken by a specific social group or class which speaks on behalf of the population as a whole.
>
> —Walter Rodney, Sixth Pan African Congress,
> *How Europe Underdeveloped Africa*

The Question of African Diaspora

It is not surprising that the failure of the national political system to study or seriously discuss the issue of reparations would lead activists to internationalize the debate. After all, obstacles or roadblocks in politics are often overcome by widening the circle of conflict,[1] and contemporary reparations activists have a recent model of success in the struggle to end Jim Crow. Moreover, it is widely acknowledged that the cold war struggle for the hearts and minds of the newly decolonized states of Africa and Asia played an influential role in ending legal segregation in the American South.[2]

Reparations raise another fundamental, and often overlooked, issue, that of identity. In broadening the conflict by mobilizing international resources, reparations activists in the United States also widen the perspectives of what constitutes reparations and who should receive them. By involving the framework of a "diaspora," reparations advocates point to the sameness of experience of persons of African descent dispersed across the globe. The focal point of that sameness is the experience of slavery and racial subordination. The notion of

123

diaspora, however, also suggests different experiences. A diasporic analysis is, by definition, a comparative analysis of different Black people in different places and often at different times.[3] Thus the concept of diaspora carries with it the presumption of a kind of unity but always in tension with the experience of separation, difference, and isolation. Implied at its root is the notion of the return to a homeland, either literally or figuratively.

Seminal scholar/activists such as W. E. B. DuBois, C. L. R. James, and Eric Williams worked within and from a diasporic perspective, but their version of the Black diaspora was one linked firmly to an evolving global system. In their minds the Black diaspora was central to the evolution and transformation of that global system. At the heart of Williams's *Capitalism and Slavery,* for example, is the notion that the first global world order emerged with slavery and the slave trade.[4] As a diasporic issue, then, reparations raise not only the subject of diasporic identity but also the issue of structural racism or global apartheid.

It is ironic that the opponents of reparations use as the justification for their opposition the belief that the slave trade brought Christianity and civilization to those Africans caught up in it. Without the slave trade, they argue, Blacks would not have been exposed to the modern world of mass democracy. In fact, the reverse argument might be made—without Black slavery, White mass democracy would have been impossible. Indeed, Orlando Patterson states,

> It is no accident that the first and greatest mass democracies of the ancient and modern worlds—Athens and the United States—share this evil in common: they were both conceived in, and fashioned by, the degradation of slaves and their descendants and the exclusion of women. The chronic, identical levels of Athenian xenophobia and misogyny, and antebellum American racism, nativism, and sexism, served a common purpose and nourished a common good: the profound commitment of both cultures to the inspired principle of participative politics.[5]

As Patterson notes, the establishment of a participative community of *us* always seemed to require *them* who must be excluded and thus define who *we* are.

Historian, Paul Gordon Lauren believes that not only did racism increase as democracy expanded but that also science advanced to serve the cause of racism. By creating and enhancing what is now widely known as *scientific racism,* science shifted racism from the dogma of mere prejudice to "a belief that the superiority or inferiority of human beings is actually determined by organic, genetically transmitted, biological differences of race."[6] Such views were not on the periphery; they were in the mainstream of nineteenth-century science.

Social science has not escaped the paradox of using the articulation of race to advance. David Goldberg contends that as we have come to conceive of social subjects principally in racial terms, it is with the institution of modernity that race was defined most fully. "Basic to modernity's self-conception," says Goldberg, "is a notion not of social subjects but of a Subject that is abstract and atomistic, general and universal, divorced from contingencies of historicity as it is from the particularities of social and political relations and identities."[7] Thus it is the liberalist commitment to an abstract individualism that poses the major hurdle for reparations advocates. Paradoxically, "the more explicitly universal modernity's commitments [are], the more open it is to and the more determined it is by the likes of racial specificity and racist exclusivity."[8]

Africa's Role in the Slave Trade

If the slave trade served to bring modernity to the West, what did it bring to Africa? Ali Mazrui, an African scholar and member of the Organization of African Unity's Eminent Persons Group on reparations, argued that the continent of Africa is owed reparations for the persistent depravation of the Black world, most notably in the forms of slavery and colonialism.[9] At the same time, African American opponents of reparations contend that Africans were complicit in the slave trade and were as guilty as the Whites who engaged in human commerce. John McWhorter, for example, stated that "the primary sources of the slave trade demonstrate with painful clarity that slaves —not some slaves, but most slaves—were obtained by African kings in intertribal wars, and were sold in masses to European merchants in exchange for material goods."[10] Armstrong Williams added that not only were various African tribes directly involved in the slave trade, but "furthermore thousands of Black Americans owned slaves during the antebellum period"[11] and thus share responsibility for the mid-Atlantic slave trade.

African complicity in the slave trade became a subject of mostly intraracial debate when Henry Louis Gates Jr.'s series *Wonders of the African World* was shown on public television in 1999. Mazrui accused Gates of absolving Whites of any responsibility for the transatlantic slave trade: "Now Skip Gates' television series virtually tells the world that the West has no case to answer. Africans sold each other. Presumably if there are to be any reparations in the trans-Atlantic slave-trade, it would have to be from Africans to Africans."[12] Mazrui recounts his astonishment at hearing a Ghanaian tourist guide on the series tell African American tourists at the Elmina slave fort that they were sold into slavery by Africans.

In his response to Mazrui's accusations, Gates acknowledged that it is "a vexed and painful issue." He attributed the statement about slave trade's not being possible without African collaboration to a Ghanaian historian on the series, but he does not believe the issue should be avoided. As he stated, "If *Wonders* succeeds in opening this deeply buried matter to sober reflection, then the series will have made an important contribution."[13]

Indeed, the intraracial dialogue appears to have begun when President Mattieu Kerekou of Benin got down on his knees at the Church of the Great Commission in Baltimore and apologized for his country's participation in the slave trade. Following his apology, the president of Benin hosted the "International Conference on Slavery and Reconciliation," at which President Jerry Rawlings of Ghana also offered an apology to African Americans and other Africans in the diaspora for his country's involvement in the slave trade. This November 1999 conference brought together the descendants of the sellers and buyers with the descendants of the victims of slavery. Participants came from Europe, Africa, and the United States (including Ohio Democratic Congressman Tony Hall). In July 2002, President Kerekou followed up with another dialogue when his country hosted the Festival of Gospel and Roots.

The Beninese ambassador to the United States also has apologized on various occasions, and his government has admitted responsibility for the export of three million slaves from its coast. Benin has even gone so far as to fund the Agency for Reconciliation and Development, which brings African Americans to Africa to invest in educational endeavors and economic development.[14]

Benin's acknowledgment of responsibility would seem to support those reparations opponents who point to African complicity in the transatlantic slave trade. At the same time, Benin's actions highlight the unwillingness of the U.S. government to accept responsibility by acknowledging a moral wrong and moving toward reconciliation.

Benin is an excellent place to begin examining Africa's role in the slave trade because it was a city-state that initially profited from it. In 1602 a Dutchman reported on Benin's large prosperous class:

> The town seemeth to be very great; when you enter into it, you go into a great broad street, not paved, which seems to be seven or eight times broader than the Warmoes street in Amsterdam; which goeth right out and never crooks . . . ; it is thought that that street is a mile long [a Dutch mile is roughly equal to four English miles] besides the suburbs. . . . When you are in the great street aforesaid, you see many great streets on the sides thereof, which also go right forth . . . the houses in this town stand in good order, one close and even with the other, as the houses in Holland stand.[15]

Benin began to decline, however, when it failed to cope with the costs of the disruption and warfare that the slave trade generated.

Other slave-trading societies in western central Africa followed a similar path, as the slave trade distorted the values central to their functioning. In traditional society, "big men" competed for prestige and authority through the number of people they controlled. It was people, not goods, that were prized, and the goods that did come through production or trade were invested in acquiring the allegiance or dependence of more people. The Atlantic slave trade then reversed this valuation process, replacing people with a system of goods not indigenously produced. This new system meant that men previously marginal to the established patterns of trade could leapfrog their way to wealth and power, but it also sowed the seeds of its own destruction. Europeans, the suppliers of these goods, increasingly demanded in return not other material goods but people. Thus African slave traders came to trade away the very source of their wealth: their people.[16]

Walter Rodney is generally credited with bringing to fore the impact of the slave trade on the "underdevelopment" of Africa.[17] For Rodney it was the difference between the potential productivity of captives in Africa and the value received in exchange for their persons that constituted Africa's exploitation. In fact, nearly one-third of his book *How Europe Underdeveloped Africa* describes the exploitative aspects of colonial rule. For example, Rodney states that "the most decisive failure of colonialism in Africa was its failure to change the technology of agricultural production." Despite colonialist claims to have modernized Africa, "the majority of Africans went into colonialism with a hoe and came out with a hoe."[18]

Rodney's work has been criticized by some people for its overreliance on Eric Williams's influential *Capitalism and Slavery*. Williams asserts that the origin of Negro slavery was economic, not racial, that Black labor was cheaper than Indian or White labor and therefore was preferred. Racial differences, Williams argues, made it easier to justify and rationalize Negro slavery. It was the wealth produced by the slave trade and Black slave labor in the colonies that provided the capital that financed the British Industrial Revolution.

Subsequent scholars have challenged both Williams and Rodney. Winthrop Jordan, for example, contends that cultural factors predisposed the English to see Africans as inferior and subhuman.[19] Economic historians also have calculated the combined profits of the slave trade and the West Indian plantations at less than 5 percent of the British national income as the Industrial Revolution began.[20] What seems undisputed is that the vast majority of eighteenth-century policymakers and commentators equated slaves with wealth and national greatness. "Their perception is confirmed," says David Brion Davis,

> by the value of slave-colony exports, by the per capita wealth of the slave colonies themselves, and by the simple fact that there was a demand for Black slaves in every colony from Canada to Chile. Until the 1820s the transatlantic flow of African slaves was at least four times greater than the total flow of white immigrants to the New World.[21]

Investment in slaves, then, was the first and largest capital investment of the early industrial era. Moreover, because slavery seemed to represent an unlimited labor supply impervious to the business cycle, it was an investment different from any other form of capital: it was "a license to steal."[22]

In his draft of the Declaration of Independence, Thomas Jefferson famously attempted to blame King George III for imposing the slave trade on the colonies,[23] but the truth was that Britain never required its colonists to buy slaves. Indeed, many complained they could not buy enough slaves at a reasonable price. "In every colony," Davis points out, "there was at least a small market for domestic servants, and in New England, New York, New Jersey, and Pennsylvania slave labor was applied to farming and to a variety of trades and productive industries. By 1750 in New York, one in ten householders owned slaves.[24]

What seems remarkable, as shown in Jefferson's draft Declaration, is the United States' unwillingness to admit the centrality of the slave economy to the colonies and the early nation. Even though Congress technically declared the slave trade illegal in 1808, the United States consistently refused to sign any meaningful international agreement to end it. By midcentury most of the slave ships not only flew the American flag but also were owned by American citizens. It is not surprising, then, that the violation of negotiated treaties actually led to an increase in the number of humans exported from Africa to the Western Hemisphere and Arabia. One contemporary estimated that the number of slaves doubled from 100,000 to 200,000 per year after the trade had been outlawed, and a more recent estimate places the peak of the transatlantic slave trade in the 1840s.[25]

Williams's and Rodney's work is important because it links modernity to the rise of racial slavery, and they are not alone in their view. Writing in 1917, W. E. B. DuBois emphasized the difference between modern slavery and ancient slavery:

> Modern world commerce, modern imperialism, the modern factory system and the modern labor problem began with the African slave trade. . . . Through the slave trade Africa lost at least 100,000,000 human beings, with all the attendant misery and economic and social disorganization. The survivor of this wholesale rape became a great international laboring force in America on which the modern capitalistic movement has been built, and out of which modern labor problems have arisen.[26]

Thus by the early eighteenth century we have the formation of a divided, racialized world system that today is referred to as *global apartheid*.[27] This global apartheid between "Europeans" and "others" has, from the earliest days, sparked global resistance.

In 1772, Arthur Young estimated that only 33 million inhabitants of the world's population of 775 million could be called free. Along with most intellectuals of his day, Adam Smith thought that slavery was unlikely to disappear for ages, if ever.[28] Nonetheless, a century later, most of the world's inhabitants could be called free, and a global antislavery movement could rightly claim the major role in slavery's demise. As W. E. B. DuBois tried to make sense of the gap between America's democratic ideals and this "peculiar" institution in *The Suppression of the African Slave Trade,* he concluded that economic necessity trumped moral and religious ideals. Much of the current historical research, however, argues the reverse.[29] In fact, rather than seeing economics and morality as dichotomous explanations, as DuBois did, some historians now study how the rise of capitalism and changes in the market contributed to changing perceptions, conventions about moral responsibility, and techniques of action that underlay the wave of change provided a new "frame" through which people viewed the institution of slavery.

In the United States and Britain, the antislavery movement was clearly a mass movement, with hundreds of thousands of people signing petitions and creating hundreds of local antislavery societies. In France, although the movement was confined to an elite, the results were equally profound.[30] The backbone of the English and American movements was religious denominations, and the networks between the two countries offered a mechanism for reciprocal influence. A vast supply of religious zeal created by the Protestant revival movements of the early nineteenth century provided a base of sentiment for antislavery ideas. The antislavery movement then invented what is today called *information politics,* promoting change through reporting facts. Not only were slave testimonials widely distributed, but even fictional accounts like *Uncle Tom's Cabin* were tremendously influential. World antislavery conferences held in London in 1840 and 1843 solidified Anglo-American cooperation even as it sharpened internal divisions within the movement. Of course, even though the American antislavery crusade culminated in the Civil War, every significant attempt to reform American society after the Civil War grew out of the abolitionist campaign. Moreover, the transnational antislavery campaign provided both a "language of politics" and organizational and tactical recipes for other transnational campaigns.[31]

Transnational Collective Action

The development of an international campaign to abolish slavery in the last century is often presented as the precursor of what is becoming commonplace today: international nongovernmental organizations or transnational social movements operating in the context of a global civil society. This transnational connection is supported by a world economy made possible by a revolution in communications technology, the same communications technology that has made possible transnational collective action and the development of the global civil society's international institutions and organizations.[32]

The strong thesis for transnational collective action makes five claims:

1. Electronic media and communication can transcend national political opportunity structures, giving way to transnational ones.
2. The national state may be losing its capacity to constrain and control transnational actors from corporations to human rights advocates.
3. As the state's capacity to control global economic forces declines, borders become blurred as individuals and groups gain access to new kinds of resources.
4. As economies globalize, cultures universalize, institutions proliferate and state sovereignty shrinks; "principled ideas" are increasingly adopted as international norms.
5. All of the above developments have prompted the generation of a dense web of new transnational organizations and movements.[33]

Pan Africanism

Although the movement to abolish slavery may be seen as the first global human rights network, its modern-day equivalent, Pan Africanism, is seldom viewed as a human rights movement. *Pan Africanism* may be defined as a body of thought and action that regards the people of African descent throughout the world as constituting a common cultural and political community by virtue of their origin in Africa and shared racial, social, and economic oppression. Furthermore, it maintains that this common oppression is best fought through united action.[34]

How does Pan Africanism fit into the new theories explaining the explosive organizational growth of such issues as human rights, the environment, women's issues, and religious fundamentalism? Is Pan Africanism a transnational advocacy network or a transnational social movement or neither?

Transnational advocacy networks (TANs) are distinguished by the centrality of principled ideas or values in motivating their formation. By contrast, transnational actors like banks and corporations are characterized by instrumental and/or material goals, and scientific groups and epistemic communities are motivated primarily by shared causal ideas. Members of TANs believe that individuals can make a difference through the creative use of information and the use of sophisticated political strategies. Generally operating through targeted campaigns, these networks create political spaces in which differently situated actors negotiate—formally or informally—the social, cultural, and political meanings of their joint enterprise.[35]

In its first phase, from 1900 to 1945, Pan Africanism appeared to share many of the characteristics of a TAN. Because channels of communication between colonial powers and their domestic subjects were blocked or ineffective, Pan African activists believed that networking with one another would advance their goal of anticolonialism and therefore turned to networks. A series of Pan African congresses were held in various locations outside Africa to form and strengthen these networks. They were made up of individuals from a variety of political ideologies and thus can be distinguished from solidarity organizations, which base their appeals on common ideological commitments.

Activists in this early stage of Pan Africanism targeted the colonial powers using tactics characteristic of TANs. By means of *information politics*, they generated politically usable information about the conditions of colonial subjects. *Symbolic politics* were prominent in the Pan African congresses after World Wars I and II. Pan Africanists also used *leverage politics* by joining powerful allies in the British labor movement. Finally, they practiced *accountability politics* by holding powerful actors to previously stated policies and principles of equality and democracy.

These early Pan Africanists allowed their personal interests determine their positions on relevant issues, rather than letting their objective interests define their positions on these issues. In contrast, supporters of the contemporary African Growth and Development Act could be charged with letting their objective interests determine their position on the issues. That is, principled activists are distinguished by the intensely self-conscious and self-reflective nature of their normative awareness.[36]

Unfortunately, when used as an instrument to examine Pan Africanism, the TAN framework has a number of weaknesses. For example, problems whose causes can be assigned to the deliberate (intentional) actions of identifiable individuals are amenable to advocacy network strategies. Accordingly, because institutional racism lacks a short and clear causal chain assigning responsibility, action against it is more difficult. Moreover, issues involving legal equality of opportunity may be harder to address in a system without strong international standards (for example, Amnesty International's refusal to challenge the system of apartheid).

These structural issues also create a problem of trust. For activists in developing countries, the issue of sovereignty is deeply embedded in the issue of structural inequality. For them, justifying external pressure or intervention in domestic affairs is much more problematic than it is for advocacy networks in developed countries. An example is the reluctance of African activists to suggest a redrawing of national borders established by colonial powers or any consensus on interventions in Angola, the Congo, or Uganda.

Is Pan Africanism better viewed as a transnational social movement than as a transnational advocacy network? Sociologist Sidney Tarrow defined *transnational social movements* as sustained and contentious interactions with opponents, both national and nonnational, by connected networks of challengers organized across national boundaries.[37] Based on this definition, environmentalism, Islamic fundamentalism, and the European and American peace movements of the 1980s are examples of transnational social movements. For Tarrow, TANs lack the categorical basis, the sustained interpersonal relations, and the exposure to similar opportunities and constraints that social movement scholars have found in domestic social networks.

Comparative work in social movement theory has synthesized recent theoretical developments, resulting in three sets of factors thought to apply internationally: (1) the structure of political opportunities and constraints confronting the movement (political opportunities); (2) the formal and informal forms of organization available to insurgents (mobilizing structures); and (3) the collective processes of interpretation, attribution, and social construction that mediate between opportunity and action (framing processes).[38]

Political opportunities may be defined as consistent—but not necessarily formal, permanent, or national—signals to social or political actors that either encourage or discourage them from using their internal resources to form social movements. These signals include the availability of access to power, a shift of alignments, the availability of influential allies, and cleavages within and among elites.[39] World Wars I and II clearly provided the signal for the most significant Pan African meetings in 1919 and 1945, respectively. Most scholars, however, have paid little attention to the impact of global political and economic processes in structuring domestic possibilities for collective action.

Mobilizing structures are collective vehicles through which people mobilize and engage in collective action. Resource mobilization theory and political process modeling have paid much attention to this factor. Comparative research has assessed the effect of both state structures and national "organizational cultures" on the form of movements in a given country. When applied to Pan Africanism, this approach is particularly helpful in examining the Universal Negro Improvement Associations (UNIA) led by Marcus Garvey. Like the Pan African Congress of 1919, Garvey's movement took advantage of the political opportunity created by World War I to organize. Yet while the choice of locating the Pan African Congress in Paris is easily explained, Garvey's choice of locating the congress in the United States and particularly in New York requires further examination. Garvey spent time in London and established the UNIA in Jamaica before moving to New York, where he was able to develop the largest Black mass movement in U.S. history. Much work remains to be done on the informal networks that Garvey and the UNIA formed, both at home and abroad.[40]

Framing is the conscious strategic effort by groups of people to fashion a shared understanding of the world and of themselves that legitimates and motivates collective action.[41] Such conscious strategic efforts include the specific metaphors, symbolic representations, and cognitive cues used to place behavior and events in an evaluative mode and to suggest alternative modes of action.

The impetus to action is as much a cultural construction as it is a function of structural vulnerability and political will. Frames promoting action stress urgency, agency, and possibility, whereas frames opposed to action emphasize jeopardy, futility, and perversity. Repertoires of organizations—which vary across groups within a particular society, among societies, and over time—are one form of cultural competence that activists may use.[42] Thus Garvey effectively used a military model of organization that resonated with returning World War I veterans. Other repertoires used were the appropriation and replication of colonial forms, organizations, protocols, uniforms, and the pompous rhetoric of White sources.

Research on Pan Africanism has generally focused on the formal ideologies rather than the collective identities, core discourses, and frames of meaning that link members of the social movement and movement networks. But it is in the discourse on collective identity that Pan Africanism reveals its weaknesses. Although *culture* is a system of meaning that people use to manage their daily worlds, it also is the basis of social and political identity that affects whether people support and act on a wide range of matters. "Natural," or inherited, identities are often the basis of aggregation in social movements. These identities are the sites of continual contestation both within movements and between insurgents and authorities.

Since social movements require solidarity in order for their members to act collectively and consistently, disagreements over group identity can be fatal. For example, the tension between the Pan African leaders W. E. B. DuBois and Marcus Garvey is often described as a conflict over racial identity.[43] Moreover, within the Pan African Congress movement, ties to colonial powers created conflict among the members. With the advent of state-led Pan Africanism as represented by Kwame Nkrumah, the first president of Ghana, geographical identity replaced racial identity as the movement's defining characteristic. This shift marked a transition from the decentered, lateral connections of DuBois's Pan African Congresses to a more centered linkage articulated primarily through a real (Ghana) or a symbolic (United States of Africa) homeland.

The rise of independent African states in the 1950s and 1960s increased African Americans' racial identity with Africa. Black power advocates like Malcolm X, Amiri Baraka, and Stokely Carmichael, along with organizations like the Student Nonviolent Coordinating Committee (SNCC) and the Black Panthers, strongly identified with these emerging African nations. When such African leaders as Kwame Nkrumah and Julius Nyerere (of Tanzania) assumed power, they moved Pan Africanism toward a geographical rather than a racial foundation. Consequently, the Pan Africanist movement led by African diasporian activists from the West working more or less as equals was transformed with the seizure of formal state power.

A Pan African network based on a rough equality between activists on the continent and those in the diaspora was replaced with one of formal inequality between African government officials who held formal state power and activists in the diaspora who held none. This shift changed also the nature of the relationship. The institutionalization of Pan Africanism in the form of the Organization of African Unity (OAU), for example, excluded any formal role for participants from the diaspora. Accordingly, at the world Black arts festival (FESTAC) in Nigeria in 1977, state delegations were given a higher status than were nonstate delegations. More important, the state delegates tended to downplay controversial issues raised by nonstate participants.[44]

Even at the sixth Pan African Congress, which was held in Tanzania in 1974 but was initiated by activists in the United States and Caribbean, nonstate participation was limited. Then at the seventh and last Pan African Congress in Uganda in 1994, Africans explicitly rejected an emphasis on developing civil society organizations, arguing that the primary goal of Pan Africanism should be the acquisition of state power.[45] Since then, African leaders have preferred to work with other Black state officials in the diaspora.[46]

The contemporary state of Pan Africanism over the last twenty years is best illustrated by two examples. In the first instance, the South African divestment movement, a strong alliance of diasporic and continental forces, was able to apply pressure on the South African government, leading to the overthrow of apartheid. In the second case, the passage of the African Growth and Opportunity Act fractured Pan African racial unity through class and status differences.

Although the modern struggle to overcome apartheid in South Africa began with the effort to impose economic sanctions at the first meeting of the United Nations' General Assembly in 1946, this effort did not reach the critical mass necessary for victory until the 1980s. The struggle included such elected officials as the presidents of the frontline African states and the Congressional Black Caucus in the United States. Black activists like those in TransAfrica (the Black lobby for Africa) and the Free South Africa movement were major components of the coalition. Even Black entertainers and athletes like tennis player Arthur Ashe were drawn into the conflict. White supporters included liberals in the United States, especially in the religious community, and leftists in South Africa, although the movement there was led by Blacks.

When Congress passed a strong economic sanctions bill over President Ronald Reagan's veto in October 1986, it marked the high point of modern diasporic politics. In fact, Reagan's overt support of white supremacy through his policy of "constructive engagement" helped unite the opposition and frame the issue as one of democracy. Jeanne Kirkpatrick, Reagan's ambassador to the United Nations, famously distinguished between totalitarian regimes and authoritarian regimes, labeling South Africa as authoritarian, stating, "Racist dictatorship is not as bad as Marxist dictatorship."[47] Ultimately, a number of factors, including the institutionalization of Black political power in the United States, the rise of a critical intellectual community around African studies programs, and the greater visibility of human rights groups in policymaking, led to success in a hostile political environment.[48]

The passage of the African Growth and Opportunity Act by the U.S. Congress presents a different example of the basic problem underlying any revival of the Pan African movement. This legislation represents a fundamental shift in American foreign policy toward Africa, replacing the economic development assistance approach with one designed to encourage private enterprise. In many ways the bill parallels the Clinton administration's "reform" of domestic welfare policy by moving welfare recipients from governmental assistance to private payrolls by means of, for example, work requirements. Of course, the Clinton administration's shift in development strategies took place in the context of a Republican-led Congress that sharply cut African economic assistance in 1995 and significant levels of economic growth in countries like Angola, Ethiopia, Rwanda, and Uganda.

The African Growth and Opportunity Act was originally introduced by Representative James McDermott (D-WA) in the spring of

1996 and a year later was backed by key members of the Congressional Black Caucus (Charles Rangel, D-NY) as well as leading Republican conservatives (Phillip Crane, R-IL). The bill's three main features —the establishment of a U.S.–African free trade area by 2020, the creation of a U.S.–African economic cooperation forum, and the creation of a U.S.–African trade and investment partnership modeled on the Organization of Petroleum Exporting Countries (OPEC)—were accompanied by the following conditions: no trade with Libya, Cuba, or Iraq; cuts in government spending, privatization of governmental services; no barriers to trade such as governmental protection regulations; liberalization of trade and movement toward the World Trade Organization; and movement toward democratic institutions and practices. In this way, the African Growth and Opportunity Act shared with welfare reform the assumption that the recipients of economic assistance rather than the structure of the political economy were responsible for their economic status.

What was most striking, however, was not the content of the bill but the split it created between traditional allies on African issues. From the earliest independence movements through the end of apartheid, African American political elites have generally been united. But this bill found Randall Robinson of TransAfrica and Ralph Nader of Public Citizen joining labor and Representative Jesse Jackson Jr. in their opposition to it. The Clinton administration counterattacked, led by Representative Charles Rangel, Assistant Secretary of State for African Affairs Susan Rice; David Dinkins and Mel Foote of the Constituency for Africa, and even Rev. Jesse Jackson Sr., who had been an early opponent of the bill. Perhaps the key voice in framing the issue for the American public came from African ambassadors, including the assistant secretary-general of the Organization of African Unity, Vijay S. Makhan, who supported the bill. In the final vote in the House, twenty-four members of the Congressional Black Caucus supported the bill and twelve opposed it.[49]

The reason for this brief discussion of the African Growth and Opportunity Act is to illustrate the difficulties of united action in the post-apartheid, post–cold war era. The old ideological divides have been complicated by class, gender, and even generational divisions. Reparations are Pan Africanism's most recent test. In the past, the reparations movement was organized and directed by Africans in the diaspora. Many of the principal figures, from Bishop Henry McNeil Turner to the activists of N'COBRA, identified themselves as Black nationalists. But when the reparations struggle expanded to include Africans in Africa, a wider normative shift was necessary. "It was the African side of the reparations movement," Mazrui observed, "which moved it from a demand of diaspora Blacks for restitution on their own countries to a new world-wide crusade for reparations for the African and Black world as a whole."[50]

The president of Nigeria, Ibrahim Babangia, took the lead in establishing a reparations movement during his tenure as head of the Organization of African Unity (OAU). The first meeting of the International Conference on Reparations was held in Lagos, Nigeria, in the winter of 1990. In 1992 the OAU formally embraced and endorsed reparations as "the last stage in the decolonization process." The meeting of African heads of state in Dakar, Senegal, formally created an international committee called the Group of Eminent Persons and charged it with determining the scope of damages and a strategy for achieving reparations. Jamaican diplomat Dr. Dudley Thompson was chosen to chair the group.[51] After a second conference in 1993, the OAU issued the Abuja Proclamation, which articulated its grievances against the United States and the Western European nations, linking slavery and colonialism:

> Emphasizing that an admission of guilt is a necessary step to reverse this situation [damage to African peoples].
>
> Emphatically convinced that what matters is not the guilt but the responsibility of those states whose economic evolution once depended on slave labour and colonialism and whose forebears participated either in selling and buying Africans, or in owning them, or in colonizing them.
>
> Convinced that the pursuit of reparations by the African peoples on the continent and in the Diaspora will be a learning experience in self-discovery and in uniting political and psychological experiences.
>
> Calls upon the international community to recognize that there is a unique and unprecedented moral debt of compensation to the Africans as the most humiliated and exploited people of the last four centuries of modern history.[52]

The UN World Conference against Racism

The United Nation's World Conference against Racism (WCAR), which met from August 31 through September 8, 2001, provides an excellent opportunity to examine the development of a Pan Africanist social movement through the issue of reparations. Billed as the largest gathering ever devoted to the discussion of race and racial discrimination, the conference was attended by 170 governments and nearly 19,000 individuals. It brought together an unprecedented group of activists (critical community) interested in conceptualizing and implementing a strategy to secure racial reparations. In writing about transnational advocacy networks, Margaret Keck and Kathryn Sikkink cite conferences and other forms of international contact as primary arenas for forming and strengthening such networks.[53]

Largely as a result of a shift in control of the UN General Assembly to "nonaligned" or "Third World" countries, between 1973 and 2003 the UN designated three decades for action to combat racism and racial discrimination. In 1978, midway through the first decade, the first World Conference was held in Geneva, Switzerland. This conference specifically addressed apartheid and, for that reason, was opposed by the United States. Delegates characterized apartheid as an "extreme form of institutionalized racism" and a crime against humanity, and reparations were not mentioned in the final conference document. In August 1983, the second World Conference against Racism was again held in Geneva, where it reviewed and assessed the activities undertaken during the first decade. The conference again devoted a good deal of attention to apartheid but also addressed acts and policies of intolerance faced by women, refugees, immigrants, and migrant workers. Item 43 in the final conference declaration states that "victims of racial discrimination should have the right to seek from tribunals just and adequate reparation or satisfaction for any damage suffered as a result of such discrimination.[54] Once again, the United States opposed the conference, and so whether it would participate in a third World Conference was a question of speculation.

The UN's decision in 1997 to convene a third World Conference against Racism reflected its growing concern with the worldwide rise in incidents of racism. The UN high commissioner for human rights, Mary Robinson, was appointed as the secretary-general of the conference, and nations, regional organizations, and nongovernmental organizations (NGOs) were asked to participate in the preparations for the conference by undertaking reviews and studies and submitting recommendations to the Preparatory Committee (Prepcom). Nongovernmental organizations were encouraged to hold forums both before and during the conference, as had been done at other recent UN global conferences such as the ones in Vienna in 1993 and Beijing in 1995. The typical procedure for past UN global conferences has been for a series of regional meetings to develop a working document that will be the foundation for discussion and action at the conference. Difficult issues (such as language) that cannot be agreed to by consensus at the regional meetings are put in brackets, and their resolution becomes as the major activity of the conference. UN documents must be agreed to by the consensus of all participating countries.

The Prepcom selected Ambassador Absa Claude Diallo of Senegal as its chair. The members of the bureau for the WCAR were Senegal, Tunisia, the Islamic Republic of Iran, Malaysia, the former Yugoslav Republic of Macedonia, Georgia, Brazil, Mexico (rapporteur), France, the United States,[55] and South Africa as ex officio.

The Prepcom selected five themes for the conference:

Theme 1: Sources, causes, forms and contemporary manifestations of racism, racial discrimination, xenophobia and related intolerance.

Theme 2: Victims of racism, racial discrimination, xenophobia and related intolerance.

Theme 3: Measures of prevention, education and protection aimed at the eradication of racism, racial discrimination, xenophobia and related intolerance.

Theme 4: Provision of effective remedies, recourses, redress, [compensatory][56] and other measures, at the national, regional and international levels.

Theme 5: Strategies to achieve full and effective equality, including international mechanisms in combating racism, racial discrimination, xenophobia and related intolerance—and follow up.[57]

Newly democratic South Africa was chosen as the host country for the conference. Table 5.1 shows the WCAR's time line.

Table 5.1
World Conference against Racism Time Line

- 1997: UN General Assembly agrees to hold a third world conference to combat racism no later than 2001.
- January 2000: "Bellagio consultation" held in Bellagio, Italy.
- May 2000: First PrepCom meeting in Geneva, Switzerland.
- July 2000: U.S. NGO Coordinating Committee meetings held in Philadelphia and Oakland, California.
- September–November 2000: U.S. Interagency Task Force "discussion group" meetings held in Atlanta, Albuquerque, Chicago, and Washington, D.C.
- October 2000: U.S. NGO Coordinating Committee meetings held in Atlanta, San Francisco, and Phoenix.
- October 2000: Regional meeting for Europe held in Strasbourg, France.
- December 2000: Regional meeting for the Americas held in Santiago, Chile.
- January 2001: Regional meeting for Africa held in Dakar, Senegal.
- February 2001: Regional meeting for Asia held in Teheran, Iran.
- May–June 2001: Second PrepCom meeting held in Geneva, Switzerland.
- July–August 2001: Third PrepCom meeting held in Geneva, Switzerland.
- August–September 2001: NGO Forum held in Durban, South Africa
- August–September 2001: World Conference against Racism held in Durban, South Africa.

Because the regional meetings offer the first and often decisive opportunity to determine a conference's major issues, we will examine the efforts of five constituencies or communities to frame the issue of reparations at the WCAR. These groups are (1) the UN itself, (2) the U.S. NGOs, (3) the African governments, (4) the U.S. government, and (5) the media.

The Prepcom decided on "United to Combat Racism: Equality, Justice, Dignity" as the slogan for the WCAR, as well as the definition of racial discrimination in article I (1) of the International Convention on the Elimination of All Forms of Racial Discrimination (CERD), which states that the term *racial discrimination* shall mean

> any distinction, exclusion, restriction or preference based on race, colour, descent, or national or ethnic origin which has the purpose or effect of nullifying or impairing the recognition, enjoyment of exercise, on an equal footing, of human rights and fundamental freedoms in the political, economic, social, cultural or any other field of public life.

Perhaps the first formal attempt to frame the conference agenda came in the first WCAR think paper, entitled "The World Conference against Racism: A Conference on Racism Worldwide?" The WCAR think papers were a joint project of the Human Rights Documentation Centre (HRDC), the International Service for Human Rights (ISHR), and the South Asia Human Rights Documentation Centre (SAHRDC). This document expressed the serious concern that the WCAR would not focus on racism worldwide. Echoing the view shared by the United States and some European governments, the authors feared that non-Western countries would use the conference to bash the West. They then tried to avoid this outcome by asking each nation to acknowledge its own struggle with discrimination as the first step in creating an atmosphere that would lead to "a more realistic and constructive manner in discussing their concerns of racism in other parts of the world."[58] While acknowledging that "the pervasiveness of racial discrimination" in both the domestic and foreign policies of Western nations deserved significant attention, "the authors believe that turning the WCAR into a geopolitical dispute may result in a significant setback for the fight against racism."

The paper, however, predicts that such an outcome is likely. First, the non-Western countries are likely "to use their numerical superiority—as they do in forums such as the Commission on Human Rights—to push through a political agenda that is concerned more with combating Western States than it is with genuinely addressing all forms of racial discrimination in all areas of the world."[59] Second, the preponderance of NGOs from Western industrialized states, with their greater resources and media contacts, are likely to focus the conference's attention on their own countries, to the delight of non-Western and developing countries. The paper concludes with a list of "forgotten issues," ranging from discrimination against Koreans in Japan to the mistreatment of indigenous people in South America.

It is quite unusual for the initial document of a global conference to predict failure and even a setback as the likely outcome. Of course, this negative framing could be seen as an attempt by the West to launch a preemptive strike at those who try to draw attention to Western racism.

In January 2000, before the first Prepcom meeting, a consultation on the WCAR was held in Bellagio, Italy, with the support of the Rockefeller Foundation. The "Bellagio consultation" included officials of the World Bank, several UN agencies, the Rockefeller Foundation, several academics, and the leaders of several influential NGOs, including the International Human Rights Law Group. The participants heard presentations on the issues of globalization, immigration, ethnic conflict, indigenous peoples, the uses of legislation and litigation with the United States serving as the model, and the role of national institutions on human rights. The Bellagio consultation recommended four themes to the WCAR, and the UN accepted all four. The only theme added after Bellagio was the third: measures of prevention, education, and protection aimed at the eradication of racism, racial discrimination, xenophobia, and related intolerance, at the national, regional, and international levels. The Bellagio consultation mentioned reparations as a subtheme under "remedies, recourse, redress, and compensatory measures." However, at the first Prepcom meeting, the word *compensatory* was put into brackets after a week of intense debate between the African countries and the European Union and the United States.[60] Thus from the very first meeting, the issue of reparations loomed over the conference, pitting Western governments against their own NGOs and the developing countries.

As might be expected, the strongest support for reparations came from the Americas regional meeting in December 2000 in Santiago, Chile, and the Africa regional meeting in January 2001 in Dakar, Senegal. The declaration agreed to by the African governments in attendance in Dakar directly links the underdevelopment of Africa to the transatlantic slave trade and colonialism. Highlighting the gap between the activists and the government officials, the delegates ignored the opening plea by the president of Senegal, Abdoulaye Wade, who not only encouraged delegates to "stop weeping over the past and build to the future" but also declared that "racism in the twenty-first century is not a big deal."[61] Perhaps wondering why Senegal chose to host the regional meeting, since "racism is almost dead," the delegates produced a declaration asking for recognition of these historic injustices and an explicit apology from ex-colonial powers or their successors. Furthermore, citing article 6 of the Convention on the Elimination of All Forms of Discrimination (CERD) and other human rights instruments, the declaration asserts the right to compensation for victims of racist policies or acts, "regardless of when they were committed." The following are the declaration's four specific recommendations to the WCAR:

33. The setting up of an International Compensation Scheme for victims of slave trade, as well as victims of any other transna-

tional racist policies and acts, in addition to the national funds or any national equivalent mechanisms aiming at fulfilling the right to compensation.

34. The setting up of a Development Reparation Fund to provide additional resources for development process in countries affected by colonialism.

35. The International Compensation Scheme and Development Reparation Fund should be financed not only from governmental sources but also by private contributions emanating in particular from those private sectors which had benefited, directly or indirectly, from transnational racist policies or acts.

36. The follow up mechanism of the World Conference will, inter alia, define the modalities of the compensation scheme for victims of slave trade and to that effect work, closely with the Eminent Persons Group established by OAU Council of Ministers' resolution CM/1339 (LIV), mandated to "set out clearly the extent of Africa's exploitation, the liability of perpetrators and the strategies for achieving reparation."[62]

Although the African declaration refers to internal ethnic conflict and the need for human rights education, the overwhelming sense is that "of a victim-oriented approach" linking most of Africa's contemporary problems to the historical legacy of transnational racist practices.[63]

The Draft Declaration and Plan of Action produced at the Americas regional meeting in Santiago calls for recognition that conquest, colonialism, and slavery created a condition of systemic discrimination "that still affects large sectors of the population." The declaration also states that slavery, the transatlantic slave trade, and other forms of servitude could today "constitute crimes against humanity." To aid in reconciliation it asks for acknowledgment

> that the enslavement and other forms of servitude of Africans and their descendants and of the indigenous peoples of the Americas, as well as the slave trade, were morally reprehensible, in some cases constituted crimes under domestic law and, if they occurred today, would constitute crimes under international law. Acknowledge that these practices have resulted in substantial and lasting economic, political and cultural damage to these peoples and that justice now requires that substantial national and international efforts be made to

repair such damage. Such reparation should be in the form of policies, programmes and measures to be adopted by the States which
benefited materially from these practices, and designed to rectify the
economic, cultural and political damage which has been inflicted on
the affected communities and peoples.[64]

Finally, the document recalls that "pursuant to international law,
persecution of a group or community with a particular identity for racial or ethnic motives, as well as institutionalized racism, are serious
violations of human rights and, in some cases, may qualify as crimes
against humanity." The Canadian government objected to applying
the modern legal concept of "crimes against humanity" to acts that
took place centuries ago. The United States also objected to character-
izing slavery as a crime against humanity or even as a crime.[65]

Once all the regional meetings had been concluded, a special committee met in March in Geneva to combine the regional drafts into one
working document. The result of the special committee's work, coming two weeks after the Americas regional meeting, was notable for
what had been excised from the regional drafts. Although there was a
separate section on indigenous peoples, as in the Santiago document,
the separate section on persons of African descent had been dropped,
and there was no mention of reparations. In fact, the entire thirty-one-
page draft mentioned "people of African descent" only twice. NGO
representatives from the Americas and Asia were so dissatisfied that
the draft was rejected and the committee was ordered to produce a
new draft at another preconference meeting in Geneva in May 2001.

At this point the United States once again tried to frame the discussion by producing a "non-paper for the WCAR" released in a de-
marche on the conference. Again stating its desire to focus on the
current form and manifestations of racism, "as it was intended to do
by the UNGA," the United States stated that it hoped the working
group would use the secretary-general's text as the basis for negotia-
tion rather than starting from scratch or working with only regional
documents. A large part of the "non-paper" is devoted to reparations:
"We simply do not believe that it is appropriate to address this history
[of slavery]—and its many and vast aspects—through such measures
as international compensatory measures." Once again, a focus on this
issue would detract, the United States insisted, from the problems

that affect peoples' lives today. The paper then brings up the views of the Senegalese president, Abdoulaye Wade, who opened the Africa regional meeting by arguing that the conference must concentrate on practical solutions to current problems. The views of the Rwandan delegate to the Dakar conference also are used to support the U.S. position. Finally, after mentioning efforts in the United States to create an African American museum and other educational activities, the non paper firmly rejects "anything that suggests present-day liability on the part of one state to another for that historical situation of slavery)."[66] The paper ends by pointing out the United States' "massive debt relief program" in Africa of more than $1 billion.

Owing to the lack of agreement on reparations and the Middle East at the second Prepcom in May, a very late third Prepcom was held in Geneva less than three weeks before the WCAR was scheduled to begin. This last-minute attempt to produce a working document for the WCAR resulted in the inclusion of a separate subsection on Africans and people of African descent. The meeting's participants also agreed on the following two paragraphs concerning reparations:

191. Urges States to take all necessary measures to address, as a matter of urgency, the pressing requirement for justice for the victims of racism, racial discrimination, xenophobia and related intolerance and to ensure that victims have full access to information, support, effective protection and national, administrative and judicial remedies, including the right to seek just and adequate reparation or satisfaction for damage, as well as legal assistance, where required.

199. Urges States to reinforce the protection against racism, racial discrimination, xenophobia and related intolerance by ensuring that all persons have access to effective and adequate remedies and enjoy the right to seek from competent national tribunals and other national institutions just and adequate reparation and satisfaction for any damage as a result of such discrimination. It further underlines the importance of access to the law and to the courts for complainants of racism and racial discrimination and draws attention to the need for judicial and other remedies to be made widely known, easily accessible, expeditious and not unduly complicated.[67]

The Prepcom, however, could not agree to include the word *compensatory* in the document, and so it was left in brackets.

Nongovernmental organizations regarded the WCAR as a political opportunity to mobilize allies and shape public opinion. Hanspeter Kriesi identified four types of formal organizations: social movement organizations (SMOs), supportive organizations, movement associations, and parties and interest groups. *SMOs* are distinguished from the other types in that they mobilize a constituency for collective action toward a political goal. *Supportive organizations* are service organizations such as churches, the media, and educational institutions that contribute to the constituency's social organization without directly taking part in the mobilization for collective action. *Movement associations* are self-help organizations, voluntary associations, or clubs that service the movement's constituency but do not contribute directly to the mobilization for action. Finally, whereas parties and interest groups pursue political goals, as SMOs do, they do not normally depend on the direct participation of their constituents to attain these goals.[68]

A Pan African Reparations Movement

One of the remarkable aspects of the push for reparations is the broad range of organizational types that came together around the issue. SMOs like N'COBRA and the Leadership Conference on Civil Rights were joined by supportive organizations connected to Fisk University and church groups like the United Church of Christ, the Mennonite Church, and the Quaker Church. Even though the U.S. government did not officially attend, several members of the Congressional Black Caucus joined the SMOs and supportive organizations in promoting reparations. Thus, the sense of collective Pan African identity served to unite a broad spectrum of organizations.

This spectrum of organizational types are differentiated further. Obviously, members of the Congressional Black Caucus differ from the mainstream of the Democratic and Republican parties in promoting reparations.[69] SMOs occupy different ideological spaces within the broader movement. Single-issue organizations such as N'COBRA and All for Reparations and Emancipation have a more nationalist perspective than that of groups like the Leadership Conference on Civil Rights or the International Human Rights Law Group (IHRLG). The more mainstream organizations brought increased legitimacy and potential allies to the campaign for reparations, while the more radical or militant groups brought a cadre of committed activists and a sense of history to the movement.

No formal hierarchal organization emerged from this mix. However, at the point of contact with opponents, that is, at the regional meetings and Prepcoms, the African / African Descendants Caucus was formed, representing all the organizations supporting reparations. Created at an earlier preparatory conference, this caucus included several hundred delegates, with fifty to two hundred attending the daily meetings in Durban, South Africa. The delegates expressed their differing views of reparations in these daily meetings. According to one observer, most of the participants from the United States saw the slavery issue as both a public apology and a precursor to reparations. Latin American delegates tended to see reparations as also providing public recognition of special racial-group interests that would reinforce their domestic politics. Some also saw reparations as a kind of international apology for slavery. Most African NGOs focused on reparations as potential redress for colonial exploitation, and delegates from Sudan and Mauritania wanted the caucus to condemn modern slavery. Of course, this latter position was the objective of the U.S. government, but the caucus delegates preferred to emphasize the transatlantic slave trade of the past.[70]

In the end, this group issued its position as "Ten Priority Action Points of Consensus":

1. The slave trade, slavery and colonialism are crimes against humanity.
2. Reparations for Africans and African Descendants.
3. Recognition of the economic basis of racism.
4. Adoption of corrective national (domestic) public policies with emphasis on environmental racism, health care and education.
5. Adoption of culture specific development policies.
6. The adoption of mechanisms to combat the interconnection of race and poverty, and the role that globalization (caused by governments and the private sector) has in this interconnection.
7. Adoption of mechanisms to combat racism in the criminal punishment (penal) system.
8. Reform of the legal system including national constitutional reforms and development of international and regional mechanisms for dismantling racism.

9. Adoption of policies specific to African and African Descendant Women that recognize and address the intersections of race and gender.
10. Support for the adoption of policies that recognize and address the intersection of race and sexual orientation.[71]

This caucus won the battle to achieve recognition as a separate subcategory in the final conference document, thereby validating its collective identity. Whether the connective structures that permitted the caucus to operate effectively will persist remains an open question.

The African/African Descendants Caucus was not the only place at which differing perspectives on reparations were aired. In addition, continental Africans met in their own caucus and took a variety of positions. Most, for example, were strongly opposed to an attack on modern-day slavery. Ironically, this led the delegates from Sudan and Mauritania to ask for support from the Descendants Caucus rather than the Continental African Caucus.

Afro-European delegates were permitted to participate in the Continental African Caucus, at which they complained that the reparations issue was too closely tied to African American interests. It therefore was left to African delegates to defeat a statement critical of the role of American NGOs in framing the reparations debate.[72] Notwithstanding, the American NGOs had their own framing debate during the WCAR preparations.

The SMOs and supportive organizations were the most active on the issue of reparations. In the United States, the lead organization in coordinating the NGOs' input into the WCAR process was the International Human Rights Law Group (IHRLG) and its executive director, Gay McDougall. Through the Bellagio consultation in January 2000, the IHRLG worked with the UN and other NGOs to create a framework for the NGOs' participation and a working agenda. As we have seen, reparations emerged from the Bellagio meeting as a controversial but not a dominant issue, but this changed over the next year.

An interim U.S. NGO Coordinating Committee for the WCAR held strategy sessions in Philadelphia and Oakland, California, in the summer of 2000. More than one hundred people from different organizations participated in the Oakland meeting, which was coordinated by the Women's Institute for Leadership Development for Human Rights (WILD) and the American Friends Service Committee. Reparations received a good deal of attention, particularly the precedents of Native American and Japanese American reparations, the Conyers bill (H.R. 40), and the need for the collaboration of groups seeking reparations. The participants adopted a procedure to select a permanent U.S. NGO Coordinating Committee.

The permanent U.S. NGO Coordinating Committee was based at the IHRLG. Along with its partners, the Leadership Conference on Civil Rights, Leadership Conference Education Fund, National Council of the Churches of Christ in the USA, and the Southern Education Foundation, Inc., the coordinating committee convened a series of U.S. leadership meetings, which were held in Atlanta, San Francisco, and Phoenix in October 2000. Local partners and hosts for the meetings were the Center for Democratic Renewal, WILD, Changemakers Foundation, World Affairs Council of Northern California, Mexican American Defense and Educational Fund, and the Inter Tribal Council of Arizona. None of these organizations had reparations as a major group goal or objective. Only the Atlanta meeting had representatives from organizations directly involved in the reparations movement: the Southern Human Rights Organizers' Conference (SHROC) and the Race Relations Institute of Fisk University. The call for reparations, however, was not limited to the representatives of those groups, and proponents of reparations spoke at each meeting.

Following the meetings, the U.S. NGO Coordinating Committee submitted a report to the U.S. government's Inter-Agency Task Force on the WCAR. That report had a section on reparations stating that "reparations for slavery and unpaid slave labor, as well as for dispossession of Indian lands, placed high on the participants' list of priority issues for the U.S. government to address." Moreover, the report added that "debt relief for 'Third World' countries, in particular those in Africa, was fully supported as a form of reparation for slavery and colonialism."[73] While the participants in the leadership meetings had no agreed-upon form for reparations to take, they expressed "disappointment at the less-than-forthcoming position of the U.S. government with respect to examining the issue of 'compensatory measures' under the agenda item relating to remedies and redress." The report concluded with a series of recommendations to the U.S. government that included an expanded policy of debt cancellation, especially in Africa; a national and international dialogue on reparations for slavery and the transatlantic slave trade; and support for the inclusion of "compensatory measures" as a subtheme on the agenda of the World Conference.[74]

The message of the U.S. leadership meetings was supported in another IHRLG report on round tables held in preparation for the WCAR and regional meetings, which was entitled "Race and Poverty in the Americas." Under the subheading of "Reparations," the report noted that there was no common understanding across the Americas of what was meant by "reparations" and suggested that achieving an NGO consensus on meaning was an important step toward intergovernmental consensus. Some of the meetings' participants emphasized that debt relief could be considered as reparations if released funds were directed toward antipoverty and antidiscrimination programs. Others stressed that the language of reparations needed to refer to "group-based" violations of human rights. Reparations were seen as essential to overcoming the systemic poverty experienced by indigenous peoples and African descendants.[75]

At the same time that the NGO Coordinating Committee was being formed in the summer of 2000, the U.S. government created an interagency task force to oversee and coordinate planning for U.S. participation in the WCAR. The task force was composed of representatives from the State Department and the Small Business Administration and was chaired by Debra Carr, a senior trial attorney in the Civil Rights Division of the Justice Department. The task force conducted a series of meetings with NGOs similar to those of the NGO Coordinating Committee, which were held in Chicago, Atlanta, and Albuquerque, as well as Washington. To date, there has been no public report on the participants in those meetings or the issues they asked the U.S. government to address in Durban.

The most complete statement made available to the public on U.S. participation is the testimony of William B. Wood, the acting assistant secretary of state for international organization affairs, before the House Subcommittee on International Operations and Human Rights on July 31, 2001. In his remarks, Wood noted that the United States cosponsored the 1998 General Assembly resolution against racism, which called for a third World Conference.[76] He also took pride in the United States' $250,000 donation to the UN Secretariat to support the conference. Although he noted the extensive consultation with NGOs and civil society coordinated by the task force, Wood did not mention the outcome of those meetings. He did state that the United States' position had been consistent in every discussion at every level. That is, that while we "acknowledge historic injustices against Africans, Native Americans and others," the focus of the work of the conference should be "on present day manifestations of racism and intolerance, and how best to combat them." "No one should doubt," Wood advised, "the profound regret of the U.S. that our Constitution and our society were ever associated with the abomination of slavery." Then Wood added an important framing perspective: "The fact that slavery was a historical phenomenon and a prevalent practice in virtually all parts of the world does not diminish that regret." After criticizing the UN Commission on Human Rights for not condemning contemporary slavery in Sudan, Wood maintained that the "selective memory and selective calls for redress are inconsistent with the goals of the WCAR." Thus, although the United States is willing to join with other WCAR participants in expressing "regret for historic injustices, such as slavery and the slave trade," it does not support the "extremes and unbalanced language relating to the transatlantic slave trade and calling for reparations or compensation."[77]

Moving to a more positive note, Wood said that the United States' emphasis has been on encouraging other states to create national legal structures providing remedies and recourse to victims of contemporary racism. He cited both High Commissioner Mary Robinson and UN Secretary-General Kofi Annan as stressing the importance of a contemporary focus. Finally, in the most direct rejection of reparations, Wood commented:

> The U.S. has consistently opposed the call for reparations for a variety of reasons, and will continue to do so. There is no consensus in the U.S. on payment of reparations. It is not clear what would be the legal or practical effect of a call for reparations for injustices more than a century old. Nor is it clear that such a call would contribute to eliminate racism in the contemporary world.[78]

The assistant secretary concluded that in "keeping with our future-oriented approach to the situation in Africa, the U.S. has been active in seeking new, more productive ways to assist Africa to develop."[79] Following Wood's testimony, Democratic Congresswoman Cynthia

McKinney of Georgia characterized the Bush administration's evasive stance toward the conference as a "clear example of their indifference to racism."[80]

By the time of the NGO forum at the WCAR, reparations had emerged as one of the two major issues of the conference,[81] and from one of the many issues highlighted by the Bellagio consultation, reparations had become one of five key areas in the NGO program of action. This program challenged Western criticism by acknowledging and condemning any current forms of enslavement in Africa. As we have seen, this position was not achieved without conflict between the African/African Descendants Caucus, which favored such a contemporary reference, and the Continental African Caucus, which a number of whose delegates opposed. The NGOs also insisted that the acceptance of a mutually agreed past could be the most significant step in developing a forward-looking agenda. Therefore, the document described four specific kinds of relief: restitution, monetary compensation, rehabilitation, and satisfaction (i.e., apology) and guarantees of no repetition. Moreover, the program recommended both interstate reparations such as debt relief and an international compensation scheme and/or development fund and intrastate reparations such as truth commissions, land grants, and monetary compensation [82]

Groups with a history of reparations activity, like N'COBRA, the Black Radical Congress, and the OAU Eminent Persons Group, were well represented in Durban. Major human rights organizations such as Human Rights Watch supported the call for reparations, but Amnesty International took no position on the issue. Several groups submitted their views on reparations in writing at the various lead-up meetings.[83] Before and during the WCAR, the NGO forum held a series of workshops devoted entirely to reparations. Many prominent advocates of reparations from the United States, the Caribbean, and Africa spoke at these workshops, including John Conyers, Manning Marable, Ray Winbush, Dudley Thompson, and Lord Anthony Gifford. Concerning reparations, the final Durban Declaration and Programme of Action adopted by the WCAR contains much of the language recommended by the African/African Descendants Caucus of the NGO forum:

99. We acknowledge and profoundly regret the massive human suffering and the tragic plight of millions of men, women and

children caused by slavery, the slave trade, the transatlantic slave trade, apartheid, colonialism and genocide, and call upon States concerned to honour the memory of the victims of past tragedies and affirm that, wherever and whenever these occurred, they must be condemned and their recurrence prevented. We regret that these practices and structures, political, socio-economic and cultural, have led to racism, racial discrimination, xenophobia and related intolerance.

100. We acknowledge and profoundly regret the untold suffering and evils inflicted on millions of men, women and children as a result of slavery, the slave trade, the transatlantic slave trade, apartheid, genocide and past tragedies. We further note that some States have taken the initiative to apologize and have paid reparation, where appropriate, for grave and massive violations committed.

The Durban Programme of Action states:

165. *Urges* States to reinforce protection against racism, racial discrimination, xenophobia and related intolerance by ensuring that all persons have access to effective and adequate remedies and enjoy the right to seek from competent national tribunals and other national institutions just and adequate reparation and satisfaction for any damage as a result of such discrimination. It further underlines the importance of access to the law and to the courts for complainants of racism and racial discrimination and draws attention to the need for judicial and other remedies to be made widely known, easily accessible, expeditious and not unduly complicated.

166. *Urges* States to adopt the necessary measures, as provided by national law, to ensure the right of victims to seek just and adequate reparation and satisfaction to redress acts of racism racial discrimination, xenophobia and related intolerance, and to design effective measures to prevent the repetition of such acts.[84]

∎

I have described the WCAR as a political opportunity for proponents of reparations and regard reparations advocates as part of a larger subcultural movement historically known as Pan Africanism. Global conferences offer opportunities for access to power, influence, resources, and media that might normally be blocked or not exist at the national and local levels. Such conferences also are an occasion for reproducing a collective identity as well as networking over an issue. In fact, concern over this collective identity may sometimes overshadow the political feasibility of the issue. According to Doug McAdam, movement scholars have, to date, grossly undervalued the impact of global political and economic processes on structuring domestic possibilities for successful collective action.[85]

At one level, the resistance of the U.S. government to world conferences on race may be seen as an attempt to close off or block political opportunities for race activists. The United States' absence from all three global conferences on race suggests that the government fears it cannot control the outcome or product of such conferences.[86] As we have seen in the case of international treaties to abolish slavery, the United States has a pattern of noncooperation. Although the postcolonial world does complicate the United States' participation globally, it is remarkable that a country that claims to be a global leader in race relations chooses not to be present at such conferences. This position has been consistent during both Democratic and Republican administrations. Moreover, it stands in contrast to the United States' participation in virtually every other global forum.

The United States' absence in Durban could certainly be seen as the NGOs' failure to mobilize enough pressure on the government. Had race activists mounted the same campaign for inclusion that feminists launched regarding the Beijing conference, the government might have acted differently.[87] Still, given the NGOs' extensive efforts regarding the WCAR, the United States' absence in Durban may be seen more as a failure of pluralist democracy. Citizens spoke but the government did not answer.

Alternatively, the refusal of NGOs and other governments promoting reparations to compromise on the word *compensatory*, for example, could be viewed as elevating collective identity or political solidarity over practical necessity. Calling for political flexibility by the NGOs and government proponents, however, is not convincing, given the firm U.S. opposition to any call for reparations from the very beginning.

In this chapter I have relied heavily on an examination of the framing process in the development of Pan Africanism as a social movement. Movement scholars have been critical of the resource mobilization perspective's lack of attention to ideas and sentiments. Pan Africanism, with its emphasis on the meaning and identity of movement participants, would appear to be an ideal candidate for scrutiny by new social movement scholars. Nonetheless, this new social movement theory has focused almost entirely on the recent social movements in Europe and North America.

The emergence of reparations as a central theme of modern Pan Africanism and, by extension, the WCAR represents a new "rhetoric of change." According to Albert Hirschman, this discourse stresses urgency, agency, and possibility and frequently overestimates the degree of political opportunity.[88] At a Black Leadership Forum conference in April 2001, Raymond Winbush, one of the major NGO proponents of reparations at the WCAR, predicted that African Americans would be granted compensation for the unpaid labor of their enslaved ancestors within the next ten years.[89]

Momentum developed not only because of the WCAR but also because of the advent of a new century and millennium. W. E. B. DuBois's prophecy that the twentieth century would be the century of the color line was extended to the twenty-first century by reparations proponents. The popularity of Randal Robinson's book *The Debt: What America Owes Blacks* was another indication that the time for action had arrived.

Perhaps the greatest sense of agency and possibility for reparations advocates came when the diaspora NGOs unified with African governments. The result was a final document that applied the international legal terminology of a "crime against humanity" to slavery and the slave trade. Adding debt relief to the call for reparations and compensatory measures ensured the support of many African governments. Finally, the addition of a section in the conference declaration on persons of African descent reinforced the notion of solidarity critical to the Pan African movement.

Of course, any "rhetoric of change" leads inevitably to a "rhetoric of rejection," and the U.S. government led the charge against reparations. Central themes of this discourse are jeopardy, futility, and perverse effects. Government officials constantly reiterate that a focus on the past would hinder, if not destroy, any opportunity for the WCAR to address current manifestations of racism. Moreover, the government insists that such efforts might even set back racial progress. UN Human Rights High Commissioner Mary Robinson and UN Secretary-General Kofi Annan were cited as supporting the U.S. view, even though both had publicly supported an examination of the issue,[90] and Senegalese President Wade added legitimacy to the U.S. position in his opening speech at the Africa regional meeting.

U.S. officials also argued that the reparations effort was futile, citing a lack of popular support for reparations at home and accusing advocates of trying to bash the West. Despite expressing regret for the past, the United States refused to apologize or endorse any language indicating that slavery or the slave trade was a "crime" or a "crime against humanity" and attempted to deflect any guilt by citing the widespread nature of the practice in the eighteenth and nineteenth centuries.

On the Media

The media's attention on the WCAR was limited largely to the period just before and during the conference. Most of the major media, including the *New York Times, Le Monde,* and *The Economist* decided that the conference was a failure even before it officially opened. The few articles on the Prepcoms and regional meetings focused on the issues of the Middle East and reparations. Moreover, the articles did not discuss the issues themselves but whether they would keep the United States from attending the conference.[91]

An article in the *New York Times* on July 30, 2001, implied that UN Secretary-General Annan agreed with the Bush administration in its desire to keep the Middle East and compensation for slavery off the agenda in Durban. Although Annan's support was important to U.S. efforts to gain legitimacy for its position, this interpretation of his speech to the Urban League is not supported by the secretary-general's actual remarks. He acknowledged that those two issues had "opened deep fissures" and that there was "an acute need for common ground." Most significantly, he stated that the WCAR "must confront the past, but "most important, it must help set a new course against racism in the future."[92] Apparently, confronting the past for the *New York Times* did not mean consideration of reparations.

In August, *Newsday* and the *Chicago Sun-Times* were accused of spreading the rumor that reparations were off the agenda in Durban. The interagency task force chair, Debra Carr, denied that the U.S. government was responsible for this disinformation.

William Raspberry of the *Washington Post* was one of the few media voices to discuss reparations, and his column elicited a great deal of response from *Post* readers. Raspberry's own position was that the government must do more to overcome the legacy of slavery, especially in education. But he believed better education should be provided for all who were failing, not because of a moral debt, but "because America needs its citizens to be educated and productive."[93] Raspberry, then, might have favored the approach taken by Martin Luther King Jr. in his "Economic Bill of Rights for the Disadvantaged."

Another *Washington Post* columnist, Courtland Milloy, specifically raised the race issue in a piece entitled "Colin Powell: Bush Man or Black Man?" Milloy talked about the pressures put on Powell by the Leadership Conference on Civil Rights and its chair, Dorothy Height, to lead the U.S. delegation to the conference. Milloy states that "of all the diplomatic dances that America's first black secretary of state has performed so far, none has ever caused him to step on the toes of his fellow blacks."[94] Thus while the conference promoted solidarity for most of the Blacks involved, it created dissonance for Powell, who initially had expressed enthusiasm for the conference.[95]

In a *New York Times* editorial, Bob Herbert took the position that the conference had been doomed to irrelevance from the start, repeating the U.S. government's criticism of African silence on the issue of present-day slavery in Sudan and Mauritania. Even though his position is an exaggeration, it fits the frame of equating the Western slave trade as part of a widespread practice that continues even today in Africa. Herbert did acknowledge that if slavery were not a crime against humanity, what was? His basic position was that "you can't fight that kind of hatred [Northern Ireland] with a resolution."[96]

The emphasis on the impact of the final document and the absence of the United States miss the most important outcomes of the WCAR. First, the WCAR debate represents a shift in the framing of the mid-1960s cycle that called for reparations for all disadvantaged Americans. The shift began with the development of the "Black manifesto" in the surge to Black power in the late 1960s. Even though this shift might be seen as reducing the chances of gaining popular support for reparations, it strengthened the collective identity of its advocates.

Moreover, the total rejection of the mid-1960s call for economic rights by liberal allies of the civil rights movement encouraged a turn inward to Black nationalism. The government's refusal to fund programs directed toward closing the economic gap also produced a shift to demands on private parties to make amends for Black oppression. Debra Friedman and Doug McAdam argue that "the more inclusive the collective identity, the harder it is to control, and thus the less powerful it is as a selective incentive."[97] Making participation more exclusive can also, however, raise the cost of participation and thus reduce membership, but to date, this has not happened with reparations.

Second, longtime reparations advocates in the United States can claim success in broadening support for their issue among mainstream civil rights and human rights organizations. Single-issue groups like N'COBRA and the All for Reparations and Emancipation saw their ranks increase as supportive organizations took up the call for reparations,[98] an action that represents the coming together of a critical community through frame alignment. Frame bridging and frame extension did not, however, need potential supporters in the mainstream organizations to depart from traditional and widely shared values.[99] In short, the members of groups like the Urban League, the NAACP, and the Leadership Conference on Civil Rights were not required to accept the nationalist leanings of the reparations organizations. Framing slavery as "a crime against humanity" promoted the solidarity of the rights-based coalitions with the reparations groups.

Third, WCAR helped move the reparations debate from the limitations on national discourse to an international arena with fewer constraints. Most important, Pan Africanist activists from the African diaspora were reconciled with African government leaders. The break that had occurred with the end of African colonialism and was manifest in the debate over the African Growth and Opportunity Act was put aside, with minor exceptions, in a united push for reparations. The African governments' push on the West for reparations for the descendants of slaves was reciprocated by the reparations activists' call for debt relief. Their combined strength served to draw attention to Africa, the neglected subject in the economic discussion of globalization.

Fourth, the intraracial dialogue on agency and responsibility for slavery illustrates the structured nature of global apartheid. Even though Arab and African participation in the slave trade cannot be denied, it does not imply equal agency, nor does it absolve the West in general or the United States in particular from responsibility. If nothing else, history shows us who the economic winners and losers were in the slave trade. Moreover, African responsibility for the slave trade is complicated by the interposition of colonialism. In fact, the damaged governance of Africa that is the colonialism's legacy is part of the continent's case for reparations.

An excellent example of how colonialism complicates the reparations discourse was the lawsuits filed on behalf of South Africa, which named more than one hundred corporations, including Citigroup, Bank of America, IBM, Eli Lilly, General Motors, and Exxon Mobil. Dumisa Buhle Ntsebeza, a human rights lawyer who spent five and a half years in prison and six in exile during the apartheid regime, joined in legal action with Ed Fagan and other lawyers who won damages against Swiss and German companies for World War II–era injustices. Two of the major lawsuits charged that the multinational companies that did business with apartheid South Africa facilitated the old regime's repressive policies and actions. A much larger suit, backed by Jubilee South Africa, was filed in November 2002 on behalf of the Khulumani group of more than thirty thousand South African apartheid-era victims. The suits were filed under the Alien Claims Tort Act, which allows foreign nationals to sue in U.S. courts for human rights abuses committed abroad.

As might be expected, the former president of South Africa, Frederik de Klerk, opposed the suits, and Archbishop Desmond Tutu, the head of the truth and reconciliation commission, supported the legal action. Tutu's commission certified some 22,000 people as victims of gross human rights violations who should be paid reparations. What is surprising is the official opposition of the current South African government. Fearing harm to the business climate, Justice Minister Penuel Maduna stated that officials were "talking to those very same companies named in the lawsuits about investing in post-apartheid South Africa."[100] In November 2004, however, a federal judge dismissed the lawsuits, ruling that they were no longer viable given the new limits that the U.S. Supreme Court has placed on suits brought under the Alien Tort Claims laws.[101]

The WCAR's success in building a collective Pan African identity around the issue of reparations came at a price. All evidence points to the success of Japanese Americans in their quest for reparations as the stimulus behind the current cycle of Black reparations, and therefore the Japanese American reparations movement may be considered a master cycle of protest.[102] Black legislators supported the Japanese American effort, and it seems likely that Japanese American activists would also be willing to support African American demands. There has been very little interaction between the two groups, however, and the call for Black reparations may prevent African American alliances with other oppressed groups in the United States. Indeed, some Afro-European delegates maintain that the focus on reparations was a result of the African American domination of the caucus agenda, even though these disagreements were eventually resolved. They were overcome by limiting the call for reparations to a general principle and omitting any discussion of particular procedural or material solutions. In fact, many people regard the declaration of slavery as a crime against humanity as only the first step in a process in which material reparations might be one remedy. In her closing statement, the president of the WCAR, the South African foreign minister Nkosazana Dalamini Zuma, stated,

> We also agreed that slavery is a crime against humanity and that an apology is necessary not for monetary gain but to restore the dignity and humanity of those who suffered . . . we agreed that a clear and unequivocal apology constitutes a starting point in a long and arduous journey of finding one another.

She added that "an apology restores the dignity, self-worth and humanity of the black body, broadly defined. We also agreed that other remedial actions would have to be adopted to correct the legacy of slavery and colonialism and all other forms of racism."[103] By refusing to acknowledge this past, the United States not only missed an opportunity to begin a sorely needed dialogue at the international level, but it also ignored and even discounted the emotional linkages of its own citizens to the larger Pan African community. While the emphasis on slavery over current discrimination or recently desegregated "Jim Crow" institutions may unnecessarily complicate the demand for accountability,[104] a focus on contemporary U.S. discrimination would have produced an agenda too tailored to African American needs.

Ultimately, the greatest cost may be borne by the U.S. government. Its consistent refusal to participate in global racism conferences and the refusal of European allies to join the United States in boycotting the Durban conference point to the United States' increasing isolationism from Europe as well as from Africa and the Third World. The UN high commissioner for human rights, Mary Robinson, observed that "the text adopted on the past is historic in that it sets out the issues in plain, unequivocal language for the first time in a document of this kind, agreed to by the international community."[105] The events of September 11, coming two days after the close of the WCAR, reconfirm the need for the United States' involvement in all international forums.

6

A True Revolution of Values

Changing the Culture and Politics of Reparations

> I shall never forget the weeping. John Washington tells of learning
> to read and write and of seeing parents, wives, husbands and chil-
> dren being separated and sold South in "I Shall Never Forget the
> Weeping."
>
> —*New York Times*[1]

> Justice is, in part, a form of remembrance.
> —W. James Booth, "The Unforgotten: Memories of Justice,"
> *American Political Science Review*[2]

An African American Memorial

In 1978, President Jimmy Carter created the President's Commission
on the Holocaust, which was chaired by Nobel laureate and Holocaust
survivor Elie Wiesel. The commission prepared a report for the president in which it recommended the establishment of a "living memorial" to the Holocaust. In 1980 a rare unanimous act of Congress had
approved the Holocaust Museum. Fully supported by Carter's succes-
sor, Ronald Reagan, the goal of the museum was "to ensure that all
Americans know of this dark chapter in human rights and human dignity."[3] The Holocaust Museum was built with a combination of public
and private funds just off the official Washington Mall but deep within
the "monumental core" of Washington between the Washington Mon-
ument and the Jefferson Memorial. It opened its doors to worldwide
acclaim in 1993.

What is remarkable about this striking museum is the lack of controversy or debate over the idea. There was no congressional debate;
instead, members of both parties lined up to express their support.
Both Carter and Reagan enthusiastically backed the museum, as have

their successors. Yet this particular memorial in Washington's "monumental core" is unique.

All the other memorials in this prized space embody the remembrance of specifically American experiences. In fact, American World War II veterans were not memorialized in this area until 2004. The Holocaust Museum is the only Mall institution to preserve the memory of a foreign experience.

The unusual support for this precedent-breaking endeavor may be explained on several levels. Israel has the overwhelming support of the U.S. government, and it publicly endorsed the Holocaust memorial in Washington. Many members of Congress, of both parties, receive political contributions from Jewish Americans, who have one of Washington's most effective lobbies. Many of the museum's initial costs were offset by private funds of more than $150 million.

The lack of public debate does not mean that the museum was without controversy. One issue, for example, was the emphasis on the Jewish part of the Holocaust story, even though according to standard estimates, non-Jewish victims of the Nazis and their collaborators amounted to some eight million people. But their story is not told in Washington as it is in the Museum of Tolerance in Los Angeles. Nonetheless, these and other debates were largely confined to the Jewish community and were not part of the public discourse.[4]

Although most memorials and monuments only symbolize the events they are meant to commemorate, the Holocaust Museum goes beyond symbolism to document the horrors of the period between 1933 and 1945. It has become a model of what a museum might accomplish as an instrument of public education. In a real sense, it refutes the views of those who deny that the Holocaust even took place or who minimize its impact. In doing so, the museum should help prevent the recurrence of such human rights violations.

But because denial of the Holocaust is not prominent in American history, why does this largely foreign event deserve such an honored place in America's public space? At a fundamental level, it reassures Americans of their role in the triumph over evil. The tour at the Holocaust Museum begins with General Dwight D. Eisenhower as the liberator, "discovering" the concentration camps at the end of the war. Even though we can claim innocence in the events leading up to the Holocaust,[5] we can take full responsibility for ending the Holocaust through our military intervention. In short, just a few years after the

Vietnam War brought our international reputation and our national self-esteem to an all-time low, we were able to remember with pride our role in ending this crime against humanity.

I believe these feelings of self-esteem help account for the long absence of a memorial in Washington or anywhere else marking the fate of Native Americans or the end of slavery. The National Museum of the American Indian (NMAI) was finally authorized by Congress and signed into law by President George H. W. Bush in 1989. The main facility located on the Washington Mall opened in 2004, and two other facilities related to the museum are now open in lower Manhattan and Suitland, Maryland. Unlike the Holocaust Museum, the NMAI was subject to considerable debate on the floor of Congress. Part of the problem was Native Americans' concern about the repatriation of human remains and sacred objects. But some of the oldest museums in America, including the Smithsonian, that have large collections of Indian artifacts had other concerns. They had obtained many of these objects through dubious means and were worried about efforts to recover them. Other issues pertained to the extent to which the reality of Indian genocide would be balanced with romantic notions of Indian incorporation, as represented by Pocahontas and Thanksgiving stories. Thus, issues of control loomed large in the debates over the museum, and the final legislation requires that a minimum of seven of the twenty-one trustees be Native Americans.

Romantic notions of the incorporation of indigenous people are countered by their location in American museums. Many of the most impressive collections of American Indian artifacts are found in natural history museums, not American history museums. Despite their cultural productions, the objects and stories of the Native Americans' everyday lives are shown alongside other "natural" phenomena such as dinosaurs, insects, and gems.[6]

The struggle to construct a national African American museum on the Mall thus must be seen in the context of the Holocaust Museum and the National Museum of the American Indian. Although the African American struggle more closely resembles that for the NMAI, there are significant differences. Blacks' involvement in the formal preservation and presentation of Black life and culture extends back at least to the first museum at a historically Black college, Howard University in 1867 and Hampton University in 1868. By 1988, 108 museums and archives in the United States and Canada were devoted to African American history and culture. Despite the existence of these material objects, however, Blacks were missing from most official accounts of American history, from Tulsa and Rosewood to the U.S. Capitol.[7] Not until the movement for Black studies in the late 1960s and early 1970s did this forgotten history begin to surface.[8]

This new scholarship helped spark interest in a national African American museum in the late 1970s. In 1981 Congress authorized the National Afro-American Museum to be located in Wilberforce, Ohio, site of the first historically Black college. The museum in Wilberforce opened in 1987, funded largely by the state of Ohio. But it did not satisfy the desires of those who wanted such an institution to be more centrally located.[9] One of the people frustrated with the invisibility of Black history in the nation's capital was Tom Mack, president of Washington's Tourmobile tour buses.

In 1984, Mack formed the National Council for Education and Economic Development (NCEED) as a base from which to develop a proposal for a national museum. After finding little support from the Smithsonian, the NAACP, or the United Negro College Fund, Mack finally found an ally in Democratic Congressman Mickey Leland of Texas. In 1986 Leland succeeded in persuading Congress to pass a resolution to build a Black museum on the Mall. Like the 1981 legislation, however, it was unfunded and nonbinding. Mack then decided to direct his efforts to the private sector but immediately confronted two problems. First, estimates placed the cost of a privately funded museum at $50 million to $100 million. Second, Mack had no ties to the large community of Black professionals represented by the African American Museums Association (AAMA). To them, Mack was an outsider who did not know or understand their business.[10] Perhaps the final blow to Mack's plan was Leland's death in an airplane crash while delivering relief supplies to Ethiopia in 1989.

Although Mack's idea remained alive, Democratic Congressman John Lewis of Georgia, with the support of the Congressional Black Caucus (CBC), offered an alternative bill. Lewis's bill would make the museum a part of the Smithsonian and locate it in the Smithsonian's existing Arts and Industries Building. Lewis also proposed an endowment fund to support the museum and expanded its focus beyond slavery to include Black achievements. The AAMA backed Lewis's proposal, and with the blessing of the Smithsonian regents, Congress approved $2 million for a feasibility study.

With this new support and a Democratic White House and Congress in 1992, the bill seemed sure to pass. Unfortunately, momentum for the Lewis bill was derailed by Mack and Gus Savage, the lame-duck chair of the CBC. Savage and Mack still believed the museum should be independent of the Smithsonian and demanded either a new building or no museum at all. By the time Savage left Congress in 1993, Jesse Helms had returned from an illness to bottle up the Lewis bill in committee.[11] The following year, Republicans swept to victory in Congress, and prospects for the bill's passage quickly diminished. Museum proponents meeting with the secretary of the Smithsonian, Ira Michael Heyman, in the spring of 1999 found him pessimistic about obtaining either the Smithsonian's or Congress's support for a renewed effort on Lewis's bill.[12]

Ironically, it was the Black Republican representative J. C. Watts Jr. from Oklahoma and the White senator Sam Brownback from Kansas who breathed new life into the museum idea. Lewis and Watts worked together on several bills related to African Americans, whereas Brownback "saw it [the museum] as a vehicle for racial reconciliation."[13] With Republican congressional support, the museum idea gained the approval of President George W. Bush, who signed a law in December 2001 creating a commission to plan the museum. In June 2003, Congress authorized $17 million in start-up funds for a Black museum to be built on or near the Mall. Other important museums devoted to Black history include the National Underground Railroad Freedom Center in Cincinnati, which opened in August 2004, the Reginald F. Lewis Museum of Maryland African American History and Culture in Baltimore, which opened in 2005, and the U.S. National Slavery Museum in Fredericksburg, Virginia, which is scheduled for completion in 2007.[14]

These museums perform an important public education function, and they also represent a form of cultural reparations, as they remember and memorialize what many people have tried to repress. For African Americans, these museums represent a shared historical experience that gives them an identity and hope that the future will be an improvement over the past. The larger community recognizes its shared past with African Americans and acknowledges their citizenship when it learns their history in a national museum.

Reparations on a Local Level

The failure of the Conyers bill to receive a hearing at the national level obscures a great deal of the discussion and debate at subnational levels. At the state and local levels, a number of reparations-related bills have passed. In October 2000, Governor Gray Davis of California signed into law two bills written by State Senator Tom Hayden which begin tracking the financial benefits accrued from slavery in the United States. The Slaveholder Insurance Policies Bill (S.B. 2199) calls on the state insurance commissioner to request insurance companies doing business in California to hand over their archival records of insurance policies held on slaves. The University of California Slavery Colloquium Bill asks the University of California to hold a research conference to explore and identify issues concerning the economic legacy of slavery in America.[15] This "legacy of slavery" conference was held in 2001 at the University of California at Santa Barbara.

By May 2002, eight insurance companies—ACEUSA, Aetna, AIG, Manhattan Life, New York Life, Penn Mutual, Providence Washington, and Royal & Sun Alliance—had found records of more than six hundred policies they once carried on slaves belonging to more than four hundred slaveholders throughout the South. All eight companies were based in nonslave states in the Northeast. The revelation that forty-three of the slaves lived in Georgia prompted the Georgia insurance commissioner, John Oxendine, to launch his own investigation of slave insurance policies in Georgia.[16]

Governor Davis commented on the report by the California Department of Insurance: "Clearly, we want to right any wrongs, and do justice to people who were taken advantage of if that is the case. And I believe that will be the case."[17] He was immediately attacked by Bill Simon, his Republican challenger in the California gubernatorial campaign, for his "divisive and politically motivated support for reparations." Simon added, "Bringing up the wounds of our country's past in a politically motivated attempt to shore up his political standing is typical of Governor Davis, who offers only politics, and no solutions."[18]

Rev. Jesse Jackson, who had supported the California legislation, called on the South Carolina General Assembly to follow California's lead. Two other states already were considering reparations legislation. In June 2001, an act was introduced in the New York assembly to establish a state commission to quantify the debt owed to African Americans and to permit certain claims.[19] Legislators in New Jersey introduced a bill in September 2002 to establish the Amistad Commission to coordinate educational and other programs on slavery and African American history.[20] The Maryland House of Delegates rejected a bill in March 2000 that would have asked Governor Parris Glendening to apologize for slavery in that state.[21]

After Governor Davis, the most prominent political leader to support a form of reparations, is Chicago Mayor Richard Daley. Following the nearly unanimous approval of a city council resolution urging Congress to study the question of reparations (i.e., the Conyers bill), the mayor stated, "We must apologize when there is apologizing to do." He added that "as a nation, we have rebuilt countries and cities, and yes we have paid dearly. It's about time that America does this."[22] Alderman Brian Doherty, who cast the only opposing vote, noted that the residents of his northwest-side ward were mostly Whites who did not participate in the slavery system and do not take responsibility for reparations. A resolution similar to the California legislation also was introduced in the Chicago City Council that asks insurance companies to report on any policies dealing with slaves.[23]

A number of other American cities have joined Chicago in supporting federal legislation to study reparations: Dallas, Washington, D.C., Cleveland, Detroit, Baltimore, and New York.[24] The Houston City Council rejected a resolution supporting the Conyers bill.[25] In response to the Chicago resolution supporting the reparations study, a resolution was proposed in East Peoria, Illinois, attacking the Conyers bill and urging the establishment of a "White Pride Day" on Lincoln's birthday to begin to eradicate the "White guilt complex."[26]

The states and cities that have passed legislation related to reparations have large and or influential African American populations, and thus they mirror Rosewood and Greenwood. Florida's large Black population was able to find allies and build a coalition of support around the Rosewood claims. Moreover, the governmental structure had a mechanism for screening claims against the state that helped shield the Rosewood claim from charges that Blacks were somehow being divisive or promoting special interests. In contrast, the Tulsa claim lacked Florida's Black political mobilization. It found no strategic allies and, almost from the outset, became a racially divisive issue. Although the actual events in Rosewood and Tulsa were quite similar, the course of reparations in each case has followed a very different path. Framing the issue as a property claim versus a claim for racial justice also was a significant factor in Rosewood and in the case of Japanese American reparations. A focus on property or land is not, however, sufficient by itself to produce a favorable outcome.

Estimates of the material harm done to African Americans range widely. In 1969 when James Forman asked American churches for $500 million in reparations, the figure was ridiculed as grossly exaggerated. Yet current estimates make Forman's demands seem like small change. Economist David Swinton suggests $500 billion in reparations after deducting for welfare programs.[27] Some reparations advocates have argued for individual payments to descendants of slaves of $98,191.25, or roughly $3 trillion, the estimated present equivalent of "forty acres and a mule." Robert Brock of the Self-Determination Committee set a higher payment of $275,000 per descendant based on unpaid slave labor.[28] Economist Robert Fogel calculated the cumulative bill for slaves' expropriated wages to be $24 billion in 1860. Depending on the amount of interest, today's debt would be between $1.6 trillion and $97 trillion.[29] According to Neal, the present value of slave labor is $1.4 trillion.[30] Jim Marketti's figures for the current value of slave labor range from $448 billion to $995 billion, depending on interest rates.[31]

Perhaps the most frequently cited work on the economic consequences of slavery and its aftermath is Roger Ransom and Richard Sutch's *One Kind of Freedom*. These economists propose that the lack of progress in the post-Emancipation era in the South was the consequence of flawed economic institutions erected to maintain Black subordination. According to their estimates, slaves received only 21.7 percent of the output produced on large plantations, and well over one-half their potential income was expropriated from them without compensation. Ransom and Sutch conservatively calculate the market value in 1860 of the two million slaves in the five cotton states (Alabama, Georgia, Louisiana, Mississippi, and South Carolina) to be $116 billion, or 45.8 percent of the total wealth held by all residents of these states. Moreover, they link the cotton planters to the extensive marketing and financial network that brought them in contact with the cotton textile manufactures of England and New England; with the importers, wholesalers, and manufacturers on the East Coast who furnished the plantation's needs; with the mule raisers of Kentucky, Missouri, and Tennessee; with the farmers of Ohio and the upper Mississippi basins who made up the deficiencies in southern supplies of barreled pork and cornmeal; and also with the bankers who provided short-term credit.[32]

The only way that this network of economic interests centering on the dominance of the planter class might have ended would have been through a redistribution of land to the freedmen at the time of Emancipation. Ransom and Sutch estimate that a farm of forty acres with one mule would have cost around $250 to $300.[33] Of course, what rose in place of slavery was a sharecropping system dependent on a single cash crop that retarded the industrialization and economic diversification of the entire South.

Among the economists working on contemporary estimates of economic reparations, Richard America has been particularly prolific. Contending that multiracial capitalist societies are especially prone to inappropriately distributed income and wealth, he calculated Black wealth in 1984 to be $208 billion of the U.S. total, or some $552 billion less than their proportion of the population. By some estimates, America asserts, unjust enrichment in the form of wealth, income, or expected lifetime earnings totals $5 trillion to $10 trillion.[34]

America favors reparations in the form of targeted programs, with high-quality preschools being a cost-effective social program. America also recommends creative antitrust legislation that would force major corporations in a socially overconcentrated industry and major corporations seeking mergers to sell units to minorities. America cites the breakup of AT&T as a precedent for such efforts.

Like America, Clarence Mumford rejects the notion of individual reparation payments of a set amount, as in the case of Japanese Americans. Citing such payments as one more national transfer program, Mumford believes that such payments would likely be absorbed in nonproductive consumption. Instead he advocates a "transformative approach" to reparations aimed at ownership parity. For example, a program might enable Black entrepreneurs and agencies to gradually increase ownership equity percentages in designated assets.[35] But such a selective form of reparations targeted to a minority of Blacks contradicts the "mass approach" of groups like N'COBRA.

Although such targeted programs are controversial, they have in fact been established. In 1998 the U.S. Department of Agriculture (USDA) settled a national class action lawsuit, claiming that it systematically discriminated against Black farmers in awarding farm loans. Citing the promise of "forty acres and a mule," U.S. District Court Judge Paul Friedman wrote: "The government broke that promise to African American farmers. Over one hundred years later, the USDA broke its promise to Mr. James Beverly [one of the original plaintiffs]."[36]

Even though the judge estimated that payments would total $2 billion and would be "virtually automatic," the reality has been different. As of August 2004, the USDA had paid $814 million to 13,445 farmers who applied for relief. More than 80,000 others were rejected, most of them because they missed the October 1999 deadline for filing a claim. Moreover, the USDA spent millions fighting each claim that was filed; about 40 percent of the claims that were filed were rejected.[37] It is estimated that some 66,000 farmers missed out because they were improperly notified of the settlement in *Pigford v. Veneman*. While the courts have rejected efforts to reopen the settlement, Black farmers are pressing Congress to act.[38]

The loss of Black-owned land is a trend of particular concern. In 1915, Blacks collectively owned 15.7 million acres of land in the United States, but by 1963, this figure had dropped to only 6 million acres. In 1920 in Illinois, for example, there were 892 Black farmers, but by 1997 there were only 123, and five years later the number had dropped to 59. African Americans now hold less than 1percent of the nation's farmland.[39]

Estimates of the material harm done to African Americans by slavery and the racial oppression that followed Emancipation range widely, but all of them dwarf any previous compensation paid by the U.S. government or private actors. Proposals for implementing a reparations payment scheme also vary widely. Virtually all envision some major government expenditures. Some, like those of Mumford and America, target income-earning assets and wealth-building capacity and would be restricted to only a few individuals. Others favor massive government-sponsored programs designed to raise educational and skill levels and, in some cases, provide housing for large numbers of African Americans. A few people recommend individual payments to all descendants of slaves, and a few maintain the historic demand for a separate Black land base or repatriation to one or more African nations. Of course, the mechanism for distributing any form of reparations is at least equally controversial, ranging from a new government agency to a national assembly of Blacks representing all sectors of the national Black community. Ultimately, none of these proposals will come to pass until we, as a nation, find the political will to confront all of our past.

Coming to Terms with a Troubled Past

Martin Luther King Jr.'s great success as a moral and political leader rested on his appeal to the civic myth that binds Americans together in a nation. According to Rodgers Smith, a *civic myth* is "used to explain why persons form a people, usually indicating how a political community originated, who is eligible for membership, who is not and why, and what the community's values and aims are."[40] King's monumental "I Have a Dream" speech, which is quoted by liberals and conservatives alike, is future oriented and hopeful and therefore inspiring. But its vision of the future is firmly anchored in a shared history that includes a troubled past. The charge that America gave its Black citizens a "bad check" marked "insufficient funds" is a reminder of that past. King called for the larger society to step forward and take responsibility for that past by fulfilling the promise of the American "idea." Essentially King was arguing that we cannot fulfill our national destiny by romanticizing or ignoring the past. Only by seizing it in all its horror and beauty can we own it. By owning it, by accepting responsibility for it as citizens, we can hope to improve it.

King's appeal is both nationalist and universalist. By pointing to the long common history shared by both White and Black Americans, King—standing symbolically at Lincoln's feet—established a shared national identity. Nonetheless, he was appealing for "civic," not "ethnic," nationalism. In practice, the two are linked. The institutions and customs of the "civic" nations grow out of and reflect particular cultural narratives, practices, and history. Thus this civic process becomes the norm, although it is not based on an empty abstraction. King was mindful of the unique history of African Americans who were denied the opportunity to integrate into the dominant culture and also prohibited from maintaining old cultures or creating new ones.

His appeal for Blacks and Whites to be permitted to pray together and go to school together is in the finest traditions of Enlightenment liberalism. It is an appeal to throw off the ascriptive blinders of the past and embrace a universal ethic of human rights. Its attempt to broaden our national community of citizens is reminiscent of Lincoln's 1858 speech:

> We have besides these men—descended by blood from our ancestors —among us perhaps half our people who are not descendants at all of these men . . . finding themselves our equals in all things. If they look back through this history to trace their connection with those days by blood, they find they have none . . . but when they look through that old Declaration of Independence . . . [they feel] . . . that it is the father of all moral principle in them, and that they have a right to claim it as though they were blood of the blood, and flesh of the flesh of the men who wrote that Declaration, and so they are."[41]

King's and Lincoln's messages are evidence that liberalism and democratic nationalism do not need to conflict, that they can be unifying and inspiring. If racism continues, however, it will be a fundamental failure of liberal democracy that cannot be ignored.

Reparations are seen as divisive by many Americans because they are framed as conflicting with these core values. Horowitz uses both liberal individualism and ascriptive nationalism to attack reparations as divisive. He acknowledges a shared history but not a shared citizenship. In the same way that the country has moved to no-fault and no-responsibility divorce,[42] Horowitz refuses to take responsibility for slavery or apartheid.

People from different racial (national) groups will share an allegiance to the larger polity only if they see it as the context in which their racial identity is nurtured rather than subordinated. Sharing the same values or principles of justice is a necessary but not a sufficient condition for political community. Calls for color blindness ignore history, and appeals to a tolerant multiculturalism leave open the question of shared identity. Although the politics of amnesty can serve current interests, memory and forgetting speak to something more elemental.[43]

In the second chapter of *The Souls of Black Folk*, "Of Dawn and Freedom," W. E. B. DuBois creates a new framework in which the plight of the freed people might be seen. He identifies three images from Sherman's March to the Sea: that of the Conqueror, the Conquered, and the Negro. The history of the post–Civil War period is that of reconciliation of the Conqueror with the Conquered at the expense of justice for the Negro. DuBois then offers an alternative vision of meaning, with two figures who are veterans of another conflict: an old male slaveholder—the broken symbol of wealth, power, and sexual domination—and an old Black woman, representing "Mammy," mother, and survivor.[44] Bridging this chasm is the work of reparations.

The Current Reparations Movement

Ultimately the success of the current reparations movement will be determined by factors that are easily theorized but very difficult to implement. As it stands, Black activists have succeeded in bringing reparations to the forefront of the Black counterpublic. As we have seen, this visibility is due to several factors, the first being the decreasing access to upward mobility by means of government assistance ranging across all three branches of government. Historically, such periods have led to heightened Black receptivity to Black nationalist concerns, with nationalist leaders and organizations occupying the leading roles in the modern reparations movement. What is new for some of these groups is the renewed attention to domestic rather than international politics. The second factor is the disillusioned liberalism of the Black middle class, which has forced it to consider options and issues outside the mainstream political discourse. Although such individuals as Randall Robinson, Charles Ogletree, and the organizers of academic reparations conferences bring greater legitimacy to the cause, they have pursued the primarily elite strategy of legal action. Similarly, while vocally supporting the call for reparations, such organizations as the NAACP and the Urban League see them as one of a host of organizational concerns with no special priority. Third, reparations have enabled their advocates to assume the moral higher ground lost after the civil rights movement. To a large extent, White opposition to an apology for slavery is a refusal to concede the higher ground. David Gresson contends that "the racial liberation movement and its companion liberation movements represented losses for white men as moral heroes; the emotional and symbolic aspects of this loss, moreover, were greater than any material loss the American dominant majority sustained." "Increasingly," Gresson points out, "whites experienced themselves as oppressed victims of an uncaring authority and cited efforts on behalf of Blacks, Hispanics, Native Americans and other ethnics as 'reverse racism'—the birth cry of modern white racial recovery rhetoric."[45] In short, the current reparations movement has achieved a rhetorical unity that has put its opponents on the defensive.

To succeed politically—either substantively or symbolically—the movement must agree on some specific goals and some specific targets. One obvious goal and target would be an apology for slavery and its consequences from Congress, the president, or both. Some reparations advocates oppose an apology because they fear it would foreclose further concessions. Yet it is difficult to imagine governmental agreement for substantive compensation without first acknowledging some moral guilt. In fact, the term *reparations* implies atonement, and responses lacking this are properly called *settlements*. The recent South African Truth Commission followed a process of recognition, responsibility, reconstruction, and then reparation.[46]

Another goal on which consensus seems to be building is for group or collective compensation from the federal government. Although some advocates still press for individual payments, it seems clear that the individual harm suffered by African Americans varied greatly. It therefore is both morally and politically more compelling to argue that development banks and educational trust funds should be set up for those most economically and educationally disadvantaged. Such an approach would avoid the issue of compensating affluent Blacks, who would still have to pay taxes to support the program. Although the issue of who will control the funds and who will qualify to apply are not insignificant, they can be surmounted and should be addressed after agreement on a general program. Such programs can and should be seen as dealing not with slavery alone but with the entire history of racism in the United States and its exercise abroad. It is true that there are no living former American slaves, but every African American has either directly or indirectly experienced racial discrimination or has been indirectly influenced by it. The failure to treat reparations as a legitimate issue acknowledges that America is far from being a "color-blind" society. The frustrated and prophetic voice of Martin Luther King Jr. recognized this nearly forty years ago:

> A true revolution of values will soon cause us to question the fairness and justice of many of our past and present policies. On the one hand

we are called to play the Good Samaritan on life's roadside, but that will be only an initial act. One day we must come to see that the whole Jericho Road must be transformed so that men and women will not be constantly beaten and robbed as they make their journey on life's highway. True compassion is more than flinging a coin to a beggar. It comes to see that an edifice which produces beggars needs restructuring.[47]

Reparations could be the beginning of a true revolution in values.

Ultimately, I agree with Henry David Thoreau that "the law will never make men free; it is men who have got to make the law free."[48] Citizenship rights have not and will not solve the problem of racial exclusion. Legal rights, even the U.S. Constitution, rest on a normative order that is determined by our culture. Cultural forces are constantly shaping and reshaping the civic myths that bind our society together and make it viable. Even such a strong, historical claim as American exceptionalism cannot be proved or falsified. Instead, I agree with Nikhil Singh that they should be understood as performative.[49] They seek to create what they purport to describe but what does not yet exist. Yet wishing or "dreaming" does not make it so. When an event like Hurricane Katrina reveals to all the world that our claims are exaggerated, if not false, it creates a political opportunity to make the claims real.

Epilogue

We Are American

The Aftermath of Hurricane Katrina

If democracy means anything morally, it signifies that the lives of all citizens matter, and that their sense of their rights must prevail.
—Judith Shklar, from Lawrie Balfour,
The Evidence of Things Not Said

That victim who is able to articulate the situation of the victim has ceased to be a victim: he, or she, has become a threat.
—James Baldwin, from Lawrie Balfour,
The Evidence of Things Not Said

Beyond the horrific images of people screaming for help from rooftops, dead bodies floating down main streets, and armed police officers turning back people trying to flee the floodwaters, one declarative statement stands out in the aftermath of Hurricane Katrina: "We are Americans."[1] That simple phrase uttered by a woman at the New Orleans Convention Center connects the struggle for reparations to the events of Hurricane Katrina. The woman at the convention center and thousands, if not millions, who witnessed the chaos during and after the hurricane expressed shock and horror at the failure of government at all levels—local, state, and federal—to meet the most basic needs of its citizens: food, water, shelter, medicine. The most basic need, the ability to survive, is society's first political obligation. The phrase "I am an American" is a direct claim of inclusion, citizenship, and, as a citizen, an expectation for these needs to be met.

The thousands of people crammed into the convention center with no air, no water, no plumbing, and little medical care were angry. Many were poor, most were Black, many were jobless, and perhaps many were uneducated and single parents, as some conservative commentators claimed. But as citizens of the United States, all of them believed that they were entitled to protection from forces beyond their control. Doesn't the basic social contract between citizens and their government call for the protection of life, limb, and property?

Even the most die-hard conservative would agree that the government is obligated to assist the elderly and the sick in times of natural disaster. Yet when Dr. Greg Henderson, a pathologist turned field medic, arrived at the convention center on the Friday after the hurricane, he was the only doctor for ten thousand people. As he reported, "They're stacking the dead on the second floor. People are having seizures in the hallway. People with open running sores, every imaginable disease and disorder, all kinds of psychiatric problems . . . people who haven't had dialysis in several days."[2] "The crowds here have gotten a bad rap," a besieged Henderson asserted. "There are not many human beings you could cram into a building with 10,000 others, in 105 degree heat, that wouldn't get just a little pissed off."[3] At Charity Hospital, nurses who hadn't bathed in days tried to sterilize themselves with hand sanitizer with only a single generator and flashlights to light their work. They wept and begged for help as two patients on the parking deck died waiting to be evacuated by help that did not come.[4]

NBC news anchor Brian Williams was present in New Orleans from the start of the story and reported from inside the Superdome for five days. "I've seen dead bodies, a lot of dead bodies. . . . I've seen harrowing desperation in the eyes of people just before their own death or the death of a loved one. I've seen things I never thought I'd see in the United States.[5]

Another medical volunteer reported an encounter with a man in his seventies who was out of medicine, and his blood sugar and blood pressure were high.

> He told me that for two nights after the floods, he had perched on a ledge so narrow that his legs dangled in the water. At one point, he said, he saw Air Force One fly over, and his hopes soared. "I waited," he said, but no help came. Finally a boat got him to a packed bridge. There, again, he waited. He shook his head in disbelief, smiling though. "Doc, they treat refugees in other countries better than they treated us."
>
> "I'm so sorry," I said. "So sorry. . . ." "Thank you, Doc. I needed to hear that. All they got to say is sorry. All they got to say is sorry."[6]

Not just the poor and minorities felt abandoned. One of New Orleans's most famous residents, novelist Anne Rice, stated, "But to my country I want to say this: During this crisis you failed us. You looked down on us; you dismissed our victims; you dismissed us."[7] You want our music, culture, and cooking, Rice reminded us, but when you saw a few troublemakers, you turned your backs. "We are a lot more than all that," she added, "and though we may seem the most exotic, the most atmospheric and, at times, the most downtrodden part of this land, we are still part of it. We are Americans. We are you."[8] When help finally did arrive, another New Orleans resident said, "I feel like an American again." He concluded, "I thought my country had abandoned me."[9]

Citizenship ties are not subject to educational requirements or marriage licenses. They are not abstract or discretionary. When the government fails at this most basic level, the political community is weakened, and no photo opportunities or presidential proclamations can restore them.

Media and commentators who began labeling those who were internally displaced by the hurricane *refugees* only made the government's failure worse. Technically, refugees are people who have fled their own country because of persecution based on race, religion, political opinion, or social group. People fleeing natural or human disasters like floods and war are more properly termed *internally displaced*. The difference is important because under international law, internally displaced persons have recognized rights and guarantees that "refugees" and "evacuees" do not. United Nations' principles clearly state: "Authorities have the duty and responsibility to assist returned and / or resettled internally displaced persons to recover, to the extent possible, their property and possessions which they left behind or were dispossessed of upon their displacement."[10] For example, low- and middle-income property owners will have particular difficulty meeting their financial obligations and will require protection from creditors.

Ironically, if those internally displaced by Hurricane Katrina were refugees legally admitted to the United States, they would automatically be entitled to counseling, housing, employment services, medical assistance, and a federally mandated series of services from resettlement organizations tracking and supporting official refugees. By contrast, those fleeing Hurricane Katrina have been moved from one temporary shelter to another, sometimes informed in midflight of his or her destination in a distant state, with no one keeping track of who has gone where. Although the Refugee Council USA, a coalition of some four hundred resettlement agencies, offered to help the Katrina victims, as I am writing this, the Bush administration was still "reviewing" its offer of assistance.[11]

The rest of the world seemed as shocked by the U.S. government's response as the residents of New Orleans were. Argentina's *Clarin* reported, "Katrina had more than the power of the wind and water, because, now, when they have subsided, it can still reveal the emptiness of an era, one that is represented by President George W. Bush." Spain's *El Pais* stated,

Up until Monday, Bush was the president of the war in Iraq and 9/11. Today, there are few doubts that he will also pass into history as the president who didn't know how to prevent the destruction of New Orleans and who abandoned its inhabitants to their fate for days. And the worst is yet to come.

Another Spanish newspaper, *La Razon*, observed, "It is clear that the USA's international image is being damaged in a way it has never known before." Suggesting that the war in Iraq and the war on terror had drained away the funds necessary to strengthen New Orleans's sea walls, Switzerland's *Le Temps* added, "would George Bush have left his holiday ranch more quickly if the disaster had not first struck the most disadvantaged populations of the black south?" Pakistan's *The Nation* wrote,

The government of the world's richest nation defied the general expectation that at the first sign of the storm it would muster an armada of ships, boats and helicopters for the rescue operation. For nearly three days it sat smugly apathetic to the people's plight, their need for food, medicine and other basic necessities.

In Kenya's *Daily Nation*, Ambrose Murunga noted, "My first reaction when television images of the survivors of Hurricane Katrina in New Orleans came through the channels was that the producers must be showing the wrong clip. The images, and even the disproportionately high number of visibly impoverished blacks among the refugees, could easily have been a re-enactment of a scene from the pigeonholed African continent."[12]

Writing in the *New York Times,* Richard Bernstein believed that the collective European response regarding the victims of Katrina seemed more muted than the response to the victims of the tsunami or the famine in Niger or the killings in Darfur. He suggested that "this relative coolness may be that these other disasters took place in poor, troubled nations, not the most powerful and richest country on earth." "The circumstances of New Orleans and Biloxi, Mississippi," Bernstein pointed out, "confirm the worst image of America that prevails in Europe, the vision of a country of staggering inequalities, indifference to the general welfare (especially during the Bush administration), and lacking in what Europeans call 'solidarity.'"[13]

In fact, the "Third World" showed solidarity with the victims of Katrina by offering aid to the United States. El Salvador, Bosnia, Kosovo, Belarus, the former Soviet republic of Georgia, Sri Lanka, Venezuela, and Cuba all offered various types of help, ranging from money to doctors to rescue specialists. More than one observer commented that Cuba had managed to evacuate more than one and a half million citizens to higher ground during a Category 5 hurricane last September that destroyed twenty thousand houses but claimed no lives.[14]

Not all White Americans, however, shared the views of Europeans, Africans, Asians, or even African Americans. Several polls indicate that even though a large majority of African Americans believed race played a role in the response to the hurricane, a majority of Whites did not. According to an ABC/7 News poll, 70 percent of Blacks but only 29 percent of Whites cited race as a factor.[15] A Pew Research Center poll found that fully two-thirds of African Americans thought that the government's response would have been faster if most of the storm's victims had been White, whereas 77 percent of Whites believed that race would not have made a difference.[16] An ABC/*Washington Post* poll reported that 76 percent of Blacks thought that race played a role in Katrina relief efforts but only 24 percent of Whites agreed.[17] According to an AP/IPSOS poll, Blacks were more critical of President George W. Bush's handling of the hurricane relief work than Whites were, by 78 to 49 percent.[18]

In another era, White refugees—French planters from Cuba and other Spanish colonies in the Caribbean—fled *to* New Orleans. After

Napoleon invaded Spain in 1809 and crowned his own brother, Joseph Bonaparte, as the king of Spain, the Spanish revolted. This nationalistic revolt spread to all the Spanish colonies, and in 1809/1810, almost all the French exiles in those colonies were expelled.[19] In 1718 France had established New Orleans as a French port, which was ceded to Spain in 1767 but returned to France in 1800.

Ironically, it was Haiti's (Saint Domingue's) struggle for independence against the French that led to the rise of New Orleans as an American city and the largest slave port in the United States. In 1800, Napoleon persuaded Charles IV of Spain to exchange Haiti for an Italian principality. But in 1804 when the French army tried to establish control over Haiti, it was defeated by Black Haitian rebels in the first successful slave revolt in the Western Hemisphere. Having his dream of a French empire in the Antilles ended by Toussaint L'Ouverture and his successors, Bonaparte committed what he ruefully called *Louisianicide* and sold the piece of land to the United States for a bargain price.[20] The Haitian revolution, followed by Thomas Jefferson's Louisiana Purchase, led to the first wave of French refugees to New Orleans.

Although Francophones and Anglophones maintained a mutual distrust for some time, one overriding factor united them: their interest in maintaining slavery. In fact, democratic politics gave them the means to unite and overcome their ethnic heterogeneity to keep free Blacks out of political life and to fight federal efforts to ban the local slave trade.

A census of New Orleans in 1806 recorded a slave population of 8,378 (49%), a White population of 6,311 (37%), and a free Black population of 2,312 (14%).[21] The Black population had developed much as it had in other Caribbean ports, with unions between European men and African or Indian women producing a "third caste" of Whites and African slaves. These relationships were institutionalized in the *placage* system, which allowed wealthy White men to set up housekeeping with a "quadroon," a light-skinned and well-bred young woman of mixed ancestry.[22] These "free people of color" formed the demographic base for the much acclaimed "Creole" culture and character of New Orleans's social life.

This same character that developed the music, cuisine, and diversity of New Orleans also helped breed its crime, disease, and vice. Rev. Theodore Clapp blamed the "floating population" of the maritime community for the town's crime. The residents' health suffered as a result of drainage problems, and epidemic diseases like yellow fever and smallpox swept through the city. The public's spirit remained weak, owing to the notion that "government" was responsible for such matters.[23]

Initially, New Orleans was unique because the slaveholding class was not a small all-powerful elite. In the early 1760s about two-thirds of households, including those of some free Blacks, owned slaves. After 1803, the number of slaveholding households fell toward the South's norm of between one-fourth and one-third, and wealth and political power were even more unequally distributed. In the end, New Orleans was not recognizably "French" or "Caribbean" or "Spanish," as its language, religion and laws had been at different periods. Instead, its classes, demographic profile, export economy, and geographic situation determined the basic character of the community and its social structure. After 1803, then, it became just another North American slave society.[24]

Let us return now to Black "refugees" streaming out of New Orleans in 2005. Police from the neighboring city of Gretna fire shots over their heads as they cross the Crescent City Connection, yelling through bullhorns for the "refugees" to return to New Orleans. They are told that there will be no Superdomes in their city. In Plaquemines Parish, school buses attempting to take storm victims to safety at the Naval Air Station/Joint Reserve Base in Belle Chasse are turned back by dozens of armed sheriff's deputies with guns drawn. In Westwego, "evacuees are told to leave immediately or go to an overcrowded shelter where they are guarded."[25]

Media reports focusing on Katrina as a "natural disaster" exacerbated by the incompetence of relief officials and politicians correctly described the effect but not the cause. Certainly, better leadership from the mayor or governor or president might have saved lives. When we look at the president's refusal to acknowledge the effects of global warming to the shift in resources from natural disasters to terrorism, the record seems clear.[26] The incompetence of the politicians at the head of the Federal Emergency Management Agency (FEMA) has become a rich source of late-night television humor. Whereas Democrats would like an independent investigation of the response to the hurricane in order to determine accountability, the Republicans insist on not "playing the blame game." In short, Katrina has become a metaphor for our discussion of reparations in particular and the role of race in America in general. Some people want to study the issue through either another Kerner Commission or a Clinton race panel. Others prefer an ahistorical approach, to look toward the future.

But both responses miss the point. The response to the hurricane revealed nothing new. In 2003, 8.2 percent of Whites, 22.5 percent of Latinos, and 24.4 percent of African Americans lived in poverty. Moreover, poverty levels have grown by 17 percent since Bush assumed office. Sixty-seven percent of New Orleans's population is Black, and 30 percent already were living below the poverty level, 84 percent of whom were Black.[27]

Crime is a part of everyday life in New Orleans, a city that has at various times led the nation in murders. Jail time does not seem to have solved the problem. From 1980 to 2000 the number of people in prison, in jail, on parole, and on probation in the United States increased by 300 percent to more than six million. In fact, the United States has become a world leader in the number of its citizens in prison, rising from 320,000 to almost two million. Blacks are overrepresented in this population, accounting for 50 percent of all prison inmates. During this period, one out of three young Black men was either locked up, on probation, or on parole. The state of Louisiana has the largest prison population in the country, with 173,000 people in state prisons. Angola Prison, the maximum-security prison sixty miles northeast of Baton Rouge, got its name from the incarceration of former slaves originally from the African nation of Angola.[28]

The diseases that always follow a natural disaster will find a health care infrastructure poorly equipped to deal with it. Louisiana is tied with Mississippi for the worst infant mortality rate in the United States, with 10 of every 1,000 babies born dying in their first year, and for Black babies the figure is 15 deaths per 1,000 births. In Costa Rica the infant mortality rate is 8 per 1,000, and in Sri Lanka the odds are better, at 13 deaths per 1,000 births.[29]

In the all-important area of transportation accessibility, New Orleans ranks first—with the exception of three cities in the New York metropolitan area—of 297 metropolitan areas nationwide of households *without* access to a car.[30]

While the isolation of the poor is hardly surprising to anyone who has visited New Orleans and seen anything outside the French Quarter, the concentration of poor Blacks in the core city is relatively new.

As late as 1950, one-third of the city's population of 570,445 (compared with 470,000 just before Katrina) was African American. New Orleans had more mixed neighborhoods than did most southern cities, including some of those now under water, like the Ninth Ward. White flight accelerated in the 1960s as suburbs were created in newly drained swamplands and as Blacks assumed a larger voice in urban politics.[31]

Even though Blacks gained more political control, the city was limited in determining its own affairs and revenue base. State commissions own the Superdome and the Ernest N. Morial Convention Center. The Louisiana legislature makes the final decision on how much room tax New Orleans hotels will charge, and the governor, not the mayor, is the primary negotiator in deals with the New Orleans Saints football team. State law caps local sales taxes and property taxes. Because of past financial problems, the federal Department of Housing and Urban Development runs the city's public housing authority.[32]

In 2002, New Orleans voters approved a citywide living wage, but a court blocked its implementation. The median income of $25,759 per year in 2004 was barely half the national average.[33] Governor Kathleen Blanco has refused to release millions of dollars of tax money collected from Harrah's New Orleans Casino, despite pleas from city officials.[34] Thus New Orleans exists in a state of neocolonialism.

In a well-staged speech on Jackson Square in New Orleans, President George W. Bush addressed both the past and the future: "Poverty has roots in a history of racial discrimination, which cut off generations from the opportunity of America." Looking forward, he stated, "We have a duty to confront this poverty with bold action . . . let us rise above the legacy of inequality."[35] Washington approved $62.3 billion to help the victims of Hurricanes Katrina, Rita, and Wilma. When added to $8.6 billion in tax breaks and programs for the region, the total is nearly $71 billion. Moreover, in the wake of Katrina, a new poll indicates that eliminating poverty has now become more important than fighting terrorism, especially for Blacks. When asked, "What do you think should be the most important priority for the United States?" 58 percent of Blacks, 43 percent of Hispanics, 40 percent of Asians, and 36 percent of Whites listed poverty as the top priority.[36] The remarkable outpouring of private contributions from Americans following Katrina also is an indication of national concern for the victims.

As we saw earlier in other polls, not all Americans link race and poverty in the way that the president's speech did. Indeed, prominent conservatives like Rush Limbaugh wondered why the president had injected race into his speech at all.[37] George Will instead blamed liberalism for creating the cultural collapse leading to poverty, observing that liberals "stopped short of indelicately noting how many of the victims were women with children but not husbands."[38] (He does not note how he discovered these figures.). Citing the outpouring of help for Katrina victims, columnist Jeff Jacoby concluded, "Yet again that racism is dead as a force in mainstream American life.[39] Walter Marschner, an appraiser in Jefferson Parish, declared, "If we can get rid of 100,000 of the lower class that are takers and not givers to the community, we'll be much better off." Marschner, who is White, added, "That might sound racist, but I don't mean it that way."[40]

Bush's speech invoking a legacy of inequality caught the attention of Black leaders as well. Bishop T. D. Jakes, who has often supported the Bush administration, noted that "African Americans are waiting to see what this administration is going to do about this crisis" and that if it is effective, Black attitudes will change.[41] But Rev. Jesse Jackson thinks that "it's a hurricane for the poor and a windfall for the rich."[42] Bush's decision to suspend the Davis-Bacon Act guaranteeing the local prevailing wage to construction workers on federally financed projects and no-bid contracts seems to support Jackson's view. Jackson compared the structure for assistance to the region—federal financial aid managed locally in the states—with the post-Reconstruction era that allowed "Jim Crow" to flourish in the South (the *Plessy* decision was based on a New Orleans case). In the twentieth century, President Franklin D. Roosevelt's New Deal programs were administered in the same way with the same results.

To date more than half—$37.5 billion—of the funding appropriated by Congress is still sitting in FEMA's account. Of the nearly $25 billion assigned to projects, only about $6.2 billion has been spent, leading some in Congress to urge reclaiming some $2.3 billion in aid.[43]

Crises, both natural and "man-made," have periodically forced Americans to confront race and racial inequality. Whether it is Black bodies swinging from trees or urban violence setting cities ablaze, their presence has been unavoidable. The liberal's traditional answer to racism has been to remove the barriers to market freedoms and private individuality. Civic republicanism wants to remove the barriers to democratic politics and public power. Although ethnic nationalism often undermines civic nationalism, it cannot permanently dominate in a nation as diverse and fluid as the United States. Who "we" are as a nation is constantly changing as waves of immigrants reach American shores.[44]

Ethnic and racial nationalism cannot dominate the polity because civic myths about the triumph over racial and ethnic prejudice are central to our definition of us. Our heterogeneity is central to our exceptionalism. The principles that apply to the market and those that apply to the nation-state historically have often been in direct conflict, as they have been in the aftermath of Katrina. Constitutionalism has arisen as the primary mechanism to constrain or limit this conflict, but the U.S. Constitution is fundamentally flawed in its efforts to address racial justice as a community. As legal scholar Mark Brandon stated,

> Who "we" are is sometimes problematic and therein lies the original failure of the Constitution; it failed to constitute slaves. That is not to say that the Constitution failed to account for slaves, nor even that it failed to bind them in some (literal) sense of the word. But it did not bind them *in a constitutional sense.* . . . This failure was deliberate and largely self-conscious. It was perpetuated both through language and by silence.[45]

In sum, slavery fatally harmed the social contract and led to the Civil War.

Brandon and others argue that the American Revolution was conservative. The colonists had not suffered a long train of abuses and wanted only the rights of British subjects. The elite remained on top, and the slaves remained on the bottom. Technically, the Constitution was illegal because the delegates to the convention were instructed to amend only the Articles of Confederation. At the conclusion of the Civil War, the Reconstruction Amendments to the Constitution violated the ratification process outlined in its article V. Many Northern states and all the Southern states except Tennessee initially rejected the Fourteenth Amendment.[46]

Reconstruction took place under military occupation, and the South was forced to ratify the amendments as a condition for readmission to the Union. Despite the belief of some that Lincoln moved to "help the freed slaves become successfully integrated into American society,"[47] he emphatically repudiated racial equality as a postwar value. Brandon contends that Lincoln disavowed even the most rudimentary of political rights for Blacks and did not take remotely seriously the idea of social equality. "From the perspective of many whites, blacks were *in* the polity but not *of* it."[48]

If Lincoln was the "Great Emancipator" but not the "Great Integrator," when were Blacks included in the body politic? Many would cite the civil rights movement as the time when African Americans finally became "first-class" citizens. In fact, the success of the civil rights movement has become the foundation for a resurgent form of American exceptionalism best represented by George W. Bush. And if American exceptionalism embodies a universalism beyond race that allows the president and his supporters to speak and act on behalf of the entire world, then an event with the repercussions of Hurricane Katrina cannot be ignored.

In the twentieth century, Martin Luther King Jr. become a symbol of our civic myths as important as Lincoln was in the nineteenth century. Indeed, King's "I Have a Dream" speech may be more familiar to schoolchildren today than Lincoln's Gettysburg Address is. Although conservatives are fond of recalling the "dream of a color-blind society," they never mention the "check marked insufficient funds." Neither do they remember their vehement opposition to King and his nonviolent protests.

King was indeed the "Great Integrator." Foreshadowing the crisis in New Orleans, he warned Americans about the danger of surrounding Negro cities with White suburbs.[49] Most important, he wanted all Americans to see that the Black revolution was much more than a struggle for the rights of Negroes, that it was the beginning of a true radical American revolution. Such a revolution would be needed to root out the triple evils of racism, poverty, and militarism that plague American life and threaten our common future. If Blacks are to be *in* and not *of* this nation, then a radical reconstruction of the values of our society itself is the real issue that we must face. Today there is no better place to begin that reconstruction than with a public discourse on racial reparations.

Notes

Notes to the Introduction

1. From James Melvin Washington, ed., *A Testament of Hope* (San Francisco: Harper & Row, 1986), p. 217.

2. "An Apology 65 Years Late," *The NewsHour with Jim Lehrer*, transcript, May 16, 1997.

3. Martha Minow, *Between Vengeance and Forgiveness: Facing History after Genocide and Mass Violence* (Boston: Beacon Press, 1998), pp. 15–17, 110.

4. Priscilla B. Hayner, *Unspeakable Truths: Confronting State Terror and Atrocity* (New York: Routledge, 2001), p. 155.

5. Janna Thompson, *Taking Responsibility for the Past: Reparation and Historical Injustice* (Malden, Mass.: Blackwell, 2002), p. xi.

6. "Journey toward Justice . . . Not Over," *USA Today*, July 9, 2003.

7. Ibid.

8. "Bush Addresses Slavery from African Port Island," *Columbia* (Mo.) *Daily Tribune*, July 8, 2003.

9. Ibid.

10. Adam Goodheart, "Slavery's Past, Paved Over or Forgotten," *New York Times*, July 13, 2003.

11. "Clinton Pays Tribute to Slaves and Their Descendants, Senegal Memorial Is Final Stop on African Tour," *Seattle Times*, April 2, 1998.

12. Ibid.

13. Ibid.

14. LaWanda Johnson, "Benin Seeks Forgiveness for Its Role in African Slave Trade," *Washington Afro-American*, October 7, 2002.

15. Kenneth O'Reilly, *Nixon's Piano: Presidents and Racial Politics from Washington to Clinton* (New York: Free Press, 1995), p. 350.

16. Minow, *Between Vengeance and Forgiveness*; Hayner, *Unspeakable Truths*; Wilmot James and Linda Van DeVijver, eds., *After the TRC: Reflections on Truth and Reconciliation in South Africa* (Athens: Ohio University Press, 2001).

17. David W. Blight, *Race and Reunion: The Civil War in American Memory* (Boston: Belknap Press, 2001), pp. 9–14.

18. Thompson, *Taking Responsibility for the Past*, pp. xix, 17, 21.

19. National guilt in Japan is widely regarded as having been absolved

by the atomic bombs dropped on Hiroshima and Nagasaki. The French believe that half the population resisted the Nazi occupation. Spain refuses to come to terms with forty years of Franco's rule, and Stalin's victims still wait to be rehabilitated. See James and Van DeVijver, *After the TRC*, p. 36.

20. Thompson, *Taking Responsibility for the Past*, pp. 68, 116.

21. Jeffrey Haydu, "Making Use of the Past: Time Periods as Cases to Compare and as Sequences of Problem Solving," *American Journal of Sociology* 104, no. 2 (1998): 339–71; William H. Sewell Jr., "Three Temporalities: Toward an Eventful Sociology," in *The Historic Turn in the Human Sciences*, edited by Terrence J. McDonald (Ann Arbor: University of Michigan Press, 1996), pp. 245–81; George Steinmetz, "Reflections on the Role of Social Narratives in Working-Class Formation: Narrative Theory in the Social Sciences," *Social Science History* 16, no. 3 (fall 1992): 489–516.

22. Margaret Keck and Kathryn Sikkink, *Activists beyond Borders* (Ithaca, N.Y.: Cornell University Press, 1998); Akira Iriye, *Global Community: The Role of International Organization in Making the Contemporary World* (Berkeley: University of California Press, 2002); John Keane, *Civil Society: Old Images, New Visions* (Stanford, Calif.: Stanford University Press, 1998); Will Kymlicha, *Multicultural Citizenship* (New York: Oxford University Press, 1995).

Notes to Chapter 1

1. Walter Jackson, *Gunnar Myrdal and America's Conscience* (Chapel Hill, N.C.: University of North Carolina Press, 1990), passim.

2. Michael C. Dawson, *Black Visions: The Roots of Contemporary African-American Political Ideologies* (Chicago: University of Chicago Press, 2001), p. 34, n.

3. *New York Times* edition, *Report of the National Advisory Commission on Civil Disorders* (New York: Dutton, 1968), p. 540.

4. Ibid., p. 413.

5. Ibid., p. 23.

6. Ibid., p. 483.

7. Ibid., p. 407.

8. Ibid., p. 410.

9. Kenneth O'Reilly, *Nixon's Piano: Presidents and Racial Politics from Washington to Clinton* (New York: Free Press, 1995), pp. 264–65.

10. Ibid.

11. Ibid.

12. Final Report of the National Commission on the Causes and Prevention of Violence, *To Establish Justice, to Insure Domestic Tranquility* (Washington, D.C.: U.S. Government Printing Office, December 1969), p. 271.

13. Andrew Hacker, *Two Nations: Black and White, Separate, Hostile, Un-*

equal (New York: Ballantine Books, 1992). Recent works supporting Hacker's argument include Linda Faye Williams, *The Constraint of Race: Legacies of White Skin Privilege in America* (University Park: Pennsylvania State University Press, 2003); Dalton Conley, *Being Black, Living in the Red* (Berkeley: University of California Press, 1999); Thomas M. Shapiro, *The Hidden Cost of Being African American* (New York: Oxford University Press, 2004).

14. Steven A. Holmes and James Bennet, "A Renewed Sense of Purpose for Clinton's Panel on Race," *New York Times*, January 14, 1998.

15. Michael A. Fletcher, "Initiative on Race Ends Short of Its Soaring Goals," *Washington Post*, September 17, 1998, p. A1.

16. Paul Bedard, "Clinton, Race Panel at Odds on Slavery," *Washington Times*, September 30, 1997, p. A1.

17. The President's Initiative on Race, *One America in the Twenty-first Century: Forging a New Future: The Advisory Board's Report to the President*, September 1998, p. 32.

18. Ibid., p. 1.

19. Ibid., p. 72, list.

20. Ibid., p. 12.

21. Holmes and Bennet, "A Renewed Sense of Purpose."

22. Commission members include John Hope Franklin (chair), Linda Chavez-Thompson, Suzan D. Johnson Cook, Thomas H. Kean, Angela E. Oh, Robert Thomas, and William F. Winter.

23. Edward G. Carmines and James A. Stimson, *Issue Evolution: Race and the Transformation of American Politics* (Princeton, N.J.: Princeton University Press, 1989), p. 44.

24. Thomas Byrne Edsall and Mary D. Edsall, *Chain Reaction* (New York: Norton, 1992), p. 262.

25. Dinesh D'Souza, *The End of Racism* (New York: Free Press, 1995), p. 274.

26. Ibid., p. 277.

27. See, for example, Patricia Hill-Collins, *Black Sexual Politics* (New York: Routledge, 2005); and Ronald W. Walters, *White Nationalism/Black Interests* (Detroit: Wayne State University Press, 2003). In examining "new" versus "old" racism, Byron D'Andra Orey found that an analysis of a survey of college students in the state of Mississippi revealed that old-fashioned racism best explains White support for the Mississippi state flag. "These findings are startling given the educational levels of the respondents," states Orey. See his "White Racial Attitudes and Support for the Mississippi State Flag," *American Politics Research*, January 2004, pp. 102–16.

28. Mark E. Brandon, *Free in the World: American Slavery and Constitutional Failure* (Princeton, N.J.: Princeton University Press, 1998), p. 68.

29. Lorenzo Morris, "The Language of Race in Public Policy," in *Critical Analyses of Issues Facing African Americans and the Nation in the Twenty-first Cen-*

tury, edited by Lorenzo Morris and Ura Jean Oyemade (Washington, D.C.: Howard University Press, 1997), pp. 33–61.

30. Albert P. Blaustein and Robert L. Zangrando, eds., *Civil Rights and the American Negro* (New York: Washington Square Press, 1968), p. 43.

31. Will Kymlicka, *Multicultural Citizenship* (New York: Oxford University Press, 1995), p. 59.

32. Morris, "The Language of Race in Public Policy," p. 46.

33. Charles W. Mills, *Blackness Visible: Essays on Philosophy and Race* (Ithaca, N.Y.: Cornell University Press, 1998), p. 146.

34. Randall L. Kennedy, "Conservatives' Selective Use of Race in the Law," *Harvard Journal of Law & Public Policy* 19 (spring 1996): 719–22.

35. *Obadele v. United States,* 52 Federal Claim.432 (2002)

36. Charles J. Ogletree Jr., "Reparations for the Children of Slaves: Litigating the Issues," 33 *University of Memphis Law Review* 245 (winter 2003): 7. Note that Ogletree states, "What will make our litigation so successful, is that all these lawyers have agreed that they will work pro bono—for free" (p. 6). See also Charles J. Ogletree Jr., "Repairing the Past: New Efforts in the Reparations Debate," 38 *Harvard Civil Rights–Civil Liberties Law Review* 279 (2003): 295.

37. See Vincene Verdun, "If the Shoe Fits, Wear It: An Analysis of Reparations to African Americans," *Tulane Law Review* 6 (February 1993); Mari J. Matsuda, "Looking to the Bottom: Critical Legal Studies and Reparations," 323 *Harvard Civil Rights–Civil Liberties Review* (spring 1987); Irma Jacqueline Ozer, "Reparations for African Americans," 479 *Harvard Law Journal* (spring 1998); Robert Westley, "Many Billions Gone: Is It Time to Consider the Case for Black Reparations," *Boston College Law Review,* December 1998; Imari A. Obadele, "Reparations Now!" *Journal of Human Rights* 5 (1988): 369–411.

38. Jon M. Van Dyke, "Reparations for the Descendants of American Slaves under International Law," in *Should America Pay?* edited by Raymond A. Winbush (New York: Amistad, 2003). See also Matsuda, "Looking to the Bottom."

39. Matsuda, "Looking to the Bottom."

40. Deadria C. Farmer-Paellmann, "Excerpt from Black Exodus: The Ex-Slave Pension Movement Reader," in Winbush, *Should America Pay?* p. 25.

41. Note that class actions are an exception but have special requirements.

42. Matsuda, "Looking to the Bottom," p. 390.

43. Matsuda, "Looking to the Bottom"; See also Eric J. Miller, "Healing the Wounds of Slavery," 24 *Boston College Third World Law Journal* 45 (winter 2004): 3; and Alfred L. Brophy, "Some Conceptual and Legal Problems in Reparations for slavery," 58 *New York University Annual Survey of American Law* 497 (winter 2003): 3–4.

44. Brophy, "Some Conceptual and Legal Problems," p. 5; and Verdun, "If the Shoe Fits, Wear It."

45. Brophy, "Some Conceptual and Legal Problems"; and Rhonda V. Magee, "The Master's Tools, from the Bottom Up," *Virginia Law Review* 79 (1993): 863.

46. Westley, "Many Billions Gone"; and Brophy, "Some Conceptual and Legal Problems."

47. Borris I. Bittker, *The Case for Black Reparations* (Boston: Beacon Press, 2003), p. 31.

48. Ibid., p. xiv.

49. Michael Janofsky, "A New Hope for Dreams Suspended by Segregation," *New York Times*, July 31, 2005, p. 1.

50. Anthony Gifford, "The Legal Basis of the Claim for Slavery Reparations," 27–SPG *Human Rights* 16, spring 2000.

51. Darcie L. Christopher, "Note: Jus Cognes, Reparation Agreements, and Holocaust Slave Labor Litigation," 31 *Law & Policy in International Business* 1227 (2000).

52. Human Rights Watch, "An Approach to Reparations," available online at www.hrw.org, accessed December 28, 2000.

53. Max du Plessis, "Historical Injustice and International Law: An Exploratory Discussion of Reparation for Slavery," *Human Rights Quarterly* 25 (2003): 633.

54. Amy Gutman, ed., *Human Rights as Politics and Idolatry* (Princeton, N.J.: Princeton University Press, 2001), p. 13; Kenneth Roth, "The Court the US Doesn't Want," *New York Times*, November 19, 1998.

55. Miller, "Healing the Wounds of Slavery," pp. 5–6.

56. Roy L. Brooks, *Atonement and Forgiveness: A New Model for Black Reparations* (Berkeley: University of California Press, 2004), pp. 98–100.

57. Ibid., pp. x, 145.

58. Ibid., pp. xi–xii.

59. Donald Robinson, *Slavery in the Structure of American Politics 1765–1820* (New York: Norton, 1979), p. 54.

60. When the United States finally ratified the International Covenant on Civil and Political Rights, the State Department prepared an introduction acknowledging that the United States had been responsible for removing and enslaving Native Americans. Former Reagan administration official Midge Decter, writing in *Commentary*, accused the State Department of "moral greed," for example, wanting the United States to be a perfect society.

61. Daniel Bell, " 'American Exceptionalism' Revisited: The Role of Civil Society," *The Public Interest* 95 (spring 1989): 41–42.

62. Ibid. , p. 49.

63. Seymour Martin Lipset, *American Exceptionalism: A Double-Edged Sword* (New York: Norton, 1996), p. 14.

64. Ibid. , pp. 143–46.

65. Niall Ferguson, *Colossus: The Rise and Fall of the American Empire* (New York: Penguin Books, 2004), p. 292 (italics added).

66. Charles P. Henry, "A World View of Race Revisited," *Journal of Negro Education,* spring 2004, pp. 137–46.

67. See Scott L. Malcolmson, *One Drop of Blood: The American Misadventure of Race* (New York: Farrar, Straus & Giroux, 2000).

68. See Philip A. Klickner with Rogers M. Smith, *The Unsteady March: The Rise and Decline of Racial Equality in America* (Chicago: University of Chicago Press, 1999).

Notes to Chapter 2

1. *United States v. Hanway,* case no. 15,299, Circuit Court, E.D. Pennsylvania, 26 F. Cas. 105: 1851 U.S. App. LEXIS 463; 9 W.L.J. 103; 2 Wall. Jr. 139.

2. Ibid., p. 4.

3. Darlene Clark Hine et al., *The African-American Odyssey,* vol. 1, *To 1877* (Upper Saddle River, N.J.: Prentice Hall, 2003), p. 109.

4. Mark E. Brandon, *Free in the World* (Princeton, N.J.: Princeton University Press, 1998), p. 33.

5. Donald Robinson, *Slavery in the Structure of American Politics* (New York: Norton, 1979), p. 7.

6. Brandon, *Free in the World,* p. 68.

7. Orlando Patterson, "Freedom, Slavery, and the Modern Construction of Rights," in *Historical Change & Human Rights,* edited by Olwen Hufton (New York: Basic Books, 1995), p. 144.

8. Nikhil Pal Singh, *Black Is a Country: Race and the Unfinished Struggle for Democracy* (Cambridge, Mass.: Harvard University Press, 2004), p. 20.

9. Robinson, *Slavery in the Structure,* pp. 12–13.

10. Ibid., p. 156.

11. Cheryl I. Harris, "Whiteness as Property," *Harvard Law Review* 106 (1993): 1721, 1744.

12. Matthew Frye Jacobson, *Whiteness of a Different Color: European Immigrants and the Alchemy of Race* (Cambridge, Mass.: Harvard University Press, 1998), p. 25.

13. Ibid.

14. Ibid., p. 7.

15. Robinson, *Slavery in the Structure,* p. 103.

16. Ibid., p. 116.

17. Ibid., pp. 116–21.

18. Lorenzo Johnson Greene, *The Negro in Colonial New England* (New York: Atheneum, 1968), p. 293.

19. Greene, *The Negro in Colonial New England*, pp. 306–7; P. Olisanwuche Esedebe, *Pan-Africanism: The Idea and Movement 1776–1963* (Washington, D.C.: Howard University Press, 1982), pp. 9–10.

20. Hine et al., *The African-American Odyssey*, pp. 108–11.

21. An article in the *Southern University Law Review* states that there were precolonial demands for reparations from African tribal leaders for the damages of the slave trade, even though there are no written records of such demands. See "Black African Reparations: Making a Claim for Enslavement and Systematic de Jure Segregation and Racial Discrimination under American and International Law," *Southern University Law Review* 25, no. 1 (1997): 261.

22. W. E. B. DuBois, *Black Reconstruction in America, 1860–1880* (New York: Atheneum, 1979), pp. 147–49. DuBois reports that although Lincoln favored a plan calling for $400 million in compensation for slave masters, he proposed nothing for slave labor.

23. Eric Foner, *Reconstruction: America's Unfinished Revolution 1863–1877* (New York: Harper & Row, 1988), p. 70–71; Kenneth M. Stampp, *The Era of Reconstruction 1865–1877* (New York: Knopf, 1965), p. 126.

24. Foner, *Reconstruction*, p. 69.

25. George R. Bentley, *History of the Freedmen's Bureau* (Philadelphia: University of Pennsylvania Press, 1955), pp. 144–46.

26. Ibid.

27. Foner, *Reconstruction*, p. 235.

28. Stampp, *The Era of Reconstruction*, p. 126.

29. Foner, *Reconstruction*, pp. 248–50.

30. Michael Reich, *Racial Inequality: A Political-Economic Analysis* (Princeton, N.J.: Princeton University Press, 1981), p. 226.

31. Linda Faye Williams, *The Constraint of Race: Legacies of White Skin Privilege in America* (University Park: Pennsylvania State University Press, 2003), pp. 48–50.

32. Noel Ignatiev, *How the Irish Became White* (New York: Routledge, 1995), p. 164.

33. Jacobson, *Whiteness of a Different Color*, pp. 164–66.

34. Albion Tourgee, quoted in Harris, "Whiteness as Property," p. 1748 (italics in original).

35. Charles A. Lofgren, *The Plessy Case: A Legal-Historical Interpretation* (New York: Oxford University Press, 1987), pp. 187–88.

36. Thomas C. Holt, "Slavery and Freedom in the Atlantic World," in *Crossing Boundaries: Comparative History of Black People in Diaspora,* edited by

Darlene Clark Hine and Jacqueline McLeod (Bloomington: Indiana University Press, 1999), pp. 160–67.

37. Roger L. Ransom and Richard Sutch, *One Kind of Freedom: The Economic Consequences of Emancipation* (Cambridge: Cambridge University Press, 2001), pp. 83–86.

38. Walter R. Vaughan, *Freedmen's Pension Bill, a Plea for American Freedmen* (Chicago, 1891), pp. 36–37.

39. Sponsors of the legislation from 1890 to 1903 include Representatives Connell, Cullom, Mason, Curtis, Pettis, Blackburn, and Hanna.

40. Mary F. Berry, "Reparations for Freedmen, 1890–1916: Fraudulent Practices or Justice Deferred?" *Journal of Negro History* 57 (1972): 221.

41. Williams, *The Constraint of Race,* p. 58. Williams notes that the survival rate for Black veterans was significantly lower than that of White veterans. Moreover, one often needed the resources to hire a lawyer to work through the pension claims bureaucracy. A particular problem for the widows and children of Black veterans was the difficulty in establishing the legality of slave marriages as well as the problem of proving the birth dates of many Blacks (pp. 60–63).

42. Williams, *The Constraint of Race,* p. 59.

43. Vaughan, *Freedmen's Pension Bill,* p. 112.

44. "Ex-Mayor Vaughan's Statement," *U.S. Department News Eagle,* Washington, D.C., December 31, 1899, Record Group 15, Ex-Slave Pension Movement, box 1, envelope 6. Note that the *U.S. Department News Eagle* is a newspaper edited by Vaughan that looks remarkably like an official government newsletter, including the eagle on the masthead.

45. S.R. 75, 56th Cong., 1st sess., January 1900, p. 2.

46. Vaughan, *Freedmen's Pension Bill,* pp. 133–35.

47. Constitution and By-Laws of the Ex-Slave Pension Association, Record Group 15, Ex-Slave Pension Movement, box 1, envelope 5.

48. A. Scales and J. W. Anderson Committee, *Ex-Slave Pension Song,* Record Group 15, Ex-Slave Pension Movement, box 1, envelope 5.

49. Letter from W. R. Vaughan, Chicago, 1892, in S.R. 75, 56th Cong., 1st sess., January 1900, p. 3.

50. Frederick Douglass, quoted in Vaughan, *Freedmen's Pension Bill,* p. 183.

51. Report of the Commissioner to General Eli Torrence, February 7, 1902, Department of the Interior, Bureau of Pensions, Record Group 15, Ex-Slave Pension Movement, box 1, envelope 6.

52. S.R. 75, 56th Cong., 1st sess., January 6, 1900.

53. "Onward to Victory!" Flyer from the Ex-Slave Mutual Relief and Bounty & Pension Association, Record Group 15, box 1, n.d.

54. Constitution and By-Laws of the Ex-Slave Pension Association, Record Group 15, Ex-Slave Pension Movement, box 1, envelope 5.

55. W. R. Vaughan, "Caution," September 23, 1897, Record Group 15, Ex-Slave Pension Movement, box 1 (italics added).

56. Letter from J. L. Davenport, acting commissioner to Thomas Ryan, acting secretary of the interior, September 13, 1902, Record Group 15, box 2, envelope 8.

57. RG 15, box 2, envelope 8, September 13, 1902.

58. Article in *Freedman's Herald,* Washington, D.C., n.d., Record Group 15, Ex-Slave Pension Movement, box 2, envelope 11.

59. EPA Newspaper, n.d., Record Group 15, Ex-Slave Pension Movement, box 2, envelope 11.

60. "Deluding the Freedmen," *Evening Star,* September 21, 1899, p. 12, Record Group 15, Ex-Slave Pension Movement, box 1.

61. Ibid.

62. "Heavy Fine or Chain Gang," *Washington, D.C. Times,* March 16, 1901, Record Group 15, Ex-Slave Pension Movement, box 1, envelope 1.

63. " 'Limit of Law Is Sufficient in this Case'—Judge Calhoun," *Atlanta Constitution* (?), n.d., Record Group 15, Ex-Slave Pension Movement, box 1, envelope 6.

64. Report of the Commissioner to General Eli Torrence, February 7, 1902, Department of the Interior, Bureau of Pensions, Record Group 15, Ex-Slave Pension Movement, box 1, envelope 6.

65. Letter from A. Parker(?), special examiner, to commissioner of pensions, March 10, 1901, Record Group 15, Ex-Slave Pension Movement, box 1, envelope 6.

66. Letter from the chief of the Law Division to the chief of S. E. Division, Department of the Interior, Bureau of Pensions, December 4, 1905, Record Group 15, Ex-Slave Pension Movement, box 1, envelope 6. Note that the act of 1884 made it a violation of federal law to impersonate a government official.

67. Letter from the chief of the Law Division to the chief of S. E. Division.

68. "Slave Pension Scheme Exposed," August 4, 1916, Record Group 15, Ex-Slave Pension Movement, box 1, envelope 6.

69. Letter from special examiner in Nashville to commissioner of pensions, October 6, 1916, Record Group 15, Ex-Slave Pension Movement.

70. Bureau of Pensions, October 6, 1916.

71. *United States v. Rev. Augustus Clark,* U.S. Court for the Eastern District of Texas, Record Group 15, Ex-Slave Pension Movement, box 1, envelope 3.

72. Berry, "Reparations for Freedmen," p. 225.

73. Ibid.

74. S.R. 75, 56th Cong., 1st sess., January 16, 1900.

75. Vaughan, *Freedmen's Pension Bill,* p. 109.

76. *United States v. Rev. Augustus Clark,* U.S. Court for the Easter District of Texas, Record Group 15, Ex-Slave Pension Movement, box 1, envelope 3.

77. Letter from Callie to Hon. H. Clay, December 13, 1900, Record Group 15, Ex-Slave Pension Movement, box 2, envelope 8.

78. Report of the commissioner to General Eli Torrence, February 7, 1902, Department of the Interior, Bureau of Pensions, Record Group 15, Ex-Slave Pension Movement, box 1, envelope 6.

79. Gerald Horne, *Fire This Time* (Charlottesville, Va.: Da Capo, 1997), p. 3.

80. King, in Thomas F. Jackson, "Reconstructing the Dream" (Ph.D. diss., Stanford University, 1993), p. 21.

81. Ibid., p. 23.

82. Ibid., p. 149.

83. Ibid., p. 384.

84. Ibid., p. 172.

85. Ibid.

86. James MacGregor Burns and Stewart Burns, *A People's Charter* (New York: Knopf, 1991), pp. 326–27.

87. Jackson, "Recasting the Dream," pp. 202–3.

88. King, in James M. Washington, ed., *A Testament of Hope* (San Francisco: Harper & Row, 1986), p. 368.

89. See, for example, David J. Garrow, *Bearing the Cross* (New York: Vintage Books, 1988); and Adam Fairclough, *To Redeem the Soul of America* (Athens: University of Georgia Press, 1987).

90. Jackson, "Recasting the Dream," p. 421.

91. Ibid., pp. 325–46.

92. King was marginalized at this conference because of his opposition to Johnson's Vietnam War policy.

93. A. Philip Randolph, Testimony to U.S. Senate, *The Federal Role in Urban Affairs*, December 1966, p. 1897.

94. Ibid, p. 1891.

95. Paula F. Pfeffer, *A. Philip Randolph, Pioneer of the Civil Rights Movement* (Albany: State University of New York Press, 1990), p. 290.

96. Wright, in Jackson, "Recasting the Dream," p. 497.

97. Garrow, *Bearing the Cross*, p. 579.

98. Ibid., p. 599.

99. Levison, in Jackson, "Recasting the Dream," p. 283.

100. Jackson, "Recasting the Dream," p. 479; also Andrew Young, *An Easy Burden* (New York: HarperCollins, 1996), p. 444.

101. PPC Declaration of 1968: (1) A meaningful job at a living wage for every employable citizen; (2) A secure and adequate income for all who cannot find jobs or for whom employment is inappropriate; (3) Access to land as a means to income and livelihood; (4) Access to capital as a means of full participation in the economic life of America; (5) Recognition by law of the right of people affected by government programs to play a truly significant role in de-

termining how they are designed and carried out. See Jackson, "Recasting the Dream," p. 445.

102. Ibid., p. 500.

103. American National Election Study, 1952–1988, tables 3.4 and 3.5.

104. See, for example, Thomas Byrne Edsall with Mary D. Edsall, *Chain Reaction* (New York: Norton, 1992).

105. Black Panther Party, Platform and Program, October 1966; Point 10: We want land, bread, housing, education, clothing, justice and peace. As our major political objective, a United Nations–supervised plebiscite to be held throughout the black colony in which only black colonial subjects will be allowed to participate, for the purpose of determining the will of black people as to their national destiny. Kathleen Cleaver and George Katsiaficas, eds., *Liberation, Imagination, and the Black Panther Party* (New York: Routledge, 2001), p. 286. Elijah Muhammad, "What Do the Muslims Want?" Point 4: We want our people in America whose parents or grandparents were descendants from slaves, to be allowed to establish a separate state or territory of their own—either on this continent or elsewhere. We believe that our former slave masters are obligated to provide such land and that the area must be fertile and mineral rich. We believe that our former slave masters are obligated to maintain and supply our needs in this separate territory for the next 20 to 25 years—until we are able to produce and supply our own needs. See John H. Bracey Jr. et al., eds., *Black Nationalism in America* (Indianapolis: Bobbs-Merrill, 1970), p. 404.

106. Arnold Schucter, *Reparations* (Philadelphia: Lippincott, 1970), pp. 2–27.

107. Vincene Verdun, "If the Shoe Fits, Wear It: An Analysis of Reparations to African Americans," 67 *Tulane Law Review* 597 (February 1993): 297.

108. "Black African Reparations," *Southern University Law Review* 25, no. 1 (1997): 261.

109. Irma Jacqueline Ozer, "Reparations for African Americans," 41 *Howard Law Journal* 479 (spring 1998): 180. Tuneen E. Chisolm, "Sweep around Your Own Front Door: Examining the Argument for Legislative African American Reparations," 147 *University of Pennsylvania Law Review* 677 (1999): 208.

110. Roy L. Brooks, ed., *When Sorry Isn't Enough: The Controversy over Apologies and Reparations for Human Injustice* (New York: New York University Press, 1999), p. 6.

111. Mari Matsuda, in Brooks, *When Sorry Isn't Enough,* p. 7.

112. Saul Levmore, "Changes, Anticipations, and Reparations," *Columbia Law Review* 99, no. 7 (November 1999): 1657–1700.

113. John Torpey, ed., *Politics and the Past* (Lanham, Md.: Rowman & Littlefield, 2003), p. 12; and Theodore J. Lowi, "American Business, Public Policy, Case Studies, and Political Theory," *World Politics* 16 (1964): 677–715.

Notes to Chapter 3

1. Thomas R. Dye, "Rosewood, Florida: The Destruction of an African American Community," *Historian: A Journal of History* 59, no. 3 (spring 1996): 608–11. Richard Newman claims that Rosewood was founded by a Black family, the Goins, who started a turpentine and lumber business and named the village "Our Town." See Newman, "Rosewood Revisited," *Transition* 0, no. 80 (1999): 36.

2. Newman, "Rosewood Revisited," p. 35.

3. Sarah Carrier, who worked as a domestic for the Taylors, and others claimed that Fannie Taylor was having an affair with a White railroad worker, who had beaten her over some domestic dispute. See Dye, "Rosewood, Florida," p. 611.

4. Michael D'Orso, *Like Judgment Day: The Ruin and Redemption of a Town Called Rosewood* (New York: Boulevard, 1996), p. 5.

5. Dye, "Rosewood, Florida," p. 616.

6. Dye, "Rosewood, Florida," p. 615; and D'Orso, *Like Judgment Day,* pp. 8–13.

7. Dye, "Rosewood, Florida," p. 614.

8. Ibid. p. 58.

9. Ibid. p. 616.

10. D'Orso, *Like Judgment Day,* chap. 11.

11. The state decided to launch a criminal investigation of Carter's murder based on Parham's testimony. See D'Orso, *Like Judgment Day,* chap. 13.

12. D'Orso, *Like Judgment Day,* chap. 15.

13. Shelia L. Croucher, *Imagining Miami: Ethnic Politics in a Postmodern World* (Charlottesville: University of Virginia Press, 1997), p. 85.

14. Croucher, *Imagining Miami,* p. 57. Marielito refers to the Cuban port of Mariel through which most of the immigrants passed during the famous boatlift of 1980.

15. Daryl Harris, "Generating Racial and Ethnic Conflict in Miami: Impact of American Foreign Policy and Domestic Racism," in *Blacks, Latinos, and Asians in Urban America: Status and Prospects for Politics and Activism,* edited by James Jennings (Westport, Conn.: Praeger, 1994), p. 84.

16. Paul A. Dunoguez, "The Right Thing to Do: Cuban American Involvement in the Rosewood Claim," unpublished seminar paper, University of California at Berkeley, December 3, 2003, pp. 13–16.

17. Ibid., pp. 21–22.

18. D'Orso, *Like Judgment Day,* pp. 192–94.

19. Special Master's Final Report, March 24, 1994, p. 1, available online at http://fn1.tfn.net/rosewood/rosewood2.txt, accessed July 22, 2003.

20. Ibid., pp. 5–8.

21. Martha Barnett, chief lobbyist for the bill and a childhood friend of Doctor's, was amazed that the caucus was initially cool to the bill.

22. Walter White, quoted in "Tulsa Race Riot: A Report by the Oklahoma Commission to Study the Tulsa Race Riot of 1921" (Oklahoma City: State of Oklahoma, 2001), p. 24. Note that even Walter White uses the term *riot* when in fact Blacks were on the defensive during the entire episode.

23. Scott L. Malcolmson, *One Drop of Blood: The American Misadventure of Race* (New York: Farrar, Straus & Giroux, 2000), p. 128; and James S. Hirsch, *Riot and Remembrance: The Tulsa Race War and Its Legacy* (Boston: Houghton Mifflin, 2002), p. 36.

24. Hirsch, *Riot and Remembrance,* p. 34.

25. Ibid. pp. 13–20.

26. Alice Lovelace, "The Tulsa Riot of 1921," available online at www .inmotion magazine.com/tulsa19.html, accessed July 9, 2003, p. 6.

27. Hirsch, *Riot and Remembrance,* p. 44.

28. Ibid., p. 45.

29. Alfred L. Brophy, *Reconstructing the Dreamland: The Tulsa Riot of 1921* (New York: Oxford University Press, 2002), p. 9.

30. "Tulsa Race Riot," pp. 51–52. Ten days before the Tulsa race riot, another front-page news story inflamed public opinion in its reporting of Negro pimps who controlled White prostitutes, as well as several roadhouses where Negroes and Whites sang and danced together (p. 55).

31. No one was really sure what happened. See "Tulsa Race Riot," p. 57.

32. The editorial and article are missing from both newspaper archives and the state archives, as are the official arrest records. See "Tulsa Race Riot," p. 58; and Hirsch, *Riot and Remembrance,* p. 81.

33. "Tulsa Race Riot," pp. 61–63.

34. Ibid., p. 64.

35. Ibid., p. 78.

36. Estimates of the number of dead vary widely. Major O. T. Johnson of the Salvation Army, for example, is reported to have said that he hired a crew of more than three dozen gravediggers who labored for several days to dig about 150 graves for Negro victims. Others report seeing bodies from Greenwood being loaded on trucks and railroad flatcars. See "Tulsa Race Riot," pp. 119–21.

37. Brophy, *Reconstructing the Dreamland,* pp. 90–93.

38. Ibid., p. 94.

39. Ibid., pp. 97–100. Non-Blacks owned a substantial amount of property in Greenwood.

40. Ibid., p. 75. Note that W. E. B. DuBois had visited Tulsa in March 1921 and had indeed promoted social equality (p. 70).

41. Brophy, *Reconstructing the Dreamland,* p. 75.

42. Hirsch, *Riot and Remembrance*, p. 196. The Tulsa riot was discussed in Kay M. Teall's *Black History in Oklahoma* and in Arthur Tolson's *Black Oklahomans: A History 1541–1972*, both published in the early 1970s. Rudia Halliburton Jr. published an article on the Tulsa race riot in the *Journal of Black Studies* in 1972 that was later expanded into a book. See Hirsch, *Riot and Remembrance*, p. 212.

43. Hirsch, *Riot and Remembrance*, pp. 201–3.

44. Ibid., p. 205.

45. Ibid., pp. 218–27.

46. Ibid., pp. 306–7.

47. "Tulsa Race Riot," p. ii.

48. Hirsch, *Riot and Remembrance*, p. 321.

49. Ibid., p. 325.

50. Philip A. Klinkner with Rogers M. Smith, *The Unsteady March: The Rise and Decline of Racial Equality in America* (Chicago: University of Chicago Press, 1999), p. 115; and Dye, "Rosewood, Florida," p. 606.

51. Hirsch, *Riot and Remembrance*, p. 239.

52. After the Civil War, a U.S. Supreme Court decision limited federal criminal liability for violations of civil rights, and an Oklahoma court decision immunizing municipalities from liability for injuries to their residents gave Greenwood residents little recourse in against the city. On state immunity, see Brophy, *Reconstructing the Dreamland*, p. 97.

Notes to Chapter 4

1. Eric K. Yamamoto, "Race Apologies," *Journal of Gender, Race and Justice* 47 (1997): 50.

2. David A. Smith, "Blair: Britain's 'Sorrow' for Shame of Slave Trade," *The Observer*, November 26, 2006.

3. Avis Thomas-Lester, "A Senate Apology for History on Lynching Vote Condemns Past Failure to Act," *Washington Post*, June 14, 2005, p. A12.

4. Ibid.

5. Margaret Kimberley, "Freedom Rider: Racist Delivers Lynching Apology," *The Black Commentator*, June 16, 2005, p. 2.

6. Sheryl Gay Stolberg, "The Senate Apologizes, Mostly," *New York Times*, June 19, 2005, p. WK3.

7. Kimberley, "Freedom Rider." Note, however, that Allen's critics did not question the motives of those lobbying for the resolution. The Committee for a Formal Apology included a number of civil rights activists as well as Representative John Lewis (D-GA). Fortunately, Allen's presidential ambitions ended when he inadvertently revealed his true feelings to an opponent's campaign worker, which were captured on a cell phone for all to judge.

8. This section is drawn largely from Leslie T. Hatamiya, *Righting a Wrong: Japanese Americans and the Passage of the Civil Liberties Act of 1988* (Stanford, Calif.: Stanford University Press, 1993).

9. Hatamiya reports that Reagan and then George H. W. Bush proposed budgets containing no redress funds for 1989 and only $20 million for 1990. Senator Daniel Inouye (D-HI), as the second-ranking Democrat on the Appropriations Committee, was able to pry loose the needed funding as an entitlement program. It took three years and included a $400 million increase over the original appropriation. See Hatamiya, *Righting a Wrong*, pp. 182–88.

10. Roy L. Brooks, ed., *When Sorry Isn't Enough: The Controversy over Apologies and Reparations for Human Injustice* (New York: New York University Press, 1999), pp. 367–69.

11. Imari Abubakari Obadele, *The New International Law Regime and United States Foreign Policy* (Baton Rouge: The Malcolm Generation, 1996), pp. 247–48.

12. Caroline Mayer, "Flier Offering Slave Reparations Solicits Personal Information" *Washington Post,* July 9, 2001, p. A2; Michelle Singletory, "The Color of Money" *Washington Post,* March 4, 2001, p. H1.

13. U.S. Internal Revenue Service, "Slavery Reparation Scams Surge, IRS Urges Taxpayers Not to File False Claims," available online at www.irs.gov, accessed January 24, 2002.

14. Amber Austin, "Activists Discuss Slave Reparations" *Associated Press,* March 7, 2001, p. A2.

15. The Afrocentric Experience, "Why Reparations?" p. 6, available online at www.swagga/com/reparation.htm, accessed October 22, 2002.

16. Ibid.

17. Ibid.

18. Ibid.

19. Ibid.

20. Michael A. Fletcher, "Call for Reparations Builds as Blacks Tally History's Toll," *Washington Post,* December 26, 2000, p. A1.

21. Adamma Ince, "Getting Back on the Bus," *Village Voice,* August 14–20, 2002, p. 3.

22. RaceRelations, "40 Acres and a Luxury Sedan," available online at Racerelations.about.com, accessed June 19, 2002.

23. CNN, "Suit Seeks Billions in Slave Reparations," available online at CNN.com/LawCenter, accessed March 28, 2002.

24. Poll, June 8–July 9, 2000, available online at ABC News.com.

25. Earl Ofari Hutchinson, *Betrayed: A History of Presidential Failure to Protect Black Lives* (Boulder, Colo.: Westview Press, 1996), p. 176.

26. Tali Mendelberg, *The Race Card: Campaign Strategy, Implicit Messages, and the Norm of Equality* (Princeton, N.J.: Princeton University Press, 2001), p. 3.

27. George Lipsitz, *The Possessive Investment in Whiteness: How White People Profit from Identity Politics* (Philadelphia: Temple University Press, 1998), p. 221.

28. Robert Chrisman and Ernest Allen Jr., "Ten Reasons: A Response to David Horowitz," *The Black Scholar,* April 3, 2001, pp. 1–10.

29. Thomas B. Edsall, " 'Poor Choice of Words,' Lott Says," *Washington Post,* December 10, 2002, p. A13.

30. Orlando Patterson, *Rituals of Blood: Consequences of Slavery in Two American Centuries* (New York: Basic Books, 1998), p. 28.

31. Ibid., p. 76.

32. Ibid., pp. 43–48.

33. Ibid., p. 210.

34. Orlando Patterson, *The Ordeal of Integration* (Washington, D.C.: Civitas / Counterpoint, 1998), pp. 9–10 (italics in original).

35. Ira Katznelson, *When Affirmative Action Was White* (New York: Norton, 2005), pp. 22–23. Note that even though Katznelson opposes reparations, he offers three proposals for affirmative action that closely resemble reparations:

- For the lag in entering the Social Security System, the excluded could be identified and they, or their heirs, could be offered one-time grants that would have to be paid into designated retirement funds.
- For the absence of access to the minimum wage, tax credits to an equivalence of the average loss could be tendered.
- For the lack of access to key programs under the GI Bill, programs of subsidized mortgages, small business loans, and educational grants could now be put in place (p. 171).

36. Dalton Conley, *Being Black, Living in the Red* (Berkeley: University of California Press, 1999), p. 1.

37. Ibid., pp. 6, 13.

38. Ibid., pp. 25–29.

39. Ibid., pp. 50–51.

40. Thomas M. Shapiro, *The Hidden Cost of Being African American* (New York: Oxford University Press, 2004) pp. 3, 107–9.

41. Michael C. Dawson, *Black Visions: The Roots of Contemporary African American Political Ideologies* (Chicago: University of Chicago Press, 2001). p. 122; John H. Bracey, ed., *Black Nationalism in America* (Indianapolis: Bobbs-Merrill, 1970), pp. lv–lx.

42. Brian Lanker, *I Dream a World: Portraits of Black Women Who Changed America* (New York: Tabori & Chang, 1989), p. 102.

43. Ida Hakim et al., *Reparations, the Cure for America's Race Problem* (Hampton, Va.: U.B. and U.S. Communications Systems, 1994), pp. 13–14.

44. Clarence J. Mumford, *Race & Civilization: Rebirth of Black Centrality* (Trenton, N.J.: Africa World Press, 2001) p. 386.

45. Hakim, *Reparations*, p. 15.

46. Herb Boyd, "State of the Black World Draws Luminaries," *New York Amsterdam News*, December 6–12, 2001, p. 5; State of Black World Conference, "Creating Our Twenty-first Century," available online at l-ncbs@lists.psu.edu, accessed April 16, 2001.

47. Hakim, *Reparations*, p. 12.

48. Randall Robinson, *The Debt: What America Owes to Blacks* (New York: Dutton, 2000), p. 100.

49. Ibid., p. 247.

50. Jennifer L. Hochschild, *Facing Up to the American Dream: Race, Class and the Soul of America* (Princeton, N.J.: Princeton University Press, 1995), p. 26.

51. Ibid., pp. 74–75.

52. Ibid., pp. 122–30. Hochschild notes that much of what makes affluent Black women feel deprived compared with others has more to do with gender than with race (p. 108).

53. Dawson, *Black Visions*, p. 309.

54. Ibid., p. 318.

55. Ibid., p. 275.

56. John McWhorter, "Why I Don't Want Reparations for Slavery," *Los Angeles Times*, July 15, 2001, p. M5.

57. Armstrong Williams, "Presumed Victims," in *Should America Pay?* edited by Raymond Winbush (New York: Amistad, 2003), pp. 165–71.

58. Dawson, *Black Visions*, p. 303. Dawson states that Black feminists face the most obstacles in disseminating their views and that the Black Marxism and the radical tradition lost much of their mass character in the 1990s.

59. Chrisman and Allen, "Ten Reasons." In his book *Uncivil Wars: The Controversy over Responsibility for Slavery* (San Francisco: Encounter Books, 2002), David Horowitz notes that he dropped the wording "bad for blacks" from the newspaper ad in order to make it less controversial. It was the original title of the piece as it appeared in Salon nine months before the college ad. Horowitz also states that forty-three of seventy-one college newspapers rejected the ad (p. 10). Even though Horowitz denies that his intention was to promote controversy, he states its positive effect: "In an eye blink, their [ads] appearance illuminated the dark places of the educational landscape and the suppression of free speech that is now routine in the academy became news" (p. 4). He also states that the "controversy provoked by the ad prompted his decision to make a 'freedom tour' of campuses and go 'in your face' to his accusers" (p. 24).

60. Andrew Brownstein, "Race, Reparations, and Free Expression," *Chron-*

icle of Higher Education, March 30, 2001, pp. A48–A50; editorial, "Walking the Fine Line of Free Speech," *Daily Californian,* March 6, 2001, p. 6.

61. John Leo, "The No Speech Culture," *U.S. News & World Report,* March 19, 2001, p. 16.

62. Brownstein, "Race, Reparations, and Free Expression." Note that the editor of the *Daily Californian,* Daniel Hernandez, is a Latino.

63. David Horowitz, "Ten Reasons Why Reparations for Blacks Is a Bad Idea for Blacks—And Racist, Too! Available online at www.adversity.net/ reparations/anti reparations ad.htm, posted March 12, 2001, and reprinted in Ronald P. Salzberger and Mary C. Turck, eds., *Reparations for Slavery* (Lanham, Md.: Rowman & Littlefield, 2004).

64. Armstrong Williams, John McWhorter, and Shelby Steele repeat many of the arguments presented by Horowitz in Winbush, *Should America Pay?* In the same volume, Christopher Hitchens offers a point-by-point response to Horowitz, agreeing with some points and disagreeing with others. For a leftist critique of reparations as undercutting class solidarity, see Adolph Reed Jr., "The Case against Reparations," *The Progressive,* December 2000, pp. 15–17.

65. For a point-by-point challenge to Horowitz, see Chrisman and Allen, "Ten Reasons."

66. On August 1, 2000, candidate George W. Bush said, "Yes, racism exists. I'm not going to be making policy based on guilt." *Time,* available online at CNN.com/Time.com. On August 27, 2001, National Public Radio reported that "President Bush is said to oppose paying slave compensation." NPR, "Making Amends," available online at www.npr.org/programs/specials/ racism/010827.reparations.htm1. On April 27, 2004, the *Boston Globe* reported that Senator John Kerry stated, "The truth is that affirmative action has kept America thinking in racial terms. . . . We cannot lecture our citizens about fairness and then disregard legitimate questions about the actual fairness of federal regulation and law." He later amended his comments to say he favored mending, not ending, affirmative action. See "Complete Biography of John Kerry," *Boston Globe,* pp. 279–80, at www.issues 2002.org/Domestic/John_ Kerry_Civil_Rights.htm#General. On August 1, 2000, Kerry said, "We should resist an 'identity politics' that confers rights and entitlements on groups and instead affirm our common rights and responsibilities as citizens." See Hyde Park declaration at www.issues2002.org/Domestic/John_Kerry_Civil_Rights .htm#General.

67. Lawrie Balfour, *The Evidence of Things Not Said: James Baldwin and the Promise of American Democracy* (Ithaca, N.Y.: Cornell University Press, 2001), pp. 3–5.

68. King, in James M. Washington, ed., *A Testament of Hope* (San Francisco: Harper & Row, 1986).

69. Balfour, *The Evidence of Things Not Said,"* p. 11.

70. Charles W. Mills, *Blackness Visible* (Ithaca, N.Y.: Cornell University Press, 1998), p. 132; Rodgers M. Smith, *Civic Ideals* (New Haven, Conn.: Yale University Press, 1997; and Balfour, *The Evidence of Things Not Said.*

71. Lawrie Balfour, "Unreconstructed Democracy: W. E. B. DuBois and the Case for Reparations," *American Political Science Review,* February 2003, p. 41.

72. Balfour, *The Evidence of Things Not Said,* p. 19.

73. Table 4.2 in Horowitz advertisement.

74. Ibid.

75. Dianne M. Pinderhughes, *Race and Ethnicity in Chicago Politics* (Urbana: University of Illinois Press, 1987), pp. 12–16.

76. Rogers M. Smith, *Civic Ideals: Conflicting Visions of Citizenship in U.S. History* (New Haven, Conn.: Yale University Press, 1997), p. 15.

77. Ibid., pp. 549–58.

78. Philip Klinkner with Rodgers M. Smith, *The Unsteady March: The Rise and Decline of Racial Equality in America* (Chicago: University of Chicago Press, 1999), pp. 3–4.

79. Derrick Bell, *Silent Covenants* (New York: Oxford University Press, 2004), p. 49.

80. Ibid., pp. 59–68.

81. James Madison and Lani Guinier suggest a type of political reparations in the form of cumulative voting and proportional representation in order to balance Black and White interests. These views, in part, led to the withdrawal of her nomination by the Clinton administration as assistant attorney general. See Lani Guinier, *The Tyranny of the Majority: Fundamental Fairness in Representative Democracy* (New York: Free Press, 1994), pp. 1–20.

Notes to Chapter 5

1. Manning Marable notes that in the early 1990s, a coalition of Jewish groups established the World Jewish Restitution Organization to locate and demand the retrieval of all wealth taken from European Jews during the Holocaust. See Manning Marable, *The Great Wells of Democracy* (New York: BasicCivitas, 2002), p. 232.

2. See, for example, Jeff Woods, *Black Struggle, Red Scare* (Baton Rouge: Louisiana State University Press, 2004); and Mary L. Dudziak, *Cold War Civil Rights* (Princeton, N.J.: Princeton University Press, 2000).

3. Thomas C. Holt, "Slavery and Freedom in the Atlantic World," in *Crossing Boundaries: Comparative History of Black People in Diaspora,* edited by Darlene Clark Hine and Jacqueline McLeod (Bloomington: Indiana University Press, 1999), pp. 35–36.

4. Ibid., pp. 40–41.

5. Orlando Patterson, *Freedom in the Making of Western Culture* (New York: Basic Books, 1991), p. 405.

6. Paul Gordon Lauren, *Power and Prejudice: The Politics and Diplomacy of Racial Discrimination* (Boulder, Colo.: Westview Press, 1996), p. 36.

7. David Theo Goldberg, *Racist Culture: Philosophy and the Politics of Meaning* (Oxford: Blackwell, 1993), pp. 1–2.

8. Ibid., p. 4.

9. Ali A. Mazrui, "Global Africa: From Abolitionists to Reparations," *African Studies Review*, December 1994, pp. 1–18.

10. John McWhorter, "Against Reparations," in *Should America Pay?* edited by Raymond Winbush (New York: Amistad, 2003), p. 185.

11. Armstrong Williams, "Presumed Victims," in *Should America Pay?* edited by Raymond Winbush (New York: Armistad, 2003), p. 166.

12. Ali A. Mazrui, "Wonders of Black Orientalism," available online at l-ncbs@lists.psu.edu, accessed November 15, 1999.

13. Henry L. Gates Jr., "A Preliminary Response to Ali Mazrui's Preliminary Critique of Wonders of the African World," available online at l-ncbs@lists.psu.edu, accessed November 13, 1999.

14. La Wanda Johnson, "Benin Seeks Forgiveness for Its Role in African Slave Trade," *Washington Afro-American*, October 7, 2002.

15. As quoted in Ronald Segal, *The Black Diaspora* (New York: Farrar, Straus & Giroux, 1995), p. 9.

16. Ibid., pp. 12–13.

17. Rodney prefers the term *underdevelopment* to *developing* because the latter assumes that Africa is meant to catch up with the West. Rodney contends that Africa is meant to remain "underdeveloped to support the continued development of the West" (p. xiv).

18. Walter Rodney, *How Europe Underdeveloped Africa: Resolutions and Selected Speeches from the Sixth Pan African Congress* (Dar es Salaam: Tanzania Publishing House, 1976), p. 219.

19. Winthrop D. Jordan, *White over Black* (Baltimore: Penguin Books, 1969), passim.

20. David Brion Davis, *Slavery and Human Progress* (New York: Oxford University Press, 1984), p. 73.

21. David Brion Davis, *The Problem of Slavery in Western Culture* (Ithaca, N.Y.: Cornell University Press, 1966), p. 135.

22. Howard Winant, *The World Is a Ghetto* (New York: Basic Books, 2001), p. 47.

23. Albert P. Blaustein and Robert L. Zangrando, *Civil Rights and the American Negro* (New York: Washington Square Press, 1968).

24. Davis, *The Problem of Slavery*, p. 135.

25. Lauren, *Power and Prejudice*, p. 29.

26. DuBois in Winant, *The World Is a Ghetto*, p. 323.

27. See Darryl C. Thomas, *The Theory and Practice of Third World Solidarity* (Westport, Conn.: Praeger, 2001), passim.

28. Seymour Drescher, "British Way, French Way: Opinion Building and Revolution in the Second French Slave Emancipation," *American Historical Review*, June 1991, p. 709.

29. Margaret Keck and Kathryn Sikkink, *Activists beyond Borders* (Ithaca, N.Y.: Cornell University Press, 1998), p. 42.

30. On the differences between the Declaration of Independence and the French Declaration of the Rights of Man and of the Citizen, see Louis Henkin, *The Age of Rights* (New York: Columbia University Press, 1990), pp. 161–67.

31. *Master frames* are the complex systems of ideas that inform entire cycles of protest. They are to movement-specific collective action frames what paradigms are to finely tuned theories. See Keck and Sikkink, *Activists beyond Borders*, p. 42.

32. Sidney Tarrow, *Power in Movement* (Cambridge: Cambridge University Press, 1998), p. 178; David S. Meyer and Sidney Tarrow, eds., *The Social Movement Society* (Boulder, Colo.: Rowman & Littlefield, 1998), p. 146.

33. Tarrow, *Power in Movement*, pp. 181–82.

34. In attempting to link Pan Africanism to the concept of the African Diaspora, Walters poses five types of Pan African relationships: (1) among African states, (2) among African states and African-origin states in the Diaspora, as in the Caribbean, (3) among African states and African-origin peoples (communities) in the Diaspora, (4) among African-origin states in the Diaspora and African-origin communities in the Diaspora, and (5) among African-origin communities in the Diaspora. See Ronald Walters, *Pan Africanism* (Detroit: Wayne State University Press, 1995).

35. Keck and Sikkink, *Activists beyond Borders*, pp. 30–32.

36. Ibid., p. 35.

37. Tarrow also notes that scholars of ethnic nationalism have ignored social movement theory. See Tarrow, *Power in Movement*, pp. 184–89, 211.

38. Doug McAdam et al., eds., *Comparative Perspectives on Social Movements* (Cambridge: Cambridge University Press, 1996), p. 2.

39. Tarrow, *Power in Movement*, p. 54.

40. George Fredrickson, *Black Liberation* (New York: Oxford University Press, 1995).

41. McAdam, *Comparative Perspectives*, p. 6.

42. Elizabeth S. Clemens, "Organizational Form as Frame," in *Perspectives on Social Movements*, edited by Doug McAdam et al. (Cambridge: Cambridge University Press, 1996), p. 211.

43. As described in his "Conservation of the Races" paper, the early DuBois had a rather mystical conception of race, whereas Garvey operated

212 Notes to Chapter 5

from a more biologically defined paradigm. Garvey's experience with mulattos in Jamaica made him suspicious of DuBois. See Robert Hill, ed., *The Marcus Garvey and Universal Negro Improvement Association Papers*, vol. 1 (Berkeley: University of California Press, 1983), p. 6.

44. Walters, *Pan Africanism*, p. 82.

45. Tajudeen Abdul-Raheem, ed., *Pan Africanism* (London: Pluto Press, 1996), p. 12.

46. In fact, the "categorical identity claims of movements often rest on the solidarity of much more intimate and specialized communities (critical communities). A critical community is a self-aware, mutually interacting group who have developed a sensitivity to some problem, an analysis of the sources of the problem and a prescription for what should be done about the problem. It is interested primarily in the development of new values and perspectives and is critical of the status quo without ties to established political institutions. This critical posture distinguishes critical communities from epistemic communities." See Thomas R. Ronchon, *Culture Moves* (Princeton, N.J.: Princeton University Press, 1998), p. 223.

Critical communities can also be distinguished from social movements that are interested in winning social and political acceptance for new values. There are many more critical communities than there are movements. For most of its existence Pan Africanism—with the notable exception of the Garvey movement—has existed as a critical community rather than a movement. In short, as with most pan movements, Pan Africanism has not moved from theory to praxis. See Louis L. Snyder, *Macro-Nationalisms* (Westport, Conn.: Greenwood Press, 1984), p. 6. The ties that link the diaspora together must be articulated and are not inevitable.

47. Donald R. Culverson, "From Cold War to Global Interdependence," in *Window on Freedom*, edited by Brenda Gayle Plummer (Chapel Hill: University of North Carolina Press, 2003), p. 232.

48. Culverson, "From Cold War"; and Francis Njuba Nesbitt, *Race for Sanctions* (Bloomington: Indiana University Press, 2004), passim.

49. Ronald Walters, "The African Growth and Opportunity Act," in *Foreign Policy and the Black (Inter)national Interest*, edited by Charles P. Henry (Albany, N.Y.: State University of New York Press, 2000).

50. Mazrui, "Global Africa," p. 4.

51. Imari Abubakari Obadele, *The New International Law Regime and United States Foreign Policy* (Baton Rouge: The Malcolm Generation, 1996), pp. 447–48.

52. Randall Robinson, *The Debt: What America Owes to Blacks* (New York: Dutton, 2000), p. 220.

53. Keck and Sikkink, *Activists beyond Borders*, p. 12.

54. Declarations and Programmes of Action adopted by the First (1978)

and the Second (1983) World Conference to Combat Racism and Racial Discrimination, p. 22, available online at www.un.org/esa/document/ecosoc mainres.htm, 1999, *United Nations*, E/CN.4/1999/WG.1/BP.1, accessed March 9.

55. Betty King, U.S. ambassador to the UN Economic and Social Council (ECOSOC), represented the United States.

56. There was no consensus on the word *compensatory*. All words with no such agreement are bracketed for later resolution.

57. International Human Rights Law Group, "Report on the World Conference against Racism, First Preparatory Committee (PrepCom) Meeting," Geneva, May 1–5, 2000.

58. "World Conference against Racism: A Conference on Racism Worldwide?" WCAR Think Paper I 2001, May 23, 2001, available online at www.hri .ca/racism/projects/think1.htm, p. 1.

59. Ibid.

60. Phillippe LeBlanc, "How Can NGOs Be Effective in the World Conference against Racism?" available online at www.hri.ca/racism/submitted/ theme/leblanc.htm, 2001, p. 1.

61. International Possibilities Unlimited, "Report on Informal Government Meeting and Africa PrepCom, February 2, 2001, e-mail from drdrobins onesprynet.com, p. 5.

62. Draft Declaration of the African Preparatory Regional Meeting for the World Conference against Racism, Racial Discrimination, Xenophobia and Related Intolerance, Dakar, Senegal, January 22–24, 2001, pp. 4–5.

63. Ibid.

64. America's draft declaration, 2001.

65. The United States' participation in the Americas regional meeting marked the first time that the country joined the Americas region at a UN global conference. Before this time the United States had participated in the Western European region.

66. Note that the leadership for an African American History Museum on the Mall in Washington came from the Congressional Black Caucus and not the Clinton or Bush administrations (see U.S. Non-Paper for the WCAR 2001).

67. Report of the PrepCom on its Third Session, *United Nations*, Geneva, Switzerland, July 30–August 10, 2001, p. 49, available online at A/CONF.189/ PC.3/11.

68. Hanspeter Kriesi, "The Impact of the National Context of Social Movements," in *Comparative Perspectives on Social Movements*, edited by Doug McAdam et al. (Cambridge: Cambridge University Press, 1996), pp. 152–53.

69. The House of Representatives passed a resolution urging the administration to boycott the WCAR. Representative Tom Lantos (D-CA) sponsored the resolution.

70. Lorenzo Morris, "Symptoms of Withdrawal," paper presented at the annual meeting of the National Conference of Black Political Scientists, Atlanta, March 9, 2002.

71. Ibid., p. 7.

72. Ibid., p. 9.

73. U.S. leadership meetings, n.d., p. 10.

74. Ibid., pp. 16–17.

75. International Human Rights Law Group, "Race and Poverty in the Americas" (Washington, D.C.: International Human Rights Law Group, August 2001), p. 9.

76. William B. Wood, *The UN World Conference against Racism,* report prepared for the House International Relations Committee, Subcommittee on International Operations and Human Rights, available online at www.state .gov/p/io/ris/rm/2001/index.cfm, July 31, 2001, p. 1.

77. Ibid., p. 3.

78. Ibid.

79. Ibid.

80. "United Nations World Conference against Racism" (Washington, D.C.: TransAfrica Forum, October 2001, p. 6.

81. The other major controversy revolved around Israel's role in the Middle East. Over the Indian government's objection, Dalits also led a successful effort to see their caste status included in the debate over forms of discrimination.

82. NGO Forum, "Program of Action for the World Conference against Racism," Durban, South Africa, August 28–September 1, 2001, pp. 37–41.

83. For example, the International Human Rights Association of American Minorities submitted a document entitled "Toward the Eradication of Racism and Racial Discrimination in the Americas." The All for Reparations and Emancipation group submitted recommendations on the issue of reparations to the WCAR.

84. NGO Forum, "Program of Action," pp. 37–41.

85. See McAdam, *Comparative Perspectives,* p. 25. Note that Malcolm X often reminded his audiences that even though Blacks were considered a minority in the United States when compared with Whites, non-Whites were the majority worldwide.

86. Steven Krasner notes that developing countries often prefer the international arena to bilateral relationships with major powers. See Steven Krasner, *Structural Conflict* (Berkeley: University of California Press, 1985).

87. Although Assistant Secretary of State William Wood noted the $250,000 the United States committed to funding the WCAR, he failed to mention the $6 million to $8 million the United States contributed to the Beijing

conference. First Lady Hillary Clinton and Secretary of State Madeline Albright headed the U.S. delegation.

88. William A. Gamson and David S. Meyer, "Framing Political Opportunity," in *Comparative Perspectives on Social Movements,* edited by Doug McAdam et al. (Cambridge: Cambridge University Press, 1996), p. 285.

89. Larry Bivens, "Slave-Reparations Debate Heating Up," *Arizona Republic,* April 21, 2001.

90. In March 2001, the *New York Times* reported that UN High Commissioner for Human Rights Mary Robinson "generally supports such demands [reparations], particularly in finding some form of recompense for slavery." Robinson stated that the "trauma is still there and it's deep, and it hasn't been properly acknowledged." She added "that this exploitation was in real terms a crime against humanity when it took place and that it had an effect into this century." See Barbara Crossette, "Global Look at Racism Hits Many Sore Points," *New York Times,* March 4, 2001.

91. Barbara Crossette, "Rights Leaders Urge Powell to Attend U.N. Racism Conference," *New York Times,* July 11, 2001; Pamela Constable, "Many Causes Set Tone for U.N. Summit on Racism," *Washington Post,* August 31, 2001, p. A14; Darryl Fears and Alan Sipress, "U.S. Warns It May Skip Conference on Racism," *Washington Post,* July 27, 2001, p. A1.

92. Elizabeth Becker, "Annan Says Race Conference Must Chart Way for Future," *New York Times,* July 31, 2001, p. F13.

93. William Raspberry, "An Education on Reparations," *Washington Post,* September 10, 2001, p. A21.

94. Courtland Milloy, "Colin Powell: Bush Man or Black Man?" *Washington Post,* July 29, 2001, p. C1.

95. Note that the secretary of state did not hear about the WCAR until January 2001, some four years after the UN General Assembly proposed the conference and seven months after the first PrepCom. See Jane Perlez, "How Powell Decided to Shun Conference," *New York Times,* September 5, 2001, p. A17.

96. Bob Herbert, "In America, Doomed to Irrelevance," *New York Times,* September 6, 2001.

97. Debra Friedman and Doug McAdam, "Collective Identity and Activism," in *Frontiers in Social Movement Theory,* edited by Aldon D. Morris and Carol McClury (New Haven, Conn.: Yale University Press, 1992), p. 165.

98. Not all race activists were pleased to come together in Durban. Dennis Brutus and Ben Cashdan challenged delegates and participants to get out of the conference center and witness the grinding poverty of Blacks and Indians in Durban's townships and throughout South Africa. They noted that while Jubilee South Africa leaders had supported the call for reparations,

South African President Thabo Mbeki had distanced himself from the reparations campaign. See Dennis Brutus and Ben Cashdan, "World Conference against Racism: South Africa between a Rock and a Hard Place," *Znet Commentary*, July 11, 2001. A number of local groups used the conference and its participants to launch a major protest march concerning South Africa's economic plight during the conference week. See Norm Dixon, "Thousands to Protest at Racism Conference," *Green Left Weekly*, August 8, 2001, p. 18.

99. Tarrow defines *frame bridging* as the least ambitious form of framing, linking two or more ideologically congruent but structurally unconnected frames regarding a particular issue or problem. *Frame amplification* tries to clarify and invigorate an interpretive frame bearing on a particular issue. *Frame extension* attempts to enlarge the movements' adherent pool by portraying its objectives or activities as similar to the values or interests of potential adherents. *Frame transformation* is the most radical form of framing, as the movement offers a radically new set of ideas and seeks to eliminate old meanings and understandings. See Sidney Tarrow, "Mentalities, Political Cultures, and Collective Action Frames," in *Frontiers in Social Movement Theory*, edited by Aldon D. Morris and Carol McClury (New Haven, Conn.: Yale University Press, 1992), p. 188.

100. Lynne Duke, "The Price of Apartheid," *Washington Post*, December 3, 2002, p. C1. See also Nicole Itano, "Should IBM and Others Pay Apartheid Bill?" *Christian Science Monitor*, November 26, 2002, p. 07.

101. "Corporate Fraud Law Upheld," *Washington Post*, November 30, 2004, p. E2. See also Daphne Eviatar, "Judgment Day—Will an Obscure Law Bring Down the Global Economy?" *Boston Globe*, December 28, 2003, p. D1.

102. Master frames affect the cyclicity and clustering of social movement activity by functioning as master algorithms that color and constrain the orientations and activities of other movements associated with it ecologically and temporally. See David A. Snow and Robert D. Benford, "Master Frames and Cycles of Protest," in *Frontiers in Social Movement Theory*, edited by Aldon D. Morris and Carol McClury (New Haven, Conn.: Yale University Press, 1992), p. 151.

103. Nkosazana Dalamini Zuma, "Closing Statement," report of the WCAR, Durban, South Africa, August 31–September 8, 2001 (A/CONF.189/12).

104. Some reparations advocates have argued that a focus on slavery weakens the case for restitution. See Boris I. Bittker, *The Case for Black Reparations* (Boston: Beacon Press, 2003); and Human Rights Watch, "An Approach to Reparations" (New York: Human Rights Watch, 2004).

105. Mary Robinson, "Closing Statement," report of the WCAR, Durban, South Africa, August 31–September 8, 2001 (A/CONF.189/12).

Notes to Chapter 6

1. *New York Times,* June 20, 2004, p. WK7.

2. *American Political Science Review,* December 2001, pp. 777–91.

3. Faith Davis Ruffins, "Culture Wars Won and Lost: Part I," *Radical History Review* 68 (1997): 83.

4. Ibid., p. 85.

5. Edwin Black reports on the pioneering work done in California on eugenics that inspired Hitler's efforts to develop a master race in his "Eugenics and the Nazis—The California Connection," *San Francisco Chronicle,* November 9, 2003, p. D1.

6. Ruffins, "Culture Wars," p. 95.

7. See Randall Robinson's account of the absence of Black labor in the building of the Capitol in *The Debt: What America Owes to Blacks* (New York: Plume, 2000), pp. 1–7.

8. A few of the important works on Black history to emerge during this period were those by John Blassingame, *The Slave Community* (New York: Oxford University Press, 1972); James H. Cone, *Black Power and Black Theology* (New York: Seabury Press, 1969); Lawrence W. Levine, *Black Culture and Black Consciousness* (New York: Oxford University Press, 1977); Eugene Genovese, *Roll, Jordan, Roll* (New York: Vintage Books, 1976); and Winthrop Jordan, *White over Black* (Baltimore: Pelican Books, 1968).

9. Perhaps the most significant factor in locating the museum in Ohio was Black political power in the state legislature and congress in the person of Louis Stokes.

10. Raoul Dennis, "Who Axed the African American Museum on the Mall?" *The Crisis,* February/March 1998, p. 10.

11. Senator Jesse Helms's opposition to the museum was seen as retaliation for Senator Carol Mosely-Braun's opposition to the routine reauthorization of a Confederate women's organization that had had a congressional seal of approval for many years. See Faith Davis Ruffins, "Culture Wars Won and Lost: Part II," *Radical History Review* 70 (1998): 95.

12. Four museum proponents, including myself, met with Heyman at the Smithsonian in the spring of 1999. This group also promoted the idea of linking a national African American museum in Washington to the preservation and memorialization of the African Burial Ground in New York City. See, for example, Brent Staples, "The Lessons of a Graveyard," *International Herald Tribune,* January 11, 2000, p. 9.

13. Lynette Clemetson, "Bush Authorizes a Black History Museum," *New York Times,* December 17, 2003.

14. Michelle Taute, "New Black History Museums," *USA Weekend,* July

16–18, 2004, pp. 20–21; and Bruce Weber, "The Road to Freedom, Revisited," *New York Times*, August 1, 2004, pp. 6–7.

15. Office of Tom Hayden, "Governor Sings Hayden Bills Researching Financial Gains from Slavery, press release, October 2, 2000; and California Department of Insurance, "Initial Statement of Reasons, file no. RH 325, January 26, 2001.

16. Alan Judd, "Georgia Orders Probe of Slave Insurance," *Atlanta Journal-Constitution*, May 4, 2002, p. A1.

17. Dan Morain, "Slave Owners and Their Insurers Are Named," *Los Angeles Times*, May 2, 2002, p. A1.

18. Ibid.

19. State of New York, 9286 A, 2001-02 Regular Session in Assembly, June 25, 2001.

20. State of New Jersey, assembly, no. 1301, 210th legislature, available online at TheBlackList@topica.com, accessed October 12, 2002.

21. William Raspberry, "When Sorry Isn't Enough," *Washington Post*, May 5, 2000, p. A27.

22. The Afrocentric Experience, "Reparations," available online at www.swagga.com, May 17, 2000; and Fran Spielman, "Daley Says He Backs Slavery Reparations," *Chicago Sun-Times*, May 10, 2000, p. 28.

23. Sabrina L. Miller and Gary Washburn, "City Mulls Law Seeking Insurers' Ties to Slavery," *Chicago Tribune*, May 30, 2002, p. 3.

24. Gwen Daye Richardson, "At Least Consider Idea of Reparations," *USA Today*, June 16, 2000, p. A19.

25. Kristen Mack, "Reparations Debate Heats Up Push for Slavery Compensation Enters Political Mainstream," *Houston Chronicle*, August 12, 2002, p. 1.

26. "Slavery Reparations Resolution Official City of East Peoria," available online at TheBlackList@topica.com, accessed September 3, 2002.

27. Robert Allen, "Past Due: The African American Quest for Reparations," *The Black Scholar*, summer 1998, p. 15.

28. Robert Brock, "Paying for Slavery," *The Economist* (U.S.), August 13, 1994, p. A28.

29. Robert Fogel, "A Price for Pain?" *The Economist* (U.S.), April 13, 2002.

30. Peter J. Meyer, review of *The Wealth of Races*, by Richard F. America, *Journal of Economic Literature*, September 1993, pp. 1472–73.

31. Robert S. Browne, "The Economic Basis for Reparations to Black America," *Review of Black Political Economy*, winter 1993, p. 99.

32. Roger L. Ransom and Richard Sutch, *One Kind of Freedom: The Economic Consequences of Emancipation* (Cambridge: Cambridge University Press, 2001), pp. 3, 52, 106.

33. Ibid., p. 82.

34. Richard F. America, *Paying the Social Debt: What White America Owes Black America* (Westport, Conn.: Praeger, 1993), pp. 18, 48, 39.

35. Clarence J. Mumford, *Race & Civilization: Rebirth of Black Centrality* (Trenton, N.J.: Africa World Press, 2001), pp. 384–92.

36. Allen G. Breed, "Blacks Dissatisfied with USDA Lawsuit Settlement," *Oakland Tribune,* September 1, 2002, p. 8.

37. Shaila K. Dewan, "Black Farmers" Refrain: Where's All Our Money?" *New York Times,* August 1, 2004, p. 12.

38. Malia Rulon, "Black Farmers Press for Compensation," *Washington Post,* February 28, 2005, p. A5. See also Mike Tierney, "Black Farmers Angry at Feds," *Atlanta Journal-Constitution,* May 5, 2005, p. E1.

39. Greg Burns, "Farms Run by African-Americans in Illinois Are 'Mighty Few' at 59," *Chicago Tribune,* June 12, 2005, p. 1.

40. Rodgers M. Smith, *Civic Ideals: Conflicting Visions of Citizenship in U.S. History* (New Haven, Conn.: Yale University Press, 1997), p. 37.

41. W. James Booth, "Communities of Memory: On Identity, Memory, and Debt," *American Political Science Review,* June 1999, p. 252.

42. Mary Ann Glendon, *Rights Talk* (New York: Free Press, 1991), p. 107.

43. W. James Booth, "The Unforgotten: Memories of Justice," *American Political Science Review,* December 2001, p. 784.

44. David W. Blight, *Race and Reunion: The Civil War in American Memory* (Boston: Belknap Press, 2001), pp. 253–54.

45. Mark Lawrence McPhail, *The Rhetoric of Racism Revisited: Reparations or Separation?* (Lanham, Md.: Rowman & Littlefield, 2002), pp. 189–90.

46. Roy L. Brooks, ed., *When Sorry Isn't Enough: The Controversy over Apologies and Reparations for Human Injustice* (New York: New York University Press, 1999), pp. 496–97.

47. Clayborne Carson, ed., *The Autobiography of Martin Luther King Jr.* (New York: Warner Books, 1998), p. 340.

48. Thoreau, quoted in Mark E. Brandon, *Free in the World: American Slavery and Constitutional Failure* (Princeton, N.J.: Princeton University Press, 1998), p. 102.

49. Nikhil Pal Singh, *Black Is a Country* (Cambridge, Mass.: Harvard University Press, 2004), pp. 18–19.

Notes to the Epilogue

1. Michael Ignatieff, "The Broken Contract," *New York Times,* September 25, 2005, p. 15.

2. Nancy Gibbs, "New Orleans Lives by the Water and Fights It . . . ," *Time,* September 12, 2005, p. 46.

3. Ibid.

4. Ibid.

5. Bill Carter, "Career-Maker for Williams as the Anchor at NBC," *New York Times,* September 4, 2005, p. A26.

6. Abraham Verghese, "Close Encounter of the Human Kind," *New York Times,* September 18, 2005, p. 192.

7. Anne Rice, "Do You Know What It Means to Lose New Orleans?" *New York Times,* September 4, 2005, p. WK11.

8. Ibid.

9. Lynne Duke and Teresa Wiltz, "A Nation's Castaways," *Washington Post,* September 4, 2005.

10. U.S. Human Rights Network, "U.S. Human Rights Network Calls for Authorities to Meet Their Legal and Moral Obligations to 'Internally Displaced Persons' in the Wake of Hurricane Katrina," September 13, 2005, available online at baraka@ushrnetwork.org.

11. Richard Bernstein, "The View from Abroad," *New York Times,* September 4, 2005, p. 12.

12. Shelby Lewis, "International Reaction to Katrina," available online at list@ncobps.org, September 6, 2005. On Cuba, see Marjorie Cohn, "The Two Americas," available online at www.truthout.org/docs, September 3, 2005.

13. Bernstein, "The View from Abroad."

14. Kevin Sullivan, "Response to Storm Shakes U.S. Image," *Oakland Tribune,* September 4, 2005; Julian Kunnie, "Wars in the Gulf: Who Cares about Poor Black People in New Orleans?" Tucson: Africana Studies, University of Arizona, n.d.; Cohn, "The Two Americas."

15. ABC/7 News Poll, broadcast on September 7, 2005.

16. Pew Research Center, "Two-in-Three Critical of Bush's Relief Efforts," available online at http://people-press.org, September 8, 2005.

17. ABC/*Washington Post* Poll, broadcast on September 28, 2005.

18. Will Lester, "Poll Shows Support for Abandoning Parts of City," *Oakland Tribune,* September 10, 2005, p. 6.

19. Thomas N. Ingersoll, *Mammon and Manon in Early New Orleans: The First Slave Society in the Deep South, 1718–1819* (Knoxville, University of Tennessee Press, 1999), p. 256.

20. Ingersoll, *Mammon and Manon,* p. 244. For the classic account of the Haitian revolution, see C. L. R. James, *Black Jacobians* (London: Secker & Warburg, 1938)

21. Ingersoll, *Mammon and Manon,* p. 248.

22. Kim Lacy Rodgers, *Righteous Lives: Narratives of the New Orleans Civil Rights Movement* (New York: New York University Press, 1993), p. 4.

23. Ingersoll, *Mammon and Manon,* pp. 251–52.

24. Ibid., pp. 119–20.

25. Chip Johnson, "Police Made Their Storm Misery Worse," available online at www.sfgate.com, September 9, 2005.

26. Sidney Blumenthal, "No One Can Say They Didn't See It Coming," available online at http://socrates.berkeley.edu/, September 3, 2005.

27. Barbara Lee, "Hurricane Exposed Two Americas," *Oakland Tribune,* September 17, 2005.

28. Eric Mann, "Letter in Support of the Movement in New Orleans and the Gulf Coast: Notes on Strategy & Tactics," September 29, 2005, pp. 13, 34, available online at www.thestrategycenter.org.

29. Nicholas D. Kristof, "A Health Care Disaster," *New York Times,* September 25, 2005, p. 11.

30. Laurie Becklund, "Listening to Katrina," *California Monthly,* November/December 2005, p. 33.

31. Rodgers, *Righteous Lives,* p. 5.

32. Robert Travis Scott, "Rebuilding Plans Confront Turf Wars, Political Strife: Racial Tension Mars Initial Discussions," *Times-Picayune,* September 18, 2005.

33. Emma Dixon, "New Orleans' Racial Divide: An Unnatural Disaster," November 18, 2005, available online at Ellarwee@aol.com.

34. Scott, "Rebuilding Plans."

35. Sophia A. Nelson, "I'm Hoping Bush Can Finish What Lincoln Started," *Washington Post,* October 23, 2005, p. B3.

36. Peter Prengaman, "Poll: Poverty Should Be Country's Top Priority," *Oakland Tribune,* October 23, 2005.

37. Nelson, "I'm Hoping Bush," p. B3.

38. George Will, "Hard Lessons for Liberals," *Oakland Tribune,* September 15, 2005.

39. Jeff Jacoby, "Katrina's Colorblind Relief," *Oakland Tribune,* September 17, 2005.

40. Brian Thevenot, "Race, Class on Everyone's Mind: Residents Visualize the Future of N.O.," *Times-Picayune,* October 2, 2005. It also was around this time that the former secretary of education Bill Bennett commented that crime would be reduced by aborting all Black babies—but he didn't mean it in a racial way!

41. Elisabeth Bumiller and Anne E. Kornblut, "Black Leaders Say Storm Forced Bush to Confront Issues of Race and Poverty," *New York Times,* September 18, 2005; see also Jesse Washington, "Blacks' Conscience Awakened," *Oakland Tribune,* September 9, 2005, p. 1.

42. Bumiller and Kornblut, "Black Leaders."

43. Cathy Booth Thomas, "Hurricane Katrina: The Cleanup," *Time,* November 28, 2005, p. 35.

44. Nikhil Pal Singh, *Black Is a Country: Race and the Unfinished Struggle for Democracy* (Cambridge, Mass.: Harvard University Press, 2004), pp. 21, 27.

45. Mark E. Brandon, *Free in the World: American Slavery and Constitutional Failure* (Princeton, N.J.: Princeton University Press, 1998), p. 28 (italics in original). Brandon takes the controversial position that the efforts of the Southern states to secede from the Union were constitutional.

46. Brandon, *Free in the World*, pp. 196–205.

47. Nelson, "I'm Hoping Bush."

48. Brandon, *Free in the World*, p. 212.

49. King in Washington; France seems to have reversed the geography, with the minorities being confined in the suburbs. See David Crary, "France, U.S. Both Face Race Conflicts," *Oakland Tribune*, November 14, 2005.

Bibliography

Books

Abdul-Raheem, Tajudeen, ed. *Pan Africanism.* London: Pluto Press, 1996.

America, Richard F. *Paying the Social Debt: What White America Owes Black America.* Westport, Conn.: Praeger, 1993.

Balfour, Lawrie. *The Evidence of Things Not Said: James Baldwin and the Promise of American Democracy.* Ithaca, N.Y.: Cornell University Press, 2001.

Bell, Derrick. *Silent Covenants.* New York: Oxford University Press, 2004.

Bentley, George R. *History of the Freedmen's Bureau.* Philadelphia: University of Pennsylvania Press, 1955.

Bittker, Boris I. *The Case for Black Reparations.* Boston: Beacon Press, 2003.

Blassingame, John. *The Slave Community.* New York: Oxford University Press, 1972.

Blaustein, Albert P., and Robert L. Zangrando, eds. *Civil Rights and the American Negro.* New York: Washington Square Press, 1968.

Blight, David W. *Race and Reunion: The Civil War in American Memory.* Cambridge, Mass.: Belknap Press, 2001.

Bracey, John H., et al., eds. *Black Nationalism in America.* Indianapolis: Bobbs-Merrill, 1970.

Brandon, Mark E. *Free in the World: American Slavery and Constitutional Failure.* Princeton, N.J.: Princeton University Press, 1998.

Brooks, Roy L. *Atonement and Forgiveness: A New Model for Black Reparations.* Berkeley: University of California Press, 2004.

Brooks, Roy L., ed. *When Sorry Isn't Enough: The Controversy over Apologies and Reparations for Human Injustice.* New York: New York University Press, 1999.

Brophy, Alfred L. *Reconstructing the Dreamland: The Tulsa Riot of 1921.* New York: Oxford University Press, 2002.

Carmines, Edward G., and James A. Stimson. *Issue Evolution: Race and the Transformation of American Politics.* Princeton, N.J.: Princeton University Press, 1989.

Carson, Clayborne, ed. *The Autobiography of Martin Luther King Jr.* New York: Warner Books, 1998.

Cleaver, Kathleen, and George Katsiaficas, eds. *Liberation, Imagination, and the Black Panther Party.* New York: Routledge, 2001.

Cone, James H. *Black Power and Black Theology.* New York: Seabury Press, 1969.

Conley, Dalton. *Being Black, Living in the Red.* Berkeley: University of California Press, 1999.

Croucher, Sheila L. *Imagining Miami: Ethnic Politics in a Postmodern World.* Charlottesville: University of Virginia Press, 1997.

Davis, David Brion. *Slavery and Human Progress.* New York: Oxford University Press, 1984.

Dawson, Michael C. *Black Visions: The Roots of Contemporary African American Political Ideologies.* Chicago: University of Chicago Press, 2001.

D'Orso, Michael. *Like Judgment Day: The Ruin and Redemption of a Town Called Rosewood.* New York: Boulevard, 1996.

D'Souza, Dinesh. *The End of Racism.* New York: Free Press, 1995.

DuBois, W. E. B. *Black Reconstruction in America, 1860–1880.* New York: Atheneum, 1979.

Dudziak, Mary L. *Cold War Civil Rights.* Princeton, N.J.: Princeton University Press, 2000.

Edsall, Thomas Byrne, with Mary D. Edsall. *Chain Reaction.* New York: Norton, 1992.

Esedebe, P. Olisanwuche. *Pan-Africanism: The Idea and Movement 1776–1963.* Washington, D.C.: Howard University Press, 1982.

Fairclough, Adam. *To Redeem the Soul of America.* Athens: University of Georgia Press, 1987.

Ferguson, Niall. *Colossus: The Rise and Fall of the American Empire.* New York: Penguin Books, 2004.

Foner, Eric. *Reconstruction: America's Unfinished Revolution 1863–1877.* New York: Harper & Row, 1988.

Fredrickson, George. *Black Liberation.* New York: Oxford University Press, 1995.

Garrow, David J. *Bearing the Cross.* New York: Vintage Books, 1988.

Genovese, Eugene. *Roll, Jordan, Roll.* New York: Vintage Books, 1976.

Glendon, Mary Ann. *Rights Talk.* New York: Free Press, 1991.

Goldberg, David Theo. *Racist Culture: Philosophy and the Politics of Meaning.* Oxford: Blackwell, 1993.

Greene, Lorenzo Johnson. *The Negro in Colonial New England.* New York: Atheneum, 1968.

Guinier, Lani. *The Tyranny of the Majority: Fundamental Fairness in Representative Democracy.* New York: Free Press, 1994.

Gutman, Amy, ed. *Human Rights as Politics and Idolatry.* Princeton, N.J.: Princeton University Press, 2001.

Hacker, Andrew. *Two Nations: Black and White, Separate, Hostile, Unequal.* New York: Ballantine Books, 1992.

Hakim, Ida, et al. *Reparations, the Cure for America's Race Problem.* Hampton, Va.: U.B. and U.S. Communications Systems, 1994.

Hatamiya, Leslie T. *Righting a Wrong: Japanese Americans and the Passage of the Civil Liberties Act of 1988.* Stanford, Calif.: Stanford University Press, 1993.

Hayner, Priscilla B. *Unspeakable Truths: Confronting State Terror and Atrocity.* New York: Routledge, 2001.

Henkin, Louis. *The Age of Rights.* New York: Columbia University Press, 1990.

Henry, Charles P., ed. *Foreign Policy and the Black (Inter)national Interest.* Albany: State University of New York Press, 2000.

Hill, Robert, ed. *The Marcus Garvey and Universal Negro Improvement Association Papers.* Vol. 1. Berkeley: University of California Press, 1983.

Hill-Collins, Patricia. *Black Sexual Politics.* New York: Routledge, 2005.

Hine, Darlene Clark, and Jacqueline McLeod, eds. *Crossing Boundaries: Comparative History of Black People in Diaspora.* Bloomington: Indiana University Press, 1999.

Hine, Darlene Clark, et al. *The African-American Odyssey.* Vol. 1: *To 1877.* Upper Saddle River, N.J.: Prentice Hall, 2003.

Hirsch, James S. *Riot and Remembrance: The Tulsa Race War and Its Legacy.* Boston: Houghton Mifflin, 2002.

Hochschild, Jennifer L. *Facing Up to the American Dream: Race, Class and the Soul of America.* Princeton, N.J.: Princeton University Press, 1995.

Horne, Gerald. *Fire This Time.* Charlottesville, Va.: Da Capo, 1997.

Hufton, Olwen, ed. *Historical Change & Human Rights.* New York: Basic Books, 1995.

Hutchinson, Earl Ofari. *Betrayed: A History of Presidential Failure to Protect Black Lives.* Boulder, Colo.: Westview Press, 1996.

Ignatiev, Noel. *How the Irish Became White.* New York: Routledge, 1995.

Ingersoll, Thomas N. *Mammon and Manon in Early New Orleans: The First Slave Society in the Deep South, 1718–1819.* Knoxville: University of Tennessee Press, 1999.

Iriye, Akira. *Global Community: The Role of International Organization in Making the Contemporary World.* Berkeley: University of California Press, 2002.

Jackson, Walter. *Gunnar Myrdal and America's Conscience.* Chapel Hill: University of North Carolina Press, 1990.

Jacobson, Matthew Frye. *Whiteness of a Different Color: European Immigrants and the Alchemy of Race.* Cambridge, Mass.: Harvard University Press, 1998.

James, C. L. R. *Black Jacobians.* London: Secker & Warburg, 1938.

James, Wilmot, and Linda Van De Vijver, eds. *After the TRC: Reflections on Truth and Reconciliation in South Africa.* Athens: Ohio University Press, 2001.

Jennings, James, ed. *Blacks, Latinos, and Asians in Urban America: Status and Prospects for Politics and Activism.* Westport, Conn.: Praeger, 1994.

Jordan, Winthrop D. *White over Black*. Baltimore: Penguin Books, 1969.

Keane, John. *Civil Society: Old Images, New Visions*. Stanford, Calif.: Stanford University Press, 1998.

Keck, Margaret, and Kathryn Sikkink. *Activists beyond Borders*. Ithaca, N.Y.: Cornell University Press, 1998.

Klickner, Philip A., with Rogers M. Smith. *The Unsteady March: The Rise and Decline of Racial Equality in America*. Chicago: University of Chicago Press, 1999.

Krasner, Steven. *Structural Conflict*. Berkeley: University of California Press, 1985.

Kymlicha, Will. *Multicultural Citizenship*. New York: Oxford University Press, 1995.

Lanker, Brian. *I Dream a World: Portraits of Black Women Who Changed America*. New York: Tabori & Chang, 1989.

Lauren, Paul Gordon. *Power and Prejudice: The Politics and Diplomacy of Racial Discrimination*. Boulder, Colo.: Westview Press, 1996.

Levine, Lawrence W. *Black Culture and Black Consciousness*. New York: Oxford University Press, 1977.

Lipset, Seymour Martin. *American Exceptionalism: A Double-Edged Sword*. New York: Norton, 1996.

Lipsitz, George. *The Possessive Investment in Whiteness: How White People Profit from Identity Politics*. Philadelphia: Temple University Press, 1998.

Lofgren, Charles A. *The Plessy Case: A Legal-Historical Interpretation*. New York: Oxford University Press, 1987.

Malcolmson, Scott L. *One Drop of Blood: The American Misadventure of Race*. New York: Farrar, Straus & Giroux, 2000.

Marable, Manning. *The Great Wells of Democracy*. New York: BasicCivitas, 2002.

Massey, Douglass S., and Nancy A. Denton. *American Apartheid: Segregation and the Making of the Underclass*. Cambridge, Mass.: Harvard University Press, 1993.

McAdam, Doug, et al., eds. *Comparative Perspectives on Social Movements*. Cambridge: Cambridge University Press, 1996.

McDonald, Terrence J., ed. *The Historic Turn in the Human Sciences*. Ann Arbor: University of Michigan Press, 1996.

McPhail, Mark Lawrence. *The Rhetoric of Racism Revisited: Reparations or Separation?* Lanham, Md.: Rowman & Littlefield, 2002.

Mendelberg, Tali. *The Race Card: Campaign Strategy, Implicit Messages, and the Norm of Equality*. Princeton, N.J.: Princeton University Press, 2001.

Meyer, David S., and Sidney Tarrow, eds. *The Social Movement Society*. Boulder, Colo.: Rowman & Littlefield, 1998.

Miller, Warren. *American National Election Study: 1952–1988*. Ann Arbor, Mich.: Institute for Social Research, 1989.

Mills, Charles W. *Blackness Visible: Essays on Philosophy and Race.* Ithaca, N.Y.: Cornell University Press, 1998.

Minow, Martha. *Between Vengeance and Forgiveness: Facing History after Genocide and Mass Violence.* Boston: Beacon Press, 1998.

Morris, Aldon D., and Carol McClury, eds. *Frontiers in Social Movement Theory.* New Haven, Conn.: Yale University Press, 1992.

Morris, Lorenzo, and Ura Jean Oyemade, eds. *Critical Analyses of Issues Facing African Americans and the Nation in the Twenty-first Century.* Washington, D.C.: Howard University Press, 1997.

Mumford, Clarence J. *Race & Civilization: Rebirth of Black Centrality.* Trenton, N.J.: Africa World Press, 2001.

National Commission on the Causes and Prevention of Violence. *Final Report: To Establish Justice, to Insure Domestic Tranquility.* Washington, D.C.: U.S. Government Printing Office, December 1969.

Nesbitt, Francis Njuba. *Race for Sanctions.* Bloomington: Indiana University Press, 2004.

New York Times Edition. *Report of the National Advisory Commission on Civil Disorders.* New York: Dutton, 1968.

Obadele, Imari Abubakari. *The New International Law Regime and United States Foreign Policy.* Baton Rouge: The Malcolm Generation, 1996.

O'Reilly, Kenneth. *Nixon's Piano: Presidents and Racial Politics from Washington to Clinton.* New York: Free Press, 1995.

Patterson, Orlando. *Freedom in the Making of Western Culture.* New York: Basic Books, 1991.

Patterson, Orlando. *The Ordeal of Integration.* Washington, D.C.: Civitas / Counterpoint, 1998.

Patterson, Orlando. *Rituals of Blood: Consequences of Slavery in Two American Centuries.* New York: Basic Books, 1998.

Pfeffer, Paula F. *A. Philip Randolph, Pioneer of the Civil Rights Movement.* Albany: State University of New York Press, 1990.

Pinderhughes, Dianne M. *Race and Ethnicity in Chicago Politics.* Urbana: University of Illinois Press, 1987.

Plummer, Brenda Gayle, ed. *Window on Freedom.* Chapel Hill: University of North Carolina Press, 2003.

Rank, Mark Robert. *One Nation, Underprivileged: Why American Poverty Affects Us All.* New York: Oxford University Press, 2004.

Ransom, Roger L., and Richard Sutch. *One Kind of Freedom: The Economic Consequences of Emancipation.* Cambridge: Cambridge University Press, 2001.

Reich, Michael. *Racial Inequality: A Political-Economic Analysis.* Princeton, N.J.: Princeton University Press, 1981.

Robinson, Donald. *Slavery in the Structure of American Politics.* New York: Norton, 1979.

Robinson, Randall. *The Debt: What America Owes to Blacks.* New York: Dutton, 2000.

Rodgers, Kim Lacy. *Righteous Lives: Narratives of the New Orleans Civil Rights Movement.* New York: New York University Press, 1993.

Ronchon, Thomas R. *Culture Moves.* Princeton, N.J.: Princeton University Press, 1998.

Salzberger, Ronald P., and Mary C. Turck, eds. *Reparations for Slavery.* Lanham, Md.: Rowman & Littlefield, 2004.

Schucter, Arnold. *Reparations.* Philadelphia: Lippincott, 1970.

Segal, Ronald. *The Black Diaspora.* New York: Farrar, Straus & Giroux, 1995.

Shapiro, Thomas M. *The Hidden Cost of Being African American.* New York: Oxford University Press, 2004.

Singh, Nikhil Pal. *Black Is a Country: Race and the Unfinished Struggle for Democracy.* Cambridge, Mass.: Harvard University Press, 2004.

Smith, Rodgers M. *Civic Ideals: Conflicting Visions of Citizenship in U.S. History.* New Haven, Conn.: Yale University Press, 1997.

Snyder, Louis L. *Macro-Nationalisms.* Westport, Conn.: Greenwood Press, 1984.

Tarrow, Sidney. *Power in Movement.* Cambridge: Cambridge University Press, 1998.

Teall, Kay M., ed. *Black History in Oklahoma: A Resource Book.* Oklahoma City: Oklahoma City Public Schools, 1971.

Thomas, Darryl C. *The Theory and Practice of Third World Solidarity.* Westport, Conn.: Praeger, 2001.

Thompson, Janna. *Taking Responsibility for the Past: Reparation and Historical Injustice.* Malden, Mass.: Blackwell, 2002.

Tolson, Arthur. *Black Oklahomans: A History 1541–1972.* New Orleans: Edwards, 1974.

Torpey, John, ed. *Politics and the Past.* Lanham, Md.: Rowman & Littlefield, 2003.

Walters, Ronald W. *Pan Africanism.* Detroit: Wayne State University Press, 1995.

Walters, Ronald W. *White Nationalism/Black Interests.* Detroit: Wayne State University Press, 2003.

Washington, James M., ed. *A Testament of Hope.* San Francisco: Harper & Row, 1986.

Weich, Ronald H., and Carlos T. Angulo. *Justice on Trial.* Washington, D.C.: Washington Leadership Conference on Civil Rights, 2000.

Williams, Linda Faye. *The Constraint of Race: Legacies of White Skin Privilege in America.* University Park: Pennsylvania State University Press, 2003.

Winbush, Raymond A., ed. *Should America Pay?* New York: Amistad, 2003.

Woods, Jeff. *Black Struggle, Red Scare.* Baton Rouge: Louisiana State University Press, 2004.

Young, Andrew. *An Easy Burden.* New York: HarperCollins, 1996.

Conference Reports and Papers

African Preparatory Regional Meeting for the World Conference against Racism, Racial Discrimination, Xenophobia and Related Intolerance. Draft Declaration. Dakar, Senegal, January 22–24, 2001.

Boyd, Herb. "State of the Black World Draws Luminaries." *New York Amsterdam News,* December 6–12, 2001.

Morris, Lorenzo. "Symptoms of Withdrawal." Paper presented at the annual meeting of the National Conference of Black Political Scientists, Atlanta, March 9, 2002.

NGO Forum. "Program of Action for the World Conference against Racism." Durban, South Africa. August 28–September 1, 2001.

Robinson, Mary. "Closing Statement." Report of the WCAR. Durban, South Africa, A/CONF.189/12. August 31–September 8, 2001.

State of Black World Conference. "Creating Our Twenty-first Century." Available online at l-ncbs@lists.psu.edu, April 16, 2001.

United Nations. First (1978) and Second (1983) World Conference to Combat Racism and Racial Discrimination. E/CN.4/1999/WG.1/BP.1. March 9, 1999.

Wood, William B. "The UN World Conference against Racism." Report to House International Relations Committee, Subcommittee on International Operations and Human Rights. Washington, D.C.: U.S. Government Printing Office, July 31, 2001.

Zuma, Nkosazana Dalamini. "Closing Statement." Report of the WCAR, Durban, South Africa. A/CONF.189/12. August 31–September 8, 2001.

Court Cases

Obadele v. United States. 52 Federal Claim.432 2002.

Randolph, A. Philip. "The Federal Role in Urban Affairs." Testimony to U.S. Senate, December 1966, 89th Cong., 2d sess.

United States v. Hanway. Case no. 15,299, Circuit Court, E.D. Pennsylvania, 26 F. Cas. 105: 1851 U.S. App. LEXIS 463; 9 W.L.J. 103; 2 Wall. Jr.

United States v. Rev. Augustus Clark. U.S. Court for the Eastern District of Texas, National Archives, Record Group 15, Ex-Slave Pension Movement, box 1, envelope 3.

Government Records

Constitution and By-Laws of the Ex-Slave Pension Association. National Archives, Record Group 15, Ex-Slave Pension Movement, box 1, envelope 5.

Constitution and By-Laws of the Ex-Slave Pension Association. National Archives, Record Group 15, Ex-Slave Pension Movement, National Archives, Record Group 15, box 1, envelope 5.

Davenport, J. L. Letter from acting commissioner to Thomas Ryan, acting secretary of the interior. September 13, 1902. National Archives, Record Group 15, box 2, envelope 8.

"Deluding the Freedmen." *Evening Star,* September 21, 1899, p. 12, National Archives, Record Group 15, Ex-Slave Pension Movement, box 1.

EPA Newspaper. n.d. National Archives, Record Group 15, Ex-Slave Pension Movement, box 2, envelope 11.

"Ex-Mayor Vaughan's Statement." *U.S. Department News Eagle.* Washington, D.C., December 31, 1899. National Archives, Record Group 15, Ex-Slave Pension Movement, box 1, envelope 6.

Ex-Slave Pension Movement. National Archives, Record Group 15, box 1, envelope 1.

Freedman's Herald. Washington, D.C. n.d. National Archives, Record Group 15, Ex-Slave Pension Movement, box 2, envelope 11.

"Heavy Fine or Chain Gang." *Washington D.C. Times,* March 16, 1901. National Archives, Record Group 15.

Letter from Callie to Hon. H. Clay, December 13, 1900. National Archives, Record Group 15, Ex-Slave Pension Movement, box 2, envelope 8.

Letter from chief of the Law Division to chief of the S.E. Division. Department of the Interior, Bureau of Pensions, December 4, 1905. National Archives, Record Group 15, Ex-Slave Pension Movement, box 1, envelope 6.

" 'Limit of Law Is Sufficient in This Case'—Judge Calhoun." *Atlanta Constitution* (?) n.d., National Archives, Record Group 15, Ex-Slave Pension Movement, box 1, envelope 6.

President's Initiative on Race. *One America in the Twenty-first Century: Forging a New Future.* Advisory Board's Report to the President, September 1998.

"Onward to Victory!" Flyer from the Ex-Slave Mutual Relief and Bounty & Pension Association, National Archives, Record Group 15, box 1, n.d.

Parker, A. Letter from (?), special examiner, to commissioner of pensions, March 10, 1901. National Archives, Record Group 15, Ex-Slave Pension Movement, box 1, envelope 6.

Report of the commissioner to General Eli Torrence, February 7, 1902. Department of the Interior, Bureau of Pensions, National Archives, Record Group 15, Ex-Slave Pension Movement, box 1, envelope 6.

Scales, A., and J. W. Anderson Committee. *Ex-Slave Pension Song.* National Archives, Record Group 15, Ex-Slave Pension Movement, box 1, envelope 5.

State of New Jersey. Assembly no. 1301, 210th legislature. Available online at TheBlackList@topica.com. Accessed October 12, 2002.

State of New York. 9286 A, 2001-02 regular session in assembly, June 25, 2001.

S.R. 75, 56th Cong., 1st sess., January 16, 1900.

Vaughan, W. R. "Caution." September 23, 1897. National Archives, Record Group 15, Ex-Slave Pension Movement, box 1.

Internet

The Afrocentric Experience. "Why Reparations?" Available online at www .swagga/com/reparation.htm. Accessed October 22, 2002.

Blumenthal, Sidney. "No One Can Say They Didn't See It Coming." Available online at http://socrates.berkeley.edu/. Accessed September 3, 2005.

Bush, George W. "Civil Rights." Available online at *Time,* CNN.com / Time .com. Accessed August 1, 2000.

Bush, George W. "Making Amends." Available online at www.npr.org/ programs/specials/racism/010827.reparations.html. Accessed August 27, 2001.

CNN. "Suit Seeks Billions in Slave Reparations." Available online at CNN .com/LawCenter. Accessed March 28, 2002.

Cohn, Marjorie. "The Two Americas." Available online at www.truthout.org/ docs. Accessed September 3, 2005.

Human Rights Watch. "An Approach to Reparations." Available online at www.hrw.org. Accessed December 28, 2000.

Dixon, Emma. "New Orleans' Racial Divide: An Unnatural Disaster." Available online at Ellarwee@aol.com. Accessed November 18, 2005.

Gates, Henry L. Jr. "A Preliminary Response to Ali Mazrui's Preliminary Critique of Wonders of the African World." Available online at l-ncbs@lists .psu.edu. Accessed November 13, 1999.

Johnson, Chip. "Police Made Their Storm Misery Worse." Available online at www.sfgate.com. Accessed September 9, 2005.

Kerry, John. "Civil Rights." Available online at www.issues2002.org/Domestic/ John_Kerry_Civil_Rights.htm#General. Accessed August 1, 2000, and April 27, 2004.

Lewis, Shelby. "International Reaction to Katrina." Available online at list@ ncobps.org. Accessed September 6, 2005.

Lovelace, Alice. "The Tulsa Riot of 1921." Available online at www.inmotion magazine.com/tulsa19.html. Accessed July 9, 2003.

Mann, Eric. "Letter in Support of the Movement in New Orleans and the Gulf Coast: Notes on Strategy & Tactics." Available online at www.thestrategy center.org. Accessed September 29, 2005.

Pew Research Center. "Two-in-Three Critical of Bush's Relief Efforts." Available online at http://people-press.org. Accessed September 8, 2005.

RaceRelations. "40 Acres and a Luxury Sedan." Available online at Race relations.about.com. Accessed June 19, 2002.

"Slavery Reparations" Resolution. Official City of East Peoria Document. Available online at TheBlackList@topica.com. Accessed September 3, 2002.

Special Master's Final Report, March 24, 1994. Available online at http://fn1.tfn.net/rosewood/rosewood2.txt. Accessed July 22, 2003.

State of New Jersey. Assembly no. 1301, 210th legislature. Available online at TheBlackList@topica.com. Accessed October 12, 2002.

U.S. Human Rights Network. "U.S. Human Rights Network Calls for Authorities to Meet Their Legal and Moral Obligations to 'Internally Displaced Persons' in the Wake of Hurricane Katrina." Available online at baraka@ushrnetwork.org. Accessed September 13, 2005.

U.S. Internal Revenue Service. "Slavery Reparation Scams Surge, IRS Urges Taxpayers Not to File False Claims." Available online at www.irs.gov. Accessed January 24, 2002.

Interviews

"An Apology 65 Years Late." Transcript. *The NewsHour with Jim Lehrer,* May 16, 1997.

Journals and Magazines

Allen, Robert. "Past Due: The African American Quest for Reparations." *The Black Scholar,* summer 1998, pp. 2–15.

Becklund, Laurie. "Listening to Katrina." *California Monthly,* November/December 2005, pp. 32–38.

Bedard, Paul. "Clinton, Race Panel at Odds on Slavery." *Washington Times,* September 30, 1997, p. A1.

Bell, Daniel. "'American Exceptionalism' Revisited: The Role of Civil Society." *The Public Interest* 95 (spring 1989): 38–56.

Berry, Mary F. "Reparations for Freedmen, 1890–1916: Fraudulent Practices or Justice Deferred?" *Journal of Negro History* 57 (1972): 219–30.

"Black African Reparations: Making a Claim for Enslavement and Systematic de Jure Segregation and Racial Discrimination under American and International Law." *Southern University Law Review* 25, no. 1 (1997): 1–41.

Booth, W. James. "Communities of Memory: On Identity, Memory, and Debt." *American Political Science Review,* June 1999, pp. 249–63.

Brophy, Alfred L. "Some Conceptual and Legal Problems in Reparations for Slavery." 58 *New York University Annual Survey of American Law,* winter 2003, pp. 497–555.

Browne, Robert S.. "The Economic Basis for Reparations to Black America." *Review of Black Political Economy,* winter 1993, pp. 99–111.

Brutus, Dennis, and Ben Cashdan. "World Conference against Racism: South Africa between a Rock and a Hard Place." *Znet Commentary,* July 11, 2001.

Chisolm, Tuneen E. "Sweep around Your Own Front Door: Examining the Argument for Legislative African American Reparations." 147 *University of Pennsylvania Law Review* 677–727.

Chrisman, Robert, and Ernest Allen Jr. "Ten Reasons: A Response to David Horowitz." *The Black Scholar,* April 3. 2001.

Christopher, Darcie L. "Cognes, Jus. Reparation Agreements. and Holocaust Slave Labor Litigation." 31 *Law & Policy in International Business* (2000): 1227–53.

Dennis, Raoul. "Who Axed the African American Museum on the Mall?" *The Crisis,* February / March 1998, pp. 8–13.

Drescher, Seymour. "British Way. French Way: Opinion Building and Revolution in the Second French Slave Emancipation." *American Historical Review,* June 1991, pp. 709–34.

du Plessis, Max. "Historical Injustice and International Law: An Exploratory Discussion of Reparation for Slavery." *Human Rights Quarterly* 25 (2003): 624–59.

Dye. Thomas R. "Rosewood. Florida: The Destruction of an African American Community." *Historian: A Journal of History,* spring 1996, pp. 605–22.

Fletcher, Michael A. "Initiative on Race Ends Short of Its Soaring Goals." *Washington Post,* September 17, 1998, p. A1.

Gibbs, Nancy. "New Orleans Lives by the Water and Fights It. . . ." *Time,* September 12, 2005, pp. 44–49.

Gifford, Anthony. "The Legal Basis of the Claim for Slavery Reparations." 27-SPG *Human Rights American Bar Association,* spring 2000, pp. 16–18.

Harris, Cheryl I. "Whiteness as Property." *Harvard Law Review* 106 (1993): 1709–91.

Haydu, Jeffrey. "Making Use of the Past: Time Periods as Cases to Compare and as Sequences of Problem Solving." *American Journal of Sociology,* September 1998, pp. 339–71.

Henry, Charles P. "A World View of Race Revisited." *Journal of Negro Education,* spring 2004, , pp. 137–46.

Kennedy, Randall L. "Conservatives' Selective Use of Race in the Law." *Harvard Journal of Law & Public Policy,* spring 1996, pp. 719–21.

Kimberley, Margaret. "Freedom Rider: Racist Delivers Lynching Apology." *The Black Commentator,* June 16, 2005. Available online at www.black commentator.com.

Levmore, Saul. "Changes. Anticipations. and Reparations." *Columbia Law Review,* November 1999, pp. 1657–1700.

Lowi, Theodore J. "American Business. Public Policy. Case Studies and Political Theory." *World Politics*, July 1964, pp. 677–715.

Matsuda. Mari J. "Looking to the Bottom: Critical Legal Studies and Reparations." 323 *Harvard Civil Rights–Civil Liberties Review*, spring 1987, pp. 323–400.

Mazrui, Ali A. "Global Africa: From Abolitionists to Reparations." *African Studies Review*, December 1994, pp. 1–18.

Meyer, Peter J. Review of *The Wealth of Races*, by Richard F. America. *Journal of Economic Literature*, September 1993.

Miller, Eric J. "Healing the Wounds of Slavery." 24 *Boston College Third World Law Journal*, winter 2004, pp. 45–79.

Obadele, Imari A. "Reparations Now!" *Journal of Human Rights* 5 (1988): 369–411.

Ogletree, Charles J. Jr. "Repairing the Past: New Efforts in the Reparations Debate." 38 *Harvard Civil Rights–Civil Liberties Law Review* (2003): 279–320.

Ogletree, Charles J. Jr. "Reparations for the Children of Slaves: Litigating the Issues." 33 *University of Memphis Law Review*, winter 2003, pp. 245–64.

Orey, Byron D'Andra. "White Racial Attitudes and Support for the Mississippi State Flag." *American Politics Research*, January 2004, pp. 102–16.

Ozer, Irma Jacqueline. "Reparations for African Americans." 41 *Howard Law Journal*, spring 1998, pp. 479–498.

"Paying for Slavery." *The Economist* (U.S.), August 13. 1994, pp. A28–29.

"A Price for Pain?" *The Economist* (U.S.), April 13, 2002.

Richard, Newman. "Rosewood Revisited." *Transition* 0, no. 80 (1999).

Ruffins, Faith Davis. "Culture Wars Won and Lost: Part I." *Radical History Review* 68 (1997): 79–100.

Ruffins, Faith Davis. "Culture Wars Won and Lost: Part II." *Radical History Review* 70 (1998): 78–101.

Steinmetz, George. "Reflections on the Role of Social Narratives in Working-Class Formation: Narrative Theory in the Social Sciences." *Social Science History*, fall 1992, pp. 489–516.

Thomas, Cathy Booth. "Hurricane Katrina: The Cleanup." *Time*, November 28, 2005, pp. 32–37.

Verdun, Vincene. "If the Shoe Fits, Wear It: An Analysis of Reparations to African Americans." *Tulane Law Review*, February 1993, pp. 597–668.

Westley, Robert. "Many Billions Gone: Is It Time to Consider the Case for Black Reparations." *Boston College Law Review*, December 1998, pp. 429–76.

Yamamoto, Eric K.. "Race Apologies" 1 *Journal of Gender, Race and Justice* (1997): 47–88.

Newspapers

Austin, Amber. "Activists Discuss Slave Reparations." *Associated Press,* March 7, 2001.

Associated Press. "Clinton Pays Tribute to Slaves and Their Descendants. Senegal Memorial Is Final Stop on African Tour." *Seattle Times,* April 2, 1998, p. A1.

Becker, Elizabeth. "Annan Says Race Conference Must Chart Way for Future." *New York Times,* July 31, 2001.

Bernstein, Richard. "The View from Abroad." *New York Times,* September 4. 2005.

Bivens, Larry. "Slave-Reparations Debate Heating Up." *Arizona Republic,* April 21, 2001.

Black, Eugene. "Eugenics and the Nazis—The California Connection." *San Francisco Chronicle,* November 19, 2003, p. D1.

Breed, Allen G. "Blacks Dissatisfied with USDA Lawsuit Settlement." *Oakland Tribune,* September 1, 2002, p. 8.

Brownstein, Andrew. "Race. Reparations. and Free Expression." *Chronicle of Higher Education,* March 30. 2001, pp. A48–50.

Bumiller, Elisabeth, and Anne E. Kornblut. "Black Leaders Say Storm Forced Bush to Confront Issues of Race and Poverty." *New York Times,* September 18, 2005.

Burns, Greg. "Farms Run by African-Americans in Illinois Are 'Mighty Few' at 59." *Chicago Tribune,* June 12, 2005, p. B1.

"Bush Addresses Slavery from African Port Island." *Columbia (Mo.) Daily Tribune,* July 8, 2003.

Carter, Bill. "Career-Maker for Williams as the Anchor at NBC." *New York Times,* September 4, 2005.

Clemetson. Lynette. "Bush Authorizes a Black History Museum." *New York Times,* December 17, 2003.

Constable, Pamela. "Many Causes Set Tone for U.N. Summit on Racism." *Washington Post,* August 31, 2001, p. A14.

"Corporate Fraud Law Upheld." *Washington Post,* November 30, 2004, p. E2.

Crary, David. "France, U.S. Both Face Race Conflicts." *Oakland Tribune,* November 14, 2005.

Crossette, Barbara. "Global Look at Racism Hits Many Sore Points." *New York Times,* March 4. 2001, p. A12.

Crossette. Barbara. "Rights Leaders Urge Powell to Attend U.N. Racism Conference." *New York Times,* July 11, 2001, p. A9.

Dewan, Shaila K. "Black Farmers' Refrain: Where's All Our Money?" *New York Times,* August 1, 2004, p. 12.

Dixon, Norm. "Thousands to Protest at Racism Conference." *Green Left Weekly,* August 8, 2001, p. 18.

Duke, Lynne. "The Price of Apartheid." *Washington Post,* December 3, 2002, p. C1.

Duke, Lynne, and Teresa Wiltz. "A Nation's Castaways." *Washington Post,* September 4, 2005.

Editorial. "Walking the Fine Line of Free Speech." *Daily Californian,* March 6, 2001, p. 6.

Edsall, Thomas B. " 'Poor Choice of Words.' Lott Says." *Washington Post,* December 10, 2002, p. A13.

Eviatar, Daphne. "Judgment Day—Will an Obscure Law Bring Down the Global Economy?" *Boston Globe,* December 28, 2003, p. D1.

Fears, Darryl, and Alan Sipress. "U.S. Warns It May Skip Conference on Racism." *Washington Post,* July 27, 2001, p. A1.

Fletcher, Michael A. "Call for Reparations Builds as Blacks Tally History's Toll." *Washington Post,* December 26, 2000, p. A1.

Goodheart, Adam. "Slavery's Past: Paved Over or Forgotten." *New York Times,* July 13, 2003.

Herbert, Bob. "In America, Doomed to Irrelevance." *New York Times,* September 6, 2001.

Holmes, Steven A., and James Bennet. "A Renewed Sense of Purpose for Clinton's Panel on Race." *New York Times,* January 14. 1998.

Ignatieff, Michael. "The Broken Contract." *New York Times,* September 25, 2005, p. 15–17.

Ince, Adamma. "Getting Back on the Bus." *Village Voice,* August 14–20, 2002.

Itano, Nicole. "Should IBM and Others Pay Apartheid Bill?" *Christian Science Monitor,* November 26. 2002, p. O7.

Jacoby, Jeff. "Katrina's Colorblind Relief." *Oakland Tribune,* September 17, 2005.

Janofsky, Michael. "A New Hope for Dreams Suspended by Segregation." *New York Times,* July 31, 2005, pp. 1, 14.

Johnson, LaWanda. "Benin Seeks Forgiveness for Its Role in African Slave Trade." *Washington Afro-American,* October 7, 2002.

"Journey toward Justice . . . Not Over." *USA Today,* July 9, 2003.

Judd, Alan. "Georgia Orders Probe of Slave Insurance." *Atlanta Journal-Constitution,* May 2, 2004, p. A1.

Kristof, Nicholas D. "A Health Care Disaster." *New York Times,* September 25. 2005.

Lee, Barbara. "Hurricane Exposed Two Americas." *Oakland Tribune,* September 17, 2005.

Leo, John. "The No Speech Culture." *U.S. News & World Report,* March 19, 2001, p. 16.

Lester, Will. "Poll Shows Support for Abandoning Parts of City." *Oakland Tribune,* September 10. 2005, p. 6.

Mack, Kristen. "Reparations Debate Heats up Push for Slavery Compensation Enters Political Mainstream." *Houston Chronicle,* August 12, 2002, p. A1.

Mayer, Caroline. "Flier Offering Slave Reparations Solicits Personal Information." *Washington Post,* July 9, 2001, p. A2.

McWhorter, John. "Why I Don't Want Reparations for Slavery." *Los Angeles Times,* July 15, 2001.

Miller, Sabrina L., and Gary Washburn. "City Mulls Law Seeking Insurers' Ties to Slavery." *Chicago Tribune,* May 30, 2002, p. M3.

Milloy, Courtland. "Colin Powell: Bush Man or Black Man?" *Washington Post,* July 29, 2001, p. C1.

Morain, Dan. "Slave Owners and Their Insurers Are Named." *Los Angeles Times,* May 2, 2000, p. A1.

Nelson, Sophia A. "I'm Hoping Bush Can Finish What Lincoln Started." *Washington Post,* October 23, 2005, p. B3.

Perlez Jane. "How Powell Decided to Shun Conference." *New York Times,* September 5, 2001.

Prengaman Peter. "Poll: Poverty Should Be Country's Top Priority." *Oakland Tribune,* October 23, 2005.

Raspberry William. "An Education on Reparations." *Washington Post,* September 10, 2001, p. A21.

Raspberry. William. "When Sorry Isn't Enough." *Washington Post,* May 5, 2000, p. A27.

Reed, Adolph, Jr. "The Case against Reparations." *The Progressive,* December 2000, pp. 15–17.

Rice, Anne. "Do You Know What It Means to Lose New Orleans?" *New York Times,* September 4. 2005, p. WK11.

Richardson, Gwen Daye. "At Least Consider Idea of Reparations." *USA Today,* June 16, 2000.

Rulon, Malia. "Black Farmers Press for Compensation." *Washington Post,* February 28, 2005, p. A5.

Scott, Robert Travis. "Rebuilding Plans Confront Turf Wars, Political Strife: Racial Tension Mars Initial Discussions." *Times-Picayune,* September 18, 2005.

Singletory, Michelle. "The Color of Money." *Washington Post,* March 4. 2001, p. H1.

Spielman, Fran. "Daley Says He Backs Slavery Reparations." *Chicago Sun-Times,* May 10, 2000, p. 28.

Staples, Brent. "The Lessons of a Graveyard." *International Herald Tribune,* November 11, 2000, p. 9.

Stolberg, Sheryl Gay. "The Senate Apologizes. Mostly." *New York Times,* June 19, 2005, p. WK3.

Sullivan, Kevin. "Response to Storm Shakes U.S. Image." *Oakland Tribune*, September 4, 2005.

Taute, Michelle. "New Black History Museums." *USA Weekend*, July 16–18, 2004, p. 20.

Thevenot, Brian. "Race, Class on Everyone's Mind: Residents Visualize the Future of N.O." *Times-Picayune*, October 2, 2005.

Thomas-Lester, Avis. "A Senate Apology for History on Lynching Vote Condemns Past Failure to Act." *Washington Post*, June 14, 2005.

Tierney, Mike. Black Farmers Angry at Feds." *Atlanta Journal-Constitution*, May 5, 2005, p. E1.

Verghese, Abraham. "Close Encounter of the Human Kind." *New York Times*, September 18, 2005, p. 192.

Washington, Jesse. "Blacks' Conscience Awakened." *Oakland Tribune*, September 9, 2005.

Weber, Bruce. "The Road to Freedom, Revisited." *New York Times*, August 1, 2004, pp. TR6–7.

Will, George. "Hard Lessons for Liberals." *Oakland Tribune*, September 15, 2005.

Reports

Applied Research Center. "Still Separate. Still Unequal." May 2000.

Human Rights Watch. "An Approach to Reparations." New York: Human Rights Watch, 2001.

International Human Rights Law Group. "Race and Poverty in the Americas." August 2000.

International Human Rights Law Group. "Report on the World Conference against Racism. First Preparatory Committee (PrepCom) Meeting." Geneva, Switzerland, May 1–5, 2000.

International Possibilities Unlimited. "Report on Informal Government Meeting and Africa PrepCom. 2001.

LeBlanc. Phillippe. "How Can NGOs Be Effective in the World Conference against Racism?" 2001.

Office of Tom Hayden. "Governor Signs Hayden Bills Researching Financial Gains from Slavery. Press release, October 2, 2000.

United Nations. "Report of the PrepCom on Its Third Session." Geneva, Switzerland. A/CONF.189/PC.3/11, July 30–August 10, 2001.

Television

ABC7/News Poll. Broadcast on September 7, 2005.

ABC / *Washington Post* Poll. Broadcast on September 28, 2005.

Poll. Available online at ABC News.com, June 8–July 9, 2000.

Unpublished Papers

Dunoguez, Paul A. "The Right Thing to Do: Cuban American Involvement in the Rosewood Claim." Unpublished seminar paper, University of California at Berkeley, December 3, 2003.

Jackson, Thomas F. "Reconstructing the Dream." Ph.D. diss., Stanford University, 1993.

Index

About the Author

Charles P. Henry is Professor of African American Studies at the University of California at Berkeley. He also is the author of *Ralph Bunche: Model Negro or American Other?* and editor of *Ralph J. Bunche: Selected Speeches and Writings and Foreign Policy and the Black (Inter)national Interest.*